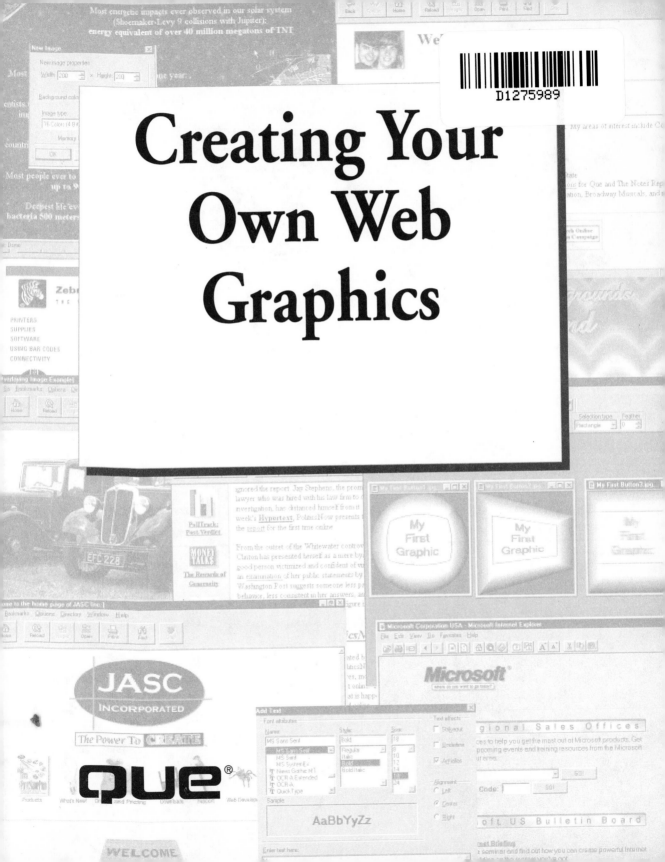

Creating Your Own Web Graphics

JASC
INCORPORATED
The Power To CREATE

que®

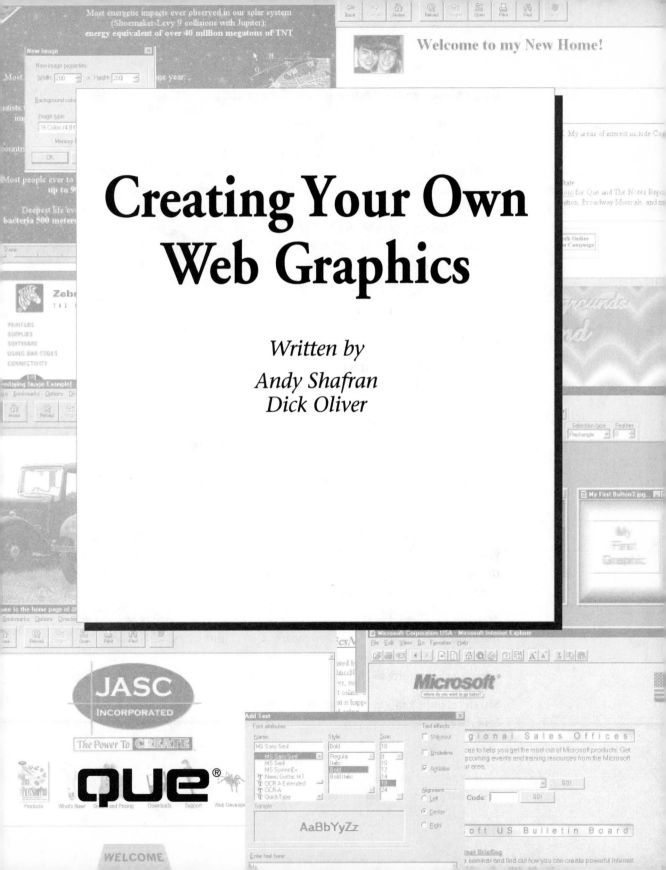

Creating Your Own Web Graphics

Written by

Andy Shafran
Dick Oliver

Creating Your Own Web Graphics

Library of Congress Catalog No.: 96-69963

ISBN: 0-7897-0912-0

98 97 96   6 5 4 3 2 1

Interpretation of the printing code: the rightmost double-digit number is the year of the book's printing; the rightmost single-digit number, the number of the book's printing. For example, a printing code of 96-1 shows that the first printing of the book occurred in 1996.

Screen reproductions in this book were created using Collage Complete from Inner Media, Inc., Hollis, NH.

Composed in *Stone Serif* and *MCPdigital* by Que Corporation

Credits

President
Roland Elgey

Publisher
Joseph B. Wikert

Publishing Manager
Jim Minatel

Title Manager
Steven M. Schafer

Editorial Services Director
Elizabeth Keaffaber

Managing Editor
Sandy Doell

Director of Marketing
Lynn E. Zingraf

Acquisitions Manager
Cheryl D. Willoughby

Product Director
Jon Steever

Production Editor
William F. McManus

Editor
Sean Dixon

Product Marketing Manager
Kim Margolius

Assistant Product Marketing Manager
Christy M. Miller

Strategic Marketing Manager
Barry Pruett

Technical Editors
Ernie Sanders
Matthew Brown

Technical Support Specialist
Nadeem Muhammed

Acquisitions Coordinator
Jane K. Brownlow

Software Relations Coordinator
Patty Brooks

Editorial Assistant
Andrea Duvall

Book Designer
Ruth Harvey

Cover Designer
Ruth Harvey

Production Team
Bryan Flores
Trey Frank
Daryl Kessler
Sossity Smith
Donna Wright

Indexer
Tim Tate

About the Authors

Andy Shafran has been writing computer books for several years. He enjoys working with the Internet, World Wide Web, and related information technologies such as Lotus Notes. Born in Columbus, Ohio, Andy recently graduated from The Ohio State University with a degree in Computer Science Engineering. He now lives in Cincinnati, the Queen City and is an avid Reds and baseball fan.

He has written several other computer books including *Creating and Enhancing Netscape Web Pages*, *Creating Your Own Netscape Web Pages*, *Enhancing Netscape Web Pages*, *The Idiot's Guide to CompuServe*, and *Easy Lotus Notes*.

When he's not busy working or writing, he enjoys live theater, particularly Broadway shows. He also loves traveling abroad and is constantly on the go to one place or another. You can talk to Andy via e-mail at **andy@shafran.com** or visit his WWW page at **http://www.shafran.com**.

Dick Oliver is the author and coauthor of numerous books on computer graphics and the Internet, including *Web Page Wizardry*, *Internet Graphics Gallery*, *Netscape Unleashed*, *Internet Explorer Unleashed*, and *Tricks of the Graphics Gurus*. He is also the president of Cedar Software, and the publisher of a paper and online newsletter called the *Nonlinear Nonsense Netletter* (**http://netletter.com**). His e-mail address is **dicko@netletter.com**. Dick lives in Elmore, Vermont, USA and commutes to work all over the world via the Internet.

Acknowledgments

I'd like to thank my wife, Liz, for helping me manage my time and responsibilities while working on this great project. All of her feedback, editing, and ideas enhanced this book significantly.

There are many other people who helped make this book a reality. Chris Anderson from JASC, Inc. collaborated on this book from the start and provided me with great resources and information to use. Dick Oliver is a terrific author who contributed his vast expertise in computer graphics to this book. Jim Minatel is a great editor at Que who guided this project with a careful hand and helped us sculpt an excellent and comprehensive guide to making Web graphics. Steve Schafer, Bill McManus, Jon Steever, Laddie Ervin, and the whole production team at Que were great to work with and provided a lot of support, assistance, and humor in the writing process.

—Andy Shafran

To my daughters, Ona (age 2) and Erica (age 4), who create their own graphics the old-fashioned way.

—Dick Oliver

We'd Like to Hear from You!

As part of our continuing effort to produce books of the highest possible quality, Que would like to hear your comments. To stay competitive, we *really* want you, as a computer book reader and user, to let us know what you like or dislike most about this book or other Que products.

You can mail comments, ideas, or suggestions for improving future editions to the address below, or send us a fax at (317) 581-4663. For the online inclined, Macmillan Computer Publishing has a forum on CompuServe (type **GO QUEBOOKS** at any prompt) through which our staff and authors are available for questions and comments. The address of our Internet site is **http://www.mcp.com** (World Wide Web).

In addition to exploring our forum, please feel free to contact me personally to discuss your opinions of this book: I'm **jsteever@que.mcp.com** on the Internet.

Thanks in advance—your comments will help us to continue publishing the best books available on computer topics in today's market.

Jon Steever
Product Development Specialist
Que Corporation
201 W. 103rd Street
Indianapolis, Indiana 46290
USA

Contents at a Glance

Introduction 1

Web Graphics Basics **11**

1 A Web Crawler's Beginning 13

2 Using and Installing
Paint Shop Pro 31

Web Graphics Basics

Making Great Images **45**

3 Creating Simple Graphics 47

4 Working with Existing Images 69

5 Scanning and Enhancing
Photos 89

6 Filters, Deformations, and
Special Effects 109

Making Great Images

Advanced Image Techniques **133**

7 Making Your Graphics Lean 135

8 The Black-and-White
Alternative 157

9 Creating Transparent GIFs 173

10 Moving Graphics:
GIF Animation 191

Advanced Techniques

**Practical Use of Images on
Your Web Pages** **209**

11 Creating Titles, Buttons, and
Bars with Paint Shop Pro 211

12 Web Graphics as Image Maps 231

13 Backgrounds and Creative
Layouts 249

14 HTML Tips for Web Images 267

Using Your Web Graphics

Appendixes **285**

A Graphical Resources on
the Web 287

B What's On the CD-ROM 291

Index 293

Appendixes

Contents

Introduction   **1**

What You'll Learn in This Book 2
Practicality is its Own Virtue 2
Who is This Book For? 3
What This Book is Not 4
How This Book Helps You Create Your Home Page 4
    Part I: Web Graphics Basics 4
    Part II: Making Great Images 5
    Part III: Advanced Image Techniques 5
    Part IV: Practical Use of Images on Your Web Pages 6
    Part V: Appendixes 6
What's on the CD-ROM? 7
Tools and Programs Used in this Book 7
    Paint Shop Pro 7
    Graphics Construction Set 7
    Map This! 8
Conventions Used in This Book 8
    On the CD-ROM 8
Keeping the Book's Content Current 9

I Web Graphics Basics   **11**

1 A Web Crawler's Beginning   **13**

Graphics Make the Web Popular 14
What are Web Graphics? 16
    Icons 17
    Photographs and Pictures 18
    Background Graphics 19
Understanding Different Web Image Types 20
    GIF 21
    JPEG 22
    PNG 23
    Other Popular Formats 24
Basic HTML Tags for Adding Images 24
    Setting Your Image Alignment 25
    Providing Alternative Text 26
    Using Images as Links 28

2 Using and Installing Paint Shop Pro   31

What is PSP? 32
Installing Paint Shop Pro 33
    Registering Paint Shop Pro 35
A Quick Tour of Paint Shop Pro 36
What Can You Do With Paint Shop Pro? 38
    Crop and Resize Graphics 42
    Add Cool Deformations 43
    Using Paint Shop Pro's Help System 44

II Making Great Images   45

3 Creating Simple Graphics   47

Making a New Image 48
    Understanding Pixel Sizing 49
    Picking the Right Background Color 53
    Choosing the Correct Number of Colors 53
Saving Your Graphic 56
    GIF Format 57
    JPEG Format 58
Drawing Shapes 59
    Choosing Colors 59
    Drawing Lines 61
    Drawing Rectangles 62
    Drawing Ovals 63
    Using the Paint Brush 64
    Brush Type 64
    Brush Size 65
    Brush Shape 65
    Paper Texture 66
Other Drawing Options 67

4 Working With Existing Images   69

Finding Graphics on the Internet 70
    Grabbing the Graphics You Find 71
    Archie and Veronica Go to the Pictures 72
Using the Graphics on the CD-ROM 77
Capturing Screen Shots 78
Modifying Graphics for Your Pages 81
    Print Graphics vs. Web Graphics 81
    Resizing Graphics 82
    Customizing Backgrounds 84
    Finishing Touches 86

5 Scanning and Enhancing Photos   89

Choosing the Most Suitable Photos 90
Scanning from Paint Shop Pro 91

Other Scanning Options 93
Correcting and Retouching Images 94
  Color Correction 95
  Brightness and Contrast Enhancement 96
  Gamma Correction 98
  Tonal Corrections 99
  Correcting Color Images Using HSL and
    RGB Controls 100
  Equalization 102
Isolating Subjects from the Background 104

6 Filters, Deformations, and Special Effects   109

Image Filters 110
Deforming Images 114
Combining and Layering Images 115
Color Effects 119
  Grey Scale and Colorize 121
  Negative and Solarize 121
  Posterize and Decrease Color Depth 124
Special Effects 127
  Drop Shadows and Highlights 127
  Creating 3D Buttons 129
  Hot Wax and Tinting 130
Plug-in Filters 131

III Advanced Image Techniques   133

7 Making Your Graphics Lean   135

Why Use Lean Files? 136
Cropping, Resizing, and Thumbnailing Images 137
  Resizing an Image 138
  Making Thumbnails 141
  Cropping 142
How Many Colors are Right for a GIF Image? 145
  How Colors Affect GIF File Size 145
  Reducing Colors 147
JPEG Compression 151
Using Interlaced and Progressive Images 154

8 The Black-and-White Alternative   157

Finding a Place for Black and White 158
When to Use B&W 160
  Artistic Emphasis and Value 160
  Theme Coordination 161
  Performance Considerations 162
Creating B&W Graphics 163
  Making New Images 163
  Converting Color Graphics To B&W 165
  Using 16 Shades of Grey 165

Overlaying Images 169
Spot Color and B&W 171

9 Creating Transparent GIFs 173

What are Transparent GIFs? 174
How Web Browsers Treat Transparent GIFs 176
Making Transparent GIFs 178
Creating a Transparent GIF from Scratch 178
Working With Existing Images 182
Setting the GIF Options 182
A Floating Photograph 183
Scanning the Picture 184
Cropping the Picture 184
Sculpting Your Image 186
Finishing Touches 188
Test Your Image 189

10 Moving Graphics: GIF Animation 191

Building a GIF Animation 192
GIF Animation Tips and Tricks 196
A Hand-Crafted Animation 199
Handling Palettes 200
Tips on Transparency 202
Doing the Loop 203
Optimizing GIF Animation for Speed and Size 204
Cropping the Crystal 205
Emptying the Pot 207

IV Practical Use of Images on Your Web Pages 209

11 Creating Titles, Buttons, and Bars with Paint Shop Pro 211

Making Your Own Buttons 212
A Blinking Button 212
Special Effect Buttons 214
Matching Titles and Bars 217
Buttons and Titles that Work Together 221
Icons and Graphical Accents 225

12 Web Graphics as Image Maps 231

How Image Maps Work 232
Differences between Server-Side and Client-Side
Image Maps 234

Creating a Client-Side Image Map 235
   Finding a Good Image 235
   Planning the Map 236
   Adding the Image to Your Web Page 238
   Mapping Your Image 238
   Adding a Default Link 244
Test the Image Map 245
Providing a Textual Alternative 245
Image Map Design Considerations 246

13 Backgrounds and Creative Layouts   249

Making Seamless Background Tiles 249
   Seamless Backgrounds By Hand 250
   Seamless Backgrounds Automatically 254
   Hand-drawn Backgrounds 257
Using Tables to Lay Out Graphics 259
   Laying It Out on the Table 259
   Nested Tables 261
Tips and Tricks for Creative Design 264

14 HTML Tips for Web Images   267

Controlling Your Image's Appearance 268
   Height and Width HTML Tags 268
   Buffering Your Image 270
   Using Tables with Graphics 271
   Introducing Frames 273
Finding the Right Image Path 274
   Link to a Sub-directory 275
   One Directory Above 275
   Link to a Different Drive 275
   Images Elsewhere on the WWW 275
   Fixing a Broken Image Pointer 278
Image Design Suggestions 279
   Image Visioning 279
   Site Consistency 280
   Color Coordination 283

V Appendixes   285

A Graphical Resources on the Web   287

Graphics Related Tools 287
Graphics and Image Information 288
WWW Browsers 288
Cool Sites I Use 289
Collections of Images to Use 289
Scanner Developers 290
Search Utilities 290

B What's on the CD-ROM   **291**

Paint Shop Pro 291
Other Graphics Programs 291
Web Graphics Collections 292
Examples from this Book 292

Index   **293**

Introduction

If HTML and modems are the lifeblood of the World Wide Web, then graphics are the soul. Graphics are the colorful and vibrant images and pictures that people place on their Web pages to add life and excitement to the standard text you normally find. Graphics come in an array of shapes and sizes. This book discusses all the important information you need to know to create incredible graphics for your Web pages. This book serves as an easy-to-use guide for creating your own Web graphics.

In this book, you will be lead painlessly through step-by-step directions for using and including great looking graphics on your Web page. You'll use a powerful graphics program called Paint Shop Pro, which is included on the CD-ROM at the back of this book, to make all of the dazzling graphics you'll need for your Web site. Making your own graphics isn't difficult—but sometimes it can be challenging to understand some of the concepts and technologies used on the World Wide Web (WWW). By the time you're finished with this book, you'll be a Web graphics expert, able to use a variety of impressive new technologies to make your Web pages stand out from millions of others that exist today.

Before you start Chapter 1, you can learn many of the important assumptions and conventions that are prevalent throughout the book by reading this Introduction. It explains how this book will teach you everything you need to know about Web graphics and why it is a vital asset to your WWW library. It will also tell you what level of Web proficiency we assumed the reader would have when we wrote this book. Finally, a summary is provided of each chapter, for quick reference, as well as an explanation of the tools and programs you will be learning. You will discover why this is the best—and only book about Web graphics you'll ever need.

Welcome to *Creating Your Own Web Graphics* and enjoy reading!

What You'll Learn in This Book

As the title of this book suggests, you bought it to learn all about creating graphics specifically for use on your Web pages. Listed below are several important concepts that you will learn while reading this book. They are all important in understanding exactly how graphics can enhance your Web site and should be reviewed. The following topics will be covered:

- **How to Make Quality Graphics**

    Just about anyone can learn to create simple images for a Web page, but making really good graphics is often more difficult. You'll learn what constitutes a high quality graphic and how easy-to-use tools can enhance even your best results.

- **Performance**

    To see colorful graphics, Web browsers have to download each image one at a time. Cutting this required download time greatly improves the usability of your Web page because the download performance increases. You'll learn several techniques that make downloading graphics much speedier.

- **Usability**

    Sometimes images serve dual purposes for your site. Besides the obvious intention of making your Web page look pretty, you may want them to serve as navigational or organizational tools, or even to add interactive animation. You'll learn how to make images work on your Web site as image maps, icons, and more.

Practicality is its Own Virtue

In this book, you'll learn how to deal with the practical issues that arise whenever you try to create graphics and add them to your Web pages. You will have to decide what type of graphics to use, what colors they should be, and how to keep their file size as small as possible.

We will not waste your time talking about obscure issues such as hue saturation, or worrying about all 16.8 million colors you can paint with. Instead, you'll find this book a practical guide to making Web graphics. This book will help you achieve all of your image-related goals in a manner easy to understand and fun to read.

Who is This Book For?

To get the most out of this book, you will have spent enough time browsing on the World Wide Web to understand some of the basic mechanics involved in creating a Web page. You should be familiar with basic HTML tags and want to learn advanced, in-depth information about working specifically with graphics on your page(s). In general, this book is geared towards the average Web browser who wants to harness some of the power of Web graphics, and for Webmasters, advanced Web developers who want to learn some of the finer intricacies of exciting and interactive Web graphics.

We've tried to gear the topics so that even new Web developers will be able to learn all about Web graphics. But, in general, knowing how the Web works and how to create a simple Web page will make it easier to read and understand this book.

The following are a couple of assumptions we made about your skill level while writing, organizing, and putting together this book. With these assumptions in mind, we tried to make this book as useful as possible without boring you with pointless details.

- **You're a Web User**—You should already be connected to the WWW at home, work, or school and understand how to use Netscape (or another browser) to comfortably surf from one site on the Internet to another.

- **You Can Build Web Pages**—This book focuses on creating and using graphics on a Web page. This book isn't an HTML reference, although we talk about many image-related HTML tags. For a more complete guide to creating Web pages, check out *Creating and Enhancing Your Netscape Web Pages, Bestseller Edition*, written by me, Andy Shafran, and available from Que. Advanced readers may want to explore *Special Edition Using HTML* by Tom Savola, or for a more picturesque guide to HTML, see *HTML Visual Quick Reference* by Dean Scharf, also published by Que.

- **You Want to Learn**—This book has been carefully planned and laid out in a way that is most useful and efficient for learning Web graphics. Working with graphics can sometimes be challenging—particularly when working with advanced options and features. However, your desire to learn graphics will make understanding even the trickiest tasks a breeze.

- **You're Running a Version of Windows**—Paint Shop Pro is only available for the PC platform. Other software products are available for

MAC users, but are not covered here. Additionally, you should be familiar with installing and running programs on your own computer.

What This Book is Not

If we were to write the definitive work on everything there is to know about Web graphics, you'd be purchasing a book 2,500 pages or more, which would be extremely boring. Rather than swamp you with comprehensive details and information about making and using Web graphics, this book describes practical and useful information for creating images.

Keep in mind that this book is geared to teach all levels of users how to build and incorporate graphics into their Web pages. While this book shows you all the finer points of using graphics efficiently and effectively on the WWW, it will not make you a professional artist or graphics designer. The focus is primarily on the regular Web developer who wants to learn how performance and advanced graphics features can truly enhance their Web page.

How This Book Helps You Create Your Home Page

In general, this book is intended to be read in the order it is written, as the subjects are presented from the easiest first, to the hardest last. It starts off with basic generalities that everyone should know when using graphics on the Web and then focuses on specific subject areas.

Feel free to use this book as a reference, or read it straight through. Remember that some chapters build on each other; but most subjects are self-contained and organized logically in the order that you're likely to need them.

For your convenience, the book is split into four sections, each containing two to four chapters. Following are listed the sections of the book along with a brief description of each chapter contained in it.

Part I: Web Graphics Basics

Part I introduces several concepts that are important to understanding Web graphics. Chapter 1, "A Web Crawler's Beginning," demonstrates how crucial graphics are to a Web page. In this chapter, I also describe the major graphical file types you will encounter and I review the basic HTML tags used when adding graphics and images to your Web page.

Chapter 2, "Using and Installing Paint Shop Pro," discusses the best software utility available for creating and working with graphics: Paint Shop Pro. I'll show you how to install a shareware version of Paint Shop Pro, using the CD-ROM included with this book, and then give you a quick tour of some basic Paint Shop Pro features that you will use regularly.

Part II: Making Great Images

Once you get your feet wet with Part I, you will start building and working with some actual images in Part II. Chapter 3, "Creating Simple Graphics," focuses on using the Paint Shop Pro drawing tools to make simple but useful graphics in both color and black-and-white. You will learn when to use each drawing tool within Paint Shop Pro and how to save your images into the different graphical formats.

There are already millions upon millions of pictures, photographs, and drawings available for you to use on your Web page. Rather than make your own graphics from scratch, Chapter 4, "Working with Existing Images," instructs you where you can find graphics that already exist. Chapter 4 also demonstrates how you can use Paint Shop Pro to modify graphics to fit your needs.

If you want to create graphics using your own photos, Chapter 5, "Scanning and Enhancing Photos," describes the process of scanning photographs and drawings into the computer to use on your Web site. Chapter 5 discusses what type of scanner to use, how the scanner works with Paint Shop Pro, and then walks you through the whole scanning process.

Finally, Chapter 6, "Filters, Deformations, and Special Effects," describes how to use several advanced Paint Shop Pro techniques to make your simple graphics look cool. You will learn all about Paint Shop Pro's special effects and image deformation functions, as well as how to change your graphics' colors and hues.

Part III: Advanced Image Techniques

Part III builds on what you learn in Parts I and II and explains how to incorporate several advanced image techniques into a Web page to enhance your page's appearance and performance. Chapter 7, "Making Your Graphics Lean," describes many different ways in which you can trim down your graphic's file size. Any one of these techniques will significantly improve performance for visitors who stop by your site. Lengthy download time for your graphics is the biggest adversary to creating a user-friendly Web page. You need to keep your files small, lean, and efficient.

Chapter 8, "The Black-and-White Alternative," discusses in-depth the advantages and disadvantages of using black-and-white images on your Web pages instead of color. You will see how Paint Shop Pro facilitates the conversion of color graphics to black-and-white and vice versa. Also, you will find out how to use a little known HTML keyword, which enables you to use both color and black-and-white images on a single page to improve effective download time for a Web page.

In Chapter 9, "Creating Transparent GIFs," a popular GIF feature that changes an image's appearance on a Web page is discussed. By making the background color of an image transparent, the image blends in harmoniously when placed on a Web page that uses many colors and background graphics.

In Chapter 10, "Moving Graphics: GIF Animation," you learn how to save multiple graphics into a single GIF file that loads and runs as a true animation in Netscape and Microsoft Internet Explorer.

Part IV: Practical Use of Images on Your Web Pages

In Part IV, the final part of this book, you will be shown how to integrate all the concepts previously covered in the book. Chapter 11, "Creating Titles, Buttons, and Bars with Paint Shop Pro," teaches you how to create color buttons to replace bulleted list items in HTML. Additionally, you will be taught how to use buttons to link Web pages to one another.

Chapter 12, "Web Graphics as Image Maps," shows you how to define different areas of an image to link to different HTML pages on the WWW. Through the use of an additional software tool called MapThis!, creating image maps is a simple and effective way of making your graphics serve as navigational maps to other spots on the Web.

To make your Web page complete, Chapter 13, "Backgrounds and Creative Layouts," discusses an extremely popular topic—using graphics in the background of a Web page. By remaining in the background, your graphics appear behind all the other images and text on your Web page. This enables you to change the style of any page just by updating the background graphic.

Finally, Chapter 14, "HTML Tips for Web Images," discusses important features of Hypertext Markup Language that affect how graphics appear on your site. This chapter introduces you to many advanced HTML tips and Web techniques that'll come in handy when creating Web sites.

Part V: Appendixes

At the end of this book are two Appendixes which contain some additional information you will find useful. Appendix A, "Graphical Resources on the Web," lists several spots on the WWW you'll want to check out to learn more about using images on your Web pages. Many sites listed in this book, as well as several others of general information, can be found in Appendix A.

Finally, Appendix B, "What's on the CD-ROM," describes the tools, graphics, and utilities that are included on the CD-ROM, contained in the back of this book.

What's on the CD-ROM?

The CD-ROM is chock full of important and useful files for creating and using your own Web graphics. On the CD-ROM, you'll find literally hundreds of different images and pictures that you can use immediately on your Web pages. The CD-ROM also contains the software tools discussed throughout the book.

Additionally, many of the samples and examples in the book are included so you can see them in color for yourself. You'll even find a vast array of general Web tools that will aid you in creating your own Web page tools, such as Web editors, multimedia clips, external WWW helper applications, and some Netscape plug-ins.

Tools and Programs Used in this Book

This book focuses on using existing programs to create and use your own graphics. Much like an artist uses a paintbrush, canvas, and palette, you'll be using several computer programs to make your own graphics. This section introduces you to the main tools that are talked about throughout this book—all of which are included on the CD-ROM.

Paint Shop Pro

Paint Shop Pro contains all the tools you'll ever need for creating, manipulating, converting, re-sizing, cropping, coloring, cutting, and transforming your Web graphics. Like a Swiss army knife, Paint Shop Pro always comes in handy when you need to make some type of change or adjustment to a graphic.

We will reference and use Paint Shop Pro (PSP) throughout this book. Check out Chapter 1, "A Web Crawler's Beginning," for more detailed information about installing and using Paint Shop Pro on your computer.

Graphics Construction Set

The Graphics Construction Set is another image management and creation tool that many people like to use. It does not compare with the flexibility and ease of use that Paint Shop Pro offers, except in the area of creating GIF animation. We'll use the Graphics Construction Set in Chapter 10, "Moving-Graphics: GIF Animation," to learn how to combine a set of images into one big file that will appear as an animation in your Web browser (Netscape or Internet Explorer).

Map This!

Another utility we'll be using is Map This!—the world's premier image map creation tool. Map This! enables you to take an existing image and draw different sections on it that will link to separate HTML files. Then Map This! creates all the HTML code required to add the image map to your Web page—with practically no hard work on your part. We'll use Map This! in Chapter 12, "Web Graphics as Image Maps."

Conventions Used in This Book

As you read through the book, you will find that several different conventions are used to highlight specific types of information that you'll want to keep an eye out for:

- All HTML codes and tags will appear in FULL MONOSPACE CAPS. This is so you can tell the difference between text that appears on-screen and text that tells Netscape what to do. Netscape doesn't care whether your HTML tags are in full caps.

- In addition, all URLs are displayed in **boldface**. You can type them directly into your Netscape window and go directly to the site referenced.

Besides these standard textual conventions, several different icons are also used throughout this book.

On the CD-ROM

You'll find the files, tools, references, and examples designated with this icon included on the CD-ROM enclosed in the back of this book. Check out Appendix B for more information on what is contained on the CD-ROM.

Tip

Text formatted in this manner offers extra information that is related to the issue being discussed. You'll find personal anecdotes and experiences, specific design techniques, and general information extras in these boxes.

Caution

Actions and commands that could make irreversible changes to your files, or potentially cause problems in the future, are displayed in this manner. Also included are possible security concerns. Make sure you read this text carefully as it could have important information that directly affects enhancing your Web page.

Note

Notes present interesting or useful information that isn't necessarily essential to the discussion. A note provides additional information that may help you avoid problems, or offers advice that relates to the topic.

Keeping the Book's Content Current

The World Wide Web and the Internet are constantly evolving. Keeping information current and relevant can sometimes be difficult when new technologies and innovations are always being introduced. Realizing this, I (Andy Shafran) have devoted a significant amount of time to building and maintaining a comprehensive Web site that keeps you, the reader of this book, informed and current. On this Web site, I'll post corrections to the book, keep a list of new and important references that are useful to readers, and add new cutting edge information that becomes available after the publication date of this book. You might learn about a new image format, a new utility that makes creating images easier, or a better way to build animation.

You'll also be able to leave your comments about the book and how you liked it. I'll keep this site current and you may want to visit it often. I think you'll find it an excellent additional value to the purchase of this book. My job as the author doesn't stop when this book gets published; through my Web site, I'll try to keep you appraised of the latest Web graphics innovations available.

Stop by the book's home page at **http://www.shafran.com/graphics**. Or, if you'd like to send me e-mail directly, I'd love to hear from you. Your input and comments are critical to making sure this book covers all the right information in an easy-to-use manner. Send mail to me at **andy@shafran.com**. ❖

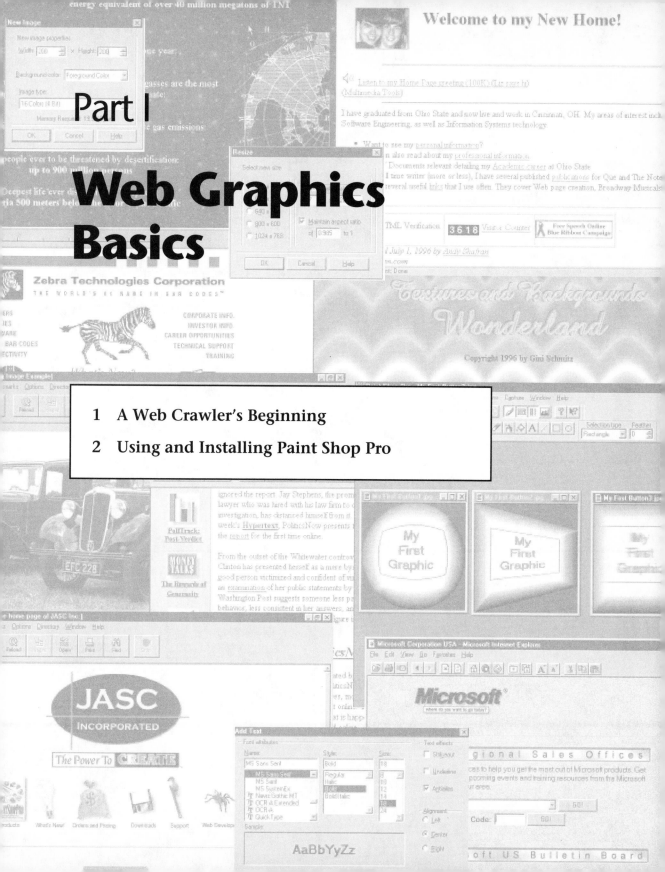

Part I

Web Graphics Basics

1   A Web Crawler's Beginning

2   Using and Installing Paint Shop Pro

CHAPTER 1

A Web Crawler's Beginning

Approximately one hundred and twenty years ago when the telephone was invented, nobody could imagine the concept of real time conversations with people from all over the city, let alone the world. People were still relying on the pony express and the telegraph to exchange communications with one another. Terms such as "telephone operator," "dial tone,"and "cordless telephone" had yet to be invented.

Soon after its invention, the telephone literally revolutionized the communications industry—and the world. Today, a new type of burgeoning technology—the Internet—is introducing completely new communications concepts that once again are revolutionizing the way we can communicate and visit with one another. Riding this wave of popularity is the World Wide Web (WWW), the Internet's graphical way to bounce from site to site and visit any Web page across the world, right from your own personal computer. The key to the popularity of the Web can be summed up in a single word—*graphics*. Graphics are the single most important feature for making the WWW fun to browse, highly informative, and extremely popular amongst all age groups and nationalities.

This chapter introduces you to many of the important features of graphics and demonstrates how they can be used with the World Wide Web. I'll introduce you to all sorts of terms you'll come across and explain why graphics are the linchpin in the WWW's popularity. This chapter will enable you to:

- **Understand the Web's Popularity**

  Graphics are only a part (a large part) of what makes the Web so popular. Understand the other issues surrounding the growth of this new technology.

■ **Define Web Graphics**

Before we can start creating our own images, it's important to understand exactly what a *Web graphic* is and how to create one.

■ **Decide What File Type to Use**

Web graphics come in two basic file types. Each has its own advantages and disadvantages in certain situations. Learn which one to use, and why.

■ **Review Image Placement HTML Tags**

You'll want to review this section to remember how to use the common image tags in HTML. It covers adding a simple image to a Web page and formatting it to your own specifications.

Graphics Make the Web Popular

The Internet has been around for many years. Originally it just connected universities and government computers together, but now encompasses businesses, organizations, and individuals from all over the world. Compared to the Internet's lengthy existence, the WWW has only been around for a few years. It was conceived in 1991 and the first graphical Web browser—Mosaic—was released in 1992. In 1994 Netscape was released. Since then the Internet's popularity has skyrocketed.

The WWW is a way for your computer to find and retrieve information from computers throughout the world. Using a Web browser, you can send out a request to an Internet site like **http://www.shafran.com** and get sent back a set of text files and graphics. It is up to your Web browser to assemble your whole page in the specified format. It is the ability to include graphics (as well as multimedia files like audio and video clips) that makes the Web popular. Without this ability, we'd all be browsing through an endless stream of boring text files—not very much fun!

You can add a photograph of yourself, include your company logo, or display famous works of art, all combined on a single Web page. That's what this book is all about—learning how to use cool and advanced graphics on your Web pages to make them more enjoyable to look at and more attractive for visitors to stop by. Don't worry if you aren't a professional artist, even simple graphics can drastically change the appearance of a Web page, with little effort on your part. Here's a simple example that will show you what I mean. Figure 1.1 shows a boring Web page for a fictional circus exhibit. It's not too exciting and probably doesn't pique your interest.

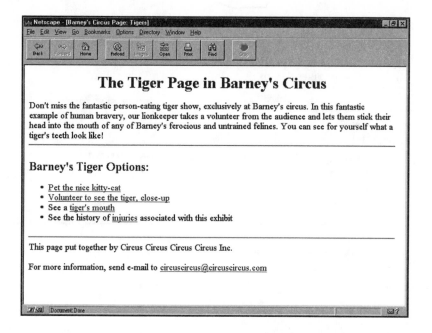

Fig. 1.1
This tiger page doesn't have a lot to offer.

By adding a single graphic to this same Web page, you get an entirely different experience (see fig. 1.2).

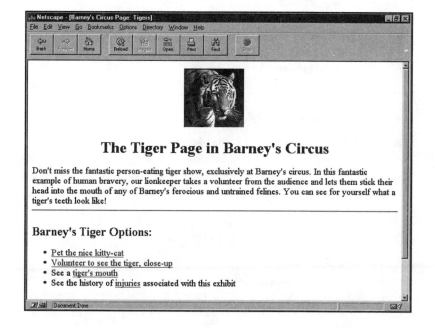

Fig. 1.2
All the text is the same, but a single graphic makes this page more attractive.

As you'll learn later in this book, the graphic in figure 1.2 was easy to use—it came from an existing collection of images found on the CD-ROM included with this book. Adding graphics is well worth your while when it comes to building your own pages—even if the graphics aren't complex.

> **NOTE**
>
> In many ways, the World Wide Web is similar to Gopher, a text-only Internet application. Like the Web, Gopher enables computers on the Internet to communicate with each other, but it can only send text files back and forth. So, using a Gopher browser, you have a lot of information at your fingertips, but it's not pretty to look at and it's not nearly as easy to use as the WWW.

Besides graphics, there are many features of the WWW that make it popular and easy to use. Below, I've compiled a list of reasons why the Web's popularity continues to rise:

- **Web Pages are Easy to Make**—Using just a few tools and the *HyperText Markup Language* (HTML), anyone can create fantastic looking pages without much difficulty. HTML is a logical formatting language—meaning you tell your Web browser how you want text and graphics to appear and the browser follows your textual commands.

- **It's Easy to Get Online**—A few years ago, connecting to the Internet was a pain in the neck. You had to learn a whole new set of technical mumbo-jumbo just to turn your computer on, let alone connect your modem, install the correct software, and worry about talking to the Internet. Nowadays, computers are much easier to use and many companies make their livelihood connecting individuals and businesses to the Web in a user-friendly manner.

- **A Lot of Information is Available**—With over 20 million Web pages in existence (that number is constantly rising), there is literally a spot for everyone and every interest on the WWW. All hobbies, professions, sports, lifestyles, and issues have their own dedicated Web site.

What are Web Graphics?

Since this book is all about Web graphics, it's important to get a handle on what graphics actually are and how graphics can be created specifically for use on the Web. Simply put, *Web Graphics* are computer saved images that are created and optimized specifically to work on a Web page. Working in conjunction with special HTML tags (which I'll talk about later this chapter), graphics can be added to any Web page in a matter of moments. However, they have to be saved in a certain format to work properly with popular Web browsers such as Netscape and Internet Explorer.

This section introduces you to three major categories of graphics that you'll encounter when exploring the Web. Each of them has its own specific traits and purpose for being included on a Web page.

Icons

The most common type of graphics you'll come across is icons. Icons are small graphics that are used to graphically represent another command or action. On the WWW, icons are often linked to other Web pages instead of regular text, serving as a graphical way to connect pages to one another. In general, icons fulfill a double duty: they enhance the appearance of a Web site and they guide visitors from one page to another. An example of how icons are used at *Politics Now* (**http://www.politicsnow.com**), an online resource for all things political, is shown in figure 1.3. Notice how they use a graph icon to represent polling data and information; a big dollar sign to link to money related issues; a voter's checkbox to link to a section where you can vote on issues online; and my favorite, a small envelope to represent sending e-mail as feedback.

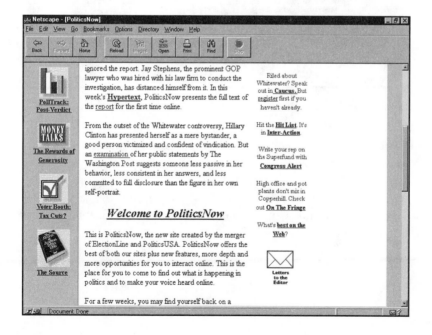

Fig. 1.3
These icons are particularly insightful and useful to visitors who stop by.

Photographs and Pictures

Most personal Web pages usually have some sort of photograph or picture included on them. For example, on my home page you can find one of my personal photographs (see fig. 1.4). To get this and similar photographs on my Web page, I had to scan them into my computer and then add the HTML to my Web page (see Chapter 5, "Scanning and Enhancing Photos"). Using Paint Shop Pro, you can control the exact size of the picture, cut away extra parts of the photo (called cropping), and even change the colors.

Here's my picture!

Fig. 1.4
You'll probably want to add a photograph of yourself to your own Web page.

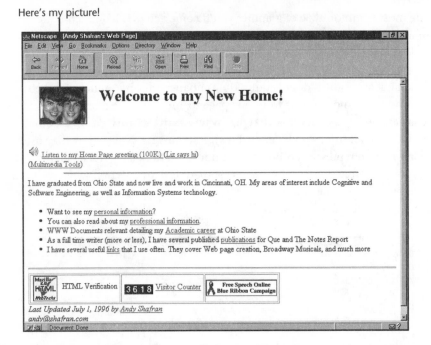

Besides adding simple photographs to Web pages, many sites choose to include custom created logos or pictures that reflect the theme of their site. For example, the Netscape home page (**http://home.netscape.com**) has a banner graphic that appears along the top of the page (see fig. 1.5). You'll learn more about creating banners and custom graphics in Chapter 3, "Creating Simple Graphics."

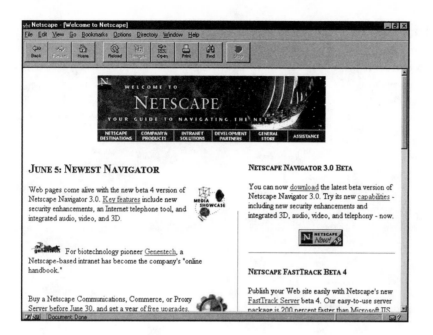

Fig. 1.5
The Netscape banner is an attractive welcoming graphic.

Web Graphics Basics

Background Graphics

Another common way to use graphics on a Web page is to add them to the background, behind the text and information that normally appear on your site. The effect is like placing a placemat beneath your plate. You can see the full plate and only that part of the background that isn't covered by the plate.

Background graphics are common tools for really adding life to Web pages. You can create and use a variety of background graphics to depict different designs, colors, and styles for your Web site. I've included literally hundreds of background images, ready to use, on the CD-ROM included with this book. Chapter 13, "Backgrounds and Creative Layouts," steps you through making your own images from scratch and shows you in more detail how they work. Figure 1.6 shows a Microsoft web page (**http://www.microsoft.com/usa**) that has a background graphic loaded behind it. Notice how the background adds texture to the normally white looking computer screen, thus adding some personality to this Web site.

Fig. 1.6
Background
graphics sit behind
text on a Web
page.

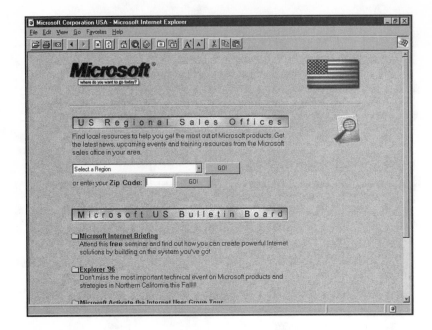

Understanding Different Web Image Types

As you can probably imagine, all images aren't necessarily saved in the same image format. Just like there are different types of graphics you can use on your Web page, there are also many different types of graphics formats that can be selected when using images on your Web pages. Graphics are saved on a computer in a standard file format so that all programs can view and manipulate them. There are literally dozens of different standards which dictate how graphics should be saved and stored on a computer disk. Most Web browsers, however, only recognize two standard graphical formats—GIF and JPEG.

In this section, I'll talk about these two popular image formats, as well as a newer format—PNG, and I will introduce you to ways you can include graphics of other formats onto your Web page.

NOTE

Although there are many different standards, most differences in the graphical formats center around file compression. When a graphic is saved onto the computer, it is transformed into a whole bunch of 1's and 0's—binary format, the language computers communicate in.

Some graphics formats simply write all of the 1's and 0's into a big file. This results in bigger files, but the computer doesn't have to work very hard to translate the binary numbers into your picture. Unfortunately, images of this type tend to have a very large file size, often taking hundreds of bytes on your computer for an image that appears very small on the computer screen.

Other formats use different methods for saving binary numbers, which result in smaller files. Using compression techniques, your computer might replace a repeating series of binary numbers with a single smaller number, resulting in a smaller file size. While you end up with smaller files, your computer tends to take a few extra moments to decompress your images before displaying them on the screen.

Most of the different formats are some combination of performance, file size, and compression techniques. It's important, though, to realize that a single graphic can be saved in many different graphics formats and each format will result in a different file size, or even quality of picture.

GIF

The most popular type of image you'll run into on the WWW is the GIF (Graphical Interchange Format). This file type was pioneered by CompuServe to provide information in a standard graphical format for its customers. GIF set an image standard nearly 10 years ago and was the first file type supported by the WWW.

The GIF image format uses a popular compression algorithm called Lempel-Ziv-Welsh, the easiest and most efficient way to compress files into the smallest possible size. The Lempel-Ziv-Welsh algorithm is the equivalent of stuffing all of your clothes into a suitcase and filling it to its limits. You are left with a reasonably sized file that is universally recognized on all computers and by almost every graphics program. By far, GIFs are the most popular image file type in the world. By compressing, and subsequently decompressing (unpacking your suitcase) your file, you don't lose any detail, all of the colors remain the same, and your image never changes its appearance from its original look. A few years ago, the developer of the GIF algorithm (CompuServe) discovered that it was using a patented formula for compression. Unisys, the patent owner, decided to enforce its ownership, causing professional graphics software developers to pay a royalty to support the GIF image type. This patent dispute brought two other image formats into the limelight—JPEG and PNG.

The drawback to using GIFs is that they are not particularly efficient when you are saving photographs, or any other images that have many different colors and shades in them. GIFs perform best when there's only a handful of different colors to display. If you scan a photograph into your computer and save it as a GIF, you'll be surprised how large your file might end up—particularly when compared to the other major WWW graphics standard—JPEG. Additionally, GIF images can only have a maximum of 256 different colors in any one file.

JPEG

A more recent development, JPEG stands for Joint Photographic Experts Group. Also commonly known as JPG, this format was developed to be significantly more efficient than GIFs in several circumstances, especially larger images with many colors. JPEG uses a more advanced compression algorithm than the GIF format, and this algorithm shrinks your graphics into a smaller file.

The JPEG compression algorithm works much differently than the GIF format but also has some drawbacks. GIFs take the original image and shrink it as tight as it can be shrunk. JPEGs use a "lossy" algorithm, which means there is some loss of detail when saving and looking at images in this format. It's the equivalent of having somebody take out a few items of clothing from your packed suitcase in order to make your suitcase smaller. As a result, JPEG files often are not as detailed as GIF images, but can offer as much as a 35% improvement in file size and compression.

Don't worry too much about losing detail during compression. When saving your JPEG, you get the option of indicating how much detail the JPEG can lose. The higher the detail, the larger the file size. At the highest quality of detail, JPEGs are about equal to GIFs as far as file size goes. You'll learn how to control these characteristics in Chapter 3, "Creating Simple Graphics."

Additionally, since JPEGs were built to handle photographs, they are much more efficient at handling lots of colors and shades. This means that JPEG files tend to be smaller and, consequently, they download quicker when browsing the WWW. This makes JPEG images more attractive to Web developers because visitors can see their images much quicker. The JPG image format supports up to 16.7 million different colors—significantly more than GIF files.

Most Web browsers support both JPEG and GIF file formats interchangeably. Both can be optimized to be more efficient when using the Web. See Chapter 7, "Making Your Graphics Lean," for more details on common performance enhancements.

PNG

Recently, a new type of image has gained popularity because of the legal issues that surrounded the use of GIFs. This new type of image is called Portable Network Graphics—PNG (pronounced *ping)*, and is slowly becoming more widely supported on the WWW.

PNG graphics offer a compromise between the GIF and JPEG formats. PNGs offer enhanced compression of images and can handle multiple colors and larger pictures well, without using a "lossy" compression scheme. PNGs represent a significant file size savings over the GIF format, but are still eclipsed by JPEG images in the file size category. PNG graphics can perform all of the same advanced tricks that you find in both JPEG and GIF file formats, making PNGs ideal vehicles for displaying graphics on the Web.

For more information on the PNG graphics type, visit my favorite PNG information center at **http://quest.jpl.nasa.gov/PNG/**. The latest version of Paint Shop Pro (Version 4.0), included on your CD-ROM, now offers full file support for the new PNG format.

> ### Note
>
> Rather than bore you with all the details, let me summarize why the PNG format was developed. Several years ago, CompuServe created GIF as its international image standard. Since CompuServe was a pioneer in the on-line world, many other companies followed its lead and began supporting the GIF standard.
>
> A few years ago, Unisys realized that CompuServe had used some of its patented computer code when developing the GIF format and decided to enforce its patent. Not wanting to be dependent on another company's patent, CompuServe (along with other independent developers on the Internet) introduced PNG as its community-wide graphics format standard. PNG has started to develop significant popularity because of its advantages over the GIF file format—such as not having to tussle with Unisys over who owns the PNG format. Nowadays, GIF and JPEG are still the first choice of developers, but PNG graphics are quickly becoming a popular alternative.

Other Popular Formats

Many other popular graphical formats are still commonly used for other applications. Don't despair if you have a set of images in another file format but want to add them to your Web pages. You have two popular options that let you use virtually any image format imaginable on your Web page:

■ **Convert to GIF or JPEG**

Using Paint Shop Pro, you can convert an image from virtually any other type into the popular GIF or JPEG file types. In Chapter 4, "Working With Existing Images," I show you how to convert graphics back and forth between file types and formats—don't worry it is very easy. That way, you can use the newly converted GIF or JPEG in your Web page just like normal.

■ **Use a Netscape Plug-in**

New Web browser technology allows you to plug-in special programs that expand the type of files you can use on your Web pages. This new technology is called plug-ins, which work directly with Netscape, the world's most popular Web browser. Using a special plug-in, you can add images of virtually any format to your Web page, without the worry of converting them from one format to another. Visit **http://www. ct.ebt.com/figinline/download.html** to learn more about FIGLeaf Inline, an exciting plug-in for Netscape. For more information on using plug-ins on your Web page, see *Enhancing Netscape Web Pages*, also published by Que.

Basic HTML Tags for Adding Images

Although this book doesn't focus on learning all the HTML tags required for building Web pages, there are several chapters which show you how to use special HTML options to increase your image's performance or appearance. It's important to have a general grasp of HTML before you start using this book, otherwise some of the tactics and techniques might be confusing or difficult to understand.

To help you out, I've included a brief review of the HTML tags required to add images to your Web page. I'll show you how to place an image on your Web page and give you some general tips to remember.

The first step is for you to obtain the image you want to use—in GIF or JPG format. Take your image and save it in the same file subdirectory as your

HTML file. Next, add the <IMG> tag to your HTML listing. If your image file name is AIRPLANE.GIF, then you add the following tag:

    <IMG SRC="AIRPLANE.GIF">

Similarly, if you had a JPG file—AIRPLANE.JPG, you'd just use this new file name instead:

    <IMG SRC="AIRPLANE.JPG">

Your Web Browser then adds the image to the Web page and displays it when you load that page. Figure 1.7 shows Netscape displaying my airplane image. Make sure you use the complete path when adding your image with HTML. For example, if this image was found in a subdirectory named PICTURES, I'd use the following tag instead:

    <IMG SRC="PICTURES\AIRPLANE.JPG">

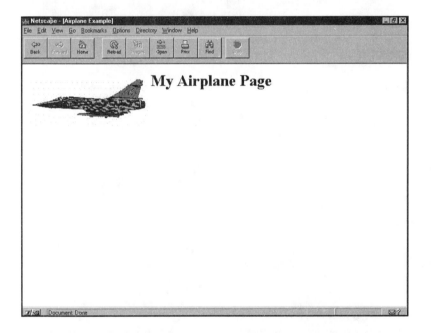

Fig. 1.7
This page is really going to fly now that it has images!

Setting Your Image Alignment

You have considerable control over how your image appears onscreen. One of the best ways to customize the appearance of your image is to set its placement alignment. You can have it line up on the left hand side of the screen (the default setting), center it, or right justify it—your choice.

All you have to do is add the ALIGN= keyword to your <IMG> tag. To center your image on the screen, you use the following tag:

```
<IMG SRC="AIRPLANE.JPG" ALIGN=CENTER>
```

Similarly, you can set the alignment to the left hand side:

```
<IMG SRC="AIRPLANE.JPG" ALIGN=LEFT >
```

or on the right hand side:

```
<IMG SRC="AIRPLANE.JPG" ALIGN=RIGHT >
```

To see how Netscape would display all three of these alignment options, take a look at figure 1.8.

Fig. 1.8
Many alignment options are at your fingertips.

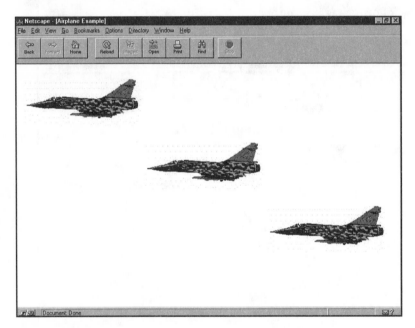

Providing Alternative Text

One of the most important enhancements you can make to your image is likely never to be seen. I'm talking about adding alternative text that appears whenever a visitor stops by who doesn't have the capability, or desire, to download and display the images you added to your Web page.

Since downloading images can sometimes take quite a while, some people instruct their Web browser *not* to automatically download and display Web images when browsing. Instead, they see a short blurb of text provided as an alternative to the image, which describes the image they could be seeing. Additionally, some Web browsers might not support all popular image types. Although JPG and GIF are common standards, new formats such as PNG, or older non-graphical browsers, might not be able to recognize your image. In fact, some WWW browsers, like Lynx, don't support graphics at all and designing a Web site that is accessible to these users isn't such a bad idea.

> **TIP**
>
> To tell Netscape *not* to automatically load images for every Web page it visits, choose Options, Auto Load Images from the menu bar. Choose it again to toggle image loading back on.

It's important to accommodate these alternative situations so that your Web page is accessible to everyone. Adding alternative text is easy: just add the ALT keyword to your image tag. So, to add a small phrase to my airplane image, I use the following tag:

```
<IMG SRC="AIRPLANE.JPG" ALT="An Airplane">
```

To see how the image appears when I browse with Netscape and the image loading is turned off, look at figure 1.9.

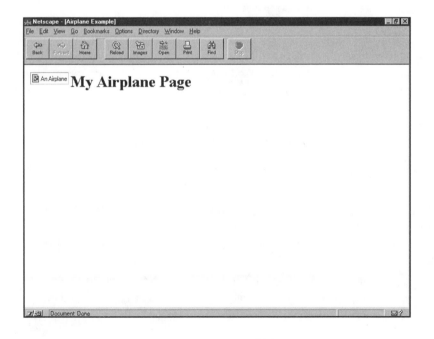

Fig. 1.9
Web pages look different when images aren't loaded.

One common practice employed when using alternative text is to add an exciting, informative phrase that makes visitors *want* to download your fully graphical page. Instead of the boring phrase I used above, try this tag instead:

```
<IMG SRC="AIRPLANE.JPG" ALT="A sizzling fighter jet! ">
```

Which description sounds more interesting to you?

In general, try to keep your Alternative text short and to the point, without using too many extraneous words.

Using Images as Links

Many people choose to use images simply as decoration on their Web page—they just want to add more life and color to an otherwise boring site. On the other hand, it is also common to link your Web site to another HTML file on the Web. This allows visitors to see your image like normal, but when they click their mouse on it, they are brought to another site.

Linking Web pages together requires using the <A HREF> tag, which stands for Hypertext Reference. You add a hypertext link to another page on the WWW by specifying its unique address, or URL (Universal Resource Locator). All this does is specify your image as the link. So, to link my airplane image to **http://www.airplane.com**, I'd use the following text:

```
<A HREF="http://www.airplane.com">
<IMG SRC="AIRPLANE.JPG" ALT="A sizzling fighter jet! ">
</A>
```

The Web browser displays the image in a similar fashion, but now a blue border appears around the image, indicating that it is now "hot," or linked to another site. When your mouse moves over the image, the pointer turns into a miniature hand and the linked Web address appears in the status bar at the bottom of the screen. Figure 1.10 shows how a linked image appears in Netscape.

You'll often find yourself linking-up Web graphics between two different pages.

Adding clickable images to Web pages is just the beginning. One advanced way you can use images is to link different parts of an image to different Web addresses. This technology, called "image maps," enables you to specify as many different areas of an image as you like. I'll step you through the whole process of creating image maps in Chapter 12, "Web Graphics as Image Maps." Figure 1.11 shows an example of the Cover Girl Web site (**http://www.covergirl.com**) using clickable image maps.

Hand

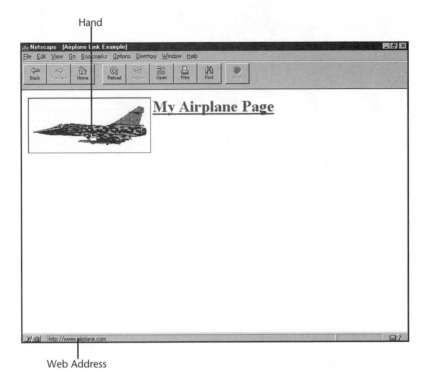

Web Address

Fig. 1.10
This airplane is now linked to another Web site.

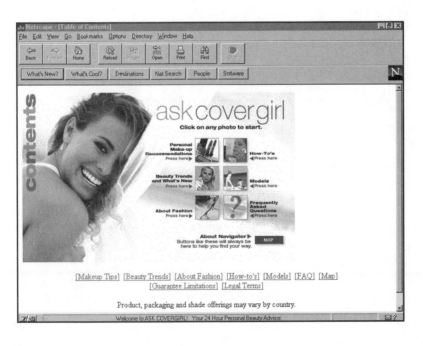

Fig. 1.11
This interactive Web site uses great images.

Web Graphics Basics

CHAPTER 2

Using and Installing Paint Shop Pro

When building a house, a construction worker uses a hammer, screwdrivers, and other related building tools. When making dinner, a chef uses the oven, pots and pans, and mixing bowls. Similarly, when creating your own graphics, you'll want to get your hands on tools that are optimized for drawing and manipulating images.

Many different tools exist to help you create your own Web graphics, but one stands out from all the rest: Paint Shop Pro. Paint Shop Pro is the best all-around computer program for everything that has to do with graphics. An award-winning piece of shareware software, Paint Shop Pro gives you 30 days to evaluate the program before deciding whether to purchase it for a fee of $54.00.

In this chapter, you will learn all about installing and using Paint Shop Pro for yourself. I've included a version of Paint Shop Pro on the CD-ROM accompanying this book so that you will have the tools needed to quickly start making your own images. I'll even take you on a quick tour of some of Paint Shop Pro's most impressive and useful features so that you can quickly become a great graphics developer. This chapter will enable you to:

■ **Understand Paint Shop Pro**

Paint Shop Pro is a robust and impressive graphics package available for Windows users. Learn what its capabilities and limitations are for you, the Web graphic developer.

■ **Install Paint Shop Pro**

Software is useless to you if it isn't installed on your computer. I'll show you how to set up PSP quickly and without hassle.

- **Tour Common Features**

  There are a handful of commands and icons that every Paint Shop Pro user should be aware of, and I'll lead you through each of them.

- **Empower your Graphics**

  Paint Shop Pro gives you unparalleled flexibility when manipulating and customizing the appearance of your graphics. Learn how to harness that power when making your own Web images.

- **Get Some Help**

  Use the impressive and robust Paint Shop Pro Help System to get all of your common questions answered.

What is PSP?

Paint Shop Pro (PSP) is a professional-caliber graphics program put together and released by JASC Inc. Paint Shop Pro provides truly impressive graphics file manipulation, editing, and conversion into over 30 different file types, with an easy-to-use and intuitive interface. JASC (**http://www.jasc.com**) is a small software company located in Minnesota which specializes in making powerful graphics and graphics management software for Windows based computers. Founded in 1991, JASC is the leader in graphics file technology and has a corner on the personal graphics utility market.

Paint Shop Pro offers all of the power and flexibility of a high-end graphics program—such as Adobe Photoshop—but with a smaller price tag. As shareware software, you can run PSP for up to 30 days before you will be required to pay $69.00 to continue running it on your computer. Adobe Photoshop, on the other hand, will cost you hundreds of dollars, and doesn't offer nearly the same value for the typical home computer user.

Note

Shareware software is an important concept for computer owners to understand. Shareware is software the developer allows you to install and evaluate for a period of time before requiring you to purchase it. This "try before you buy" methodology enables you to pick and choose among software you like, instead of making you purchase a program first, only to discover it doesn't fit your needs.

Shareware software has a limited free trial period. After your trial expires, you must either delete the software from your computer or pay the registration fee to the

---

company who developed the program. If you continue to use the software after the evaluation period expires, you are guilty of pirating valuable software.

Although people don't usually get arrested for using shareware beyond its expiration date, it's not a good practice. Shareware authors spend many hours developing and marketing their product. By supporting their products, you encourage them to continue to update and release their software as shareware, for everybody to use. If you think a registration fee is too high or you don't like the software, simply don't use the program and delete it from your computer—it's that easy.

In this chapter, I talk about Paint Shop Pro, version 4.0. Created especially for Windows 95, Paint Shop Pro 4.0 is an efficient and well designed tool that all Web developers should have at their fingertips. Other versions of PSP are also available for Windows 3.1 users. Unfortuantely, a Macintosh version is not available. Whether you want to scan and save a new image, or simply change the colors on your Web page's banner, Paint Shop Pro will enable you to do virtually anything you want.

> **Note**
>
> In this book, I use Paint Shop Pro 4.0 for Windows 95. Other versions of PSP have similar capabilities, but screenshots and windows may look slightly different.

Installing Paint Shop Pro

Paint Shop Pro 4.0 can be found on the CD-ROM included in the back of this book. Insert the CD into your drive and explore it using your favorite WWW browser, such as Netscape or Internet Explorer. Versions for Windows 95 and Windows 3.1 can also be found.

On the CD

Start the installation process by running the Paint Shop Pro executable file found on the CD-ROM. After telling PSP where to install on your hard drive, all the work is taken care of by PSP. Once you finish the installation, you can run Paint Shop Pro immediately. From your Windows 95 Start menu, choose Programs | Paint Shop Pro | Paint Shop Pro 4 to start the program. You can see what Paint Shop Pro should look like when running in figure 2.1. You can now use Paint Shop Pro for 30 days, until your shareware time limit expires.

Don't fret if you don't use Windows 95. I've included an older version of Paint Shop Pro for Windows 3.1 users. Use the Windows File Manger to explore the CD-ROM—or browse with your WWW Browser.

Fig. 2.1

Paint Shop Pro looks like your standard Windows application.

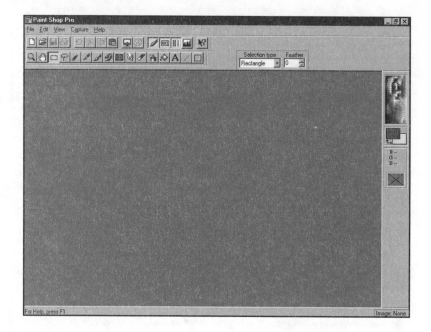

Computer software is often enhanced, with new versions coming out regularly. Since this book was published, a new version of Paint Shop Pro may have been released, with even more features and enhancements. When writing this book, I used Paint Shop Pro 4.0. Possibly, another more recent version has been released and is available for downloading for free at the JASC home page. Visit JASC at **http://www.jasc.com** to see the latest and greatest version of Paint Shop Pro available for downloading (see fig. 2.2).

While there, you might want to check out some of JASC's other graphics-related products. JASC offers a wide variety of tools for managing and creating all sorts of graphics files. You'll also find some of them on the CD-ROM included with this book. Check out Appendix B, "What's on the CD-ROM?," for a complete listing. Feel free to explore the CD to your heart's content!

Fig. 2.2
The JASC home page is the clearinghouse for everything pertaining to Paint Shop Pro.

Registering Paint Shop Pro

Once you've decided you want to register Paint Shop Pro, prepare to open your wallet. At the time of this writing, Paint Shop Pro 4.0 costs $69.00. Although this may seem like a steep price, if you are serious about creating and manipulating graphics, it's well worth it. Paint Shop Pro is the most affordable graphics program available that offers sophisticated functionality, technical support, and ease of use.

The easiest way to register Paint Shop Pro is to order it on-line at **http:// www.jasc.com/order.html**. With existing user encryption-secure techniques, you can safely charge PSP to a major credit card in a matter of moments. The PSP on-line order form is shown in figure 2.3.

> ### Caution
>
> Sending your credit card over the Internet is only secure if you are using Netscape 1.1 or better, or Internet Explorer 2.0 or better. These encryption techniques provided by Netscape and Microsoft provide for complete data encryption so that prying eyes won't be able to filch your credit card number for unsavory purposes.

Fig. 2.3

JASC makes it easy for you to order Paint Shop Pro.

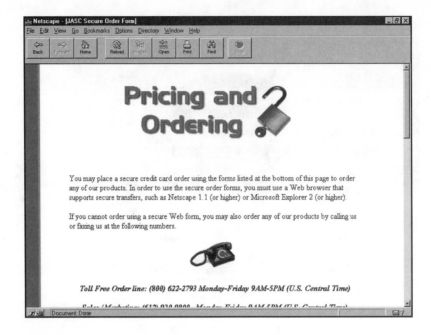

Note

If you prefer to order Paint Shop Pro the old-fashioned way (via telephone), or you don't have a secure Web browser, call 1-800-622-2793 or 612-930-9800 and you can talk directly to a sales representative.

A Quick Tour of Paint Shop Pro

Now that you have Paint Shop Pro installed and running on your computer, let's start using it and take a look around. If you are using the shareware version, each and every time you start Paint Shop Pro you will be reminded how much time you have left until the shareware license expires. Click the OK button to continue, and you will see the main Paint Shop Pro window.

As you'll quickly notice, most of the screen is blank, wide open for you to start building and creating your own Web graphics. There are several tool bars and icon sets lining the top and right hand side of your screen that you'll want to take special notice of. These icon sets, called toolbars, or palettes in Paint Shop Pro, enable you to perform many common commands at the click of your mouse button. In fact, several commands are only available through their respective icons. In this section, I'll show you each toolbar (or palette), followed by an overview of what each toolbar is used for.

Fig. 2.4
The Toolbar.

First off is the Toolbar (see fig 2.4). The Toolbar is a set of miniature icons that represent common commands you often use. Commands such as opening, closing, and viewing graphics are all accessible as an icon in the Toolbar, as well as icons that toggle on and off the Style Bar, Color Palette, and Tool Palette (discussed below). The Toolbar can be toggled on and off by choosing View | Toolbar from the Paint Shop Pro menu bar.

Fig. 2.5
The Tool Palette.

The Tool Palette contains the main set of commands that you'll use to draw, paint, and add new shapes and text to your fantastic Web images (see fig. 2.5). In the Tool Palette, you can select a rectangle, circle, or polygon to draw; you can fill in your shape with a particular color or pattern; you can select part of your image to crop or paint with a paintbrush; you can even erase bits and pieces of your image with the small icon that resembles a pencil eraser.

You'll use the Tool Palette for virtually all of your creative needs when modifying your images. The Tool Palette can be toggled on and off by choosing View | Tool Palette from the Paint Shop Pro menu bar, or by clicking the Toggle Tool Palette icon from the Toolbar (see fig. 2.4).

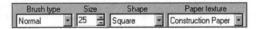

Fig. 2.6
The Style Bar.

The small set of selections in the Style Bar (see fig. 2.6) dynamically change depending on which icon in the Tool Palette (see fig. 2.5) you select. Sometimes the Style Bar is a single set of options; other times you have three or four characteristics to choose from. For example, when you click the Paint Brush icon from the Tool Palette, you have four options to choose from— Brush Type, Size, Shape, and Paper texture. These four available options are shown in figure 2.6.

Always keep an eye on what options are available in the Style Bar when you are drawing or editing a graphic. You will likely get additional flexibility with the Style Bar options, which determine how your Tool draws or makes changes to the graphic. The Style Bar can be toggled on and off by choosing View | Style Bar from the Paint Shop Pro menu bar or by clicking the Toggle Style Bar icon from the Toolbar (refer to fig. 2.4).

Fig. 2.7
The Color Palette.

Down the right-hand side of the screen you'll notice the Color Palette (see fig. 2.7). From the Color Palette, you can choose which colors you are going to draw with when adding shapes, text, or painting onto your image. Move your mouse over the vast array of colors at the top of the Color Palette. You can click any particular color to make it your current drawing color. Paint Shop Pro lets you choose from literally millions of different colors and shades to draw with.

 The Color Palette can be toggled on and off by choosing View | Color Palette from the Paint Shop Pro menu bar or by clicking on the Toggle Color Palette icon from the Toolbar.

What Can You Do With Paint Shop Pro?

Now that you are familiar with how to install Paint Shop Pro and you're finished with your quick PSP tour, let's take a few moments to learn how to use some of the most important and useful features of Paint Shop Pro.

I spend practically this whole book talking about the use of different Paint Shop Pro features for customizing a graphic, converting file formats, or building a new image from scratch. However, this section will help give you a broader overview of the types of features you can expect from Paint Shop Pro later in this book. Besides bland features such as opening and saving your images, Paint Shop Pro enables you to crop part of an image, change colors instantly, and even deform your images according to interesting characteristics.

Let's get started by creating a new image from scratch. Choose File | New from the Paint Shop Pro menu bar or click the New File icon to bring up the New Image dialog box shown in figure 2.8.

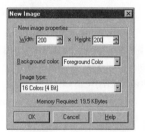

Fig. 2.8
Here's where all of your images start.

From the New Image dialog box, you can select the size of your new image in pixel coordinates. Your computer screen's height and width is measured in pixels, not inches or centimeters. I'll talk more about pixels in the next chapter, so for now enter 200 for both the height and width, click the OK button and a medium sized empty box should appear (see fig. 2.9).

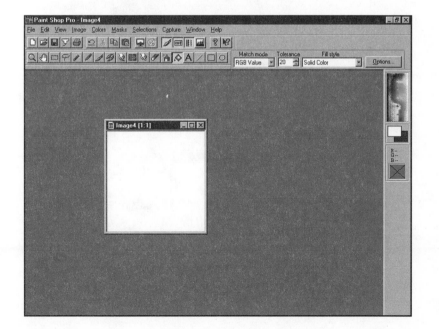

Fig. 2.9
On my screen, a 200 × 200 pixel box takes up about 1/8th of the screen.

Web Graphics Basics

Once your drawing space is ready to go, click the Rectangle icon from the Tool Palette (refer to fig. 2.5). Then select a color from the Color Palette (refer to fig. 2.7). I chose a shade of blue for my image. Now use the mouse to draw a rectangle on the screen. This is done by clicking with the left mouse button and dragging the mouse until you get a rectangle, then releasing the mouse button. A rectangle should appear.

Next, click the Text icon from the Tool Palette with your mouse and try picking out a different color from the Color Palette. Click inside your new image to bring up the Add Text dialog box shown in figure 2.10. Type some sample text you want to add to your image and then choose the text attributes you want to use. You can select text alignment, font, and display attributes from here. I chose a font that appears in **boldface** and in the font size of 18 points for this example. Once finished, click the OK button and your text will be added to your graphic. Click the right mouse to apply the text to your graphic. Figure 2.11 shows what your image should look like so far.

Fig. 2.10

You can control how text appears in your image here.

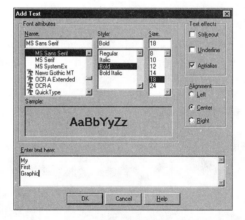

Fig. 2.11

Not too complicated, this image is just the beginning of what PSP offers.

Just to give you a taste of what to expect in this book, let's try something cool with this simple graphic. Choose Colors | Increase Color Depth | 16 Million Colors from the menu bar. You just made 16 million colors available for you to use in your image—more than you can use on your own image, but just enough for Paint Shop Pro to do some awesome things. Now click another color from the Color Palette—I'll use a shade of green for this example. Make sure you set the new color to be in the background by selecting it with your right mouse button.

Finally, choose Image | Special Effect | Buttonize from the menu bar. In the Buttonize dialog box that appears, choose the edge size of the button you want to create (I picked 18) and click the OK button. Suddenly your image is transformed into something cool and unique. Figure 2.12 shows your new dynamic image—it looks just like a button!

Fig. 2.12
This is just the tip of the iceberg when it comes to building graphics!

Of course, you can save your image for future use. Click File | Save As from the menu bar to bring up the Save As dialog box shown in figure 2.13. Type your file name in the File Name box, and image format type in the Save As Type box, then click Save—I'll use a JPG for this example so it can be directly added to my Web pages.

Fig. 2.13
You can save your image in 30 different graphical formats.

Crop and Resize Graphics

With a sample image under your belt, you are starting to realize just how powerful Paint Shop Pro really is when it comes to using graphics for your Web page. Two features you'll find yourself using often are cropping and resizing images.

Cropping an image is the process of selecting a particular area of a picture and using only that specific area—cropping deletes everything outside of the selected area! For example, you might take a picture of a person and crop their upper body—so that you don't see their pelvis, legs, or feet. You might only have room to use part of the image, or you simply don't want the full-size image.

Caution

Be careful not to save a cropped version of an image over the original. When cropping an image and saving the results, use File | Save As to bring up the Save As dialog box and give your newly cropped image a different name.

To crop an image, click the selection tool from the Tool Palette. Click your left mouse button on the image to draw a rectangle over the part you wish to crop and keep. Then choose Image | Crop from the menu bar, and voila, your image is cropped. Now you can save your newly cropped image, or manipulate it for other uses.

Similarly, resizing an image entails changing the general size and appearance of your graphic. When you create your images, you indicate how many pixels wide and tall the image should be, but you can re-adjust these measurements at any time. Choose Image | Resize from the menu bar to bring up the Resize dialog box shown in figure 2.14.

Fig. 2.14
Images can be set to all sorts of different sizes.

You can resize your image to any of the standard, screen-size values on the left hand side of the window, or you can set your image to be a particular height and width—just like you did when creating it originally. Don't be afraid to test all sorts of different combinations, you might be surprised with the results!

> **Caution**
>
> If you are unhappy with a change you make, choose Edit | Undo from the menu bar and Paint Shop Pro quickly reverts your image back to the original size, or pre-crop state. Be aware that you cannot undo an undo command. Changes undone have to be re-applied. You can only undo the last change.

Add Cool Deformations

In the sample graphic you just created, I showed you how to add a cool special effect to your image. Buttonizing an image is one of several different styles and effects you can add to your image. One of the best new features of Paint Shop Pro is the ability to deform the appearance of your standard images to come up with something a little unique and creative. Select different deformations from the Image | Deformations menu bar selection. You can choose from nearly a dozen different deformations that Paint Shop Pro will automatically make for you, including making your image a circle or pentagon, adding a windblown appearance, or changing the angle at which your image appears.

Figure 2.15 shows three examples of deformations to my original image created earlier.

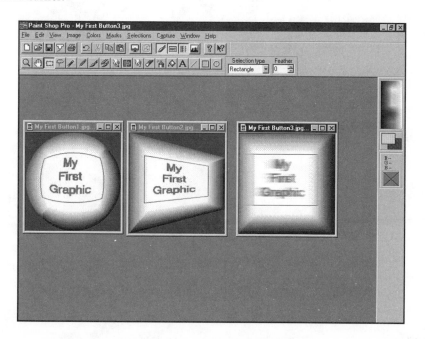

Fig. 2.15
The Deformations you're seeing are: Circle, Horizontal Perspective, and Wind.

Using Paint Shop Pro's Help System

As you read through this book, you'll find many of Paint Shop Pro's advanced features discussed in significant detail. In addition to the Paint Shop Pro manuals (which are excellently written), you'll use this book to guide you through deformations, special effects, saving and loading new images, and much more.

In addition to using this book and the reference manuals, Paint Shop Pro comes with a comprehensive and extremely useful interactive help system. Nearly any topic you can think of that is related to making or configuring images is discussed. Paint Shop Pro functionality and many tips are also discussed in the Help System.

To access the on-line interactive help, choose Help | Help Topics from the menu bar. Figure 2.16 shows the Help Index in action.

Fig. 2.16
Paint Shop Pro's Help system is a fantastic resource for creating graphics.

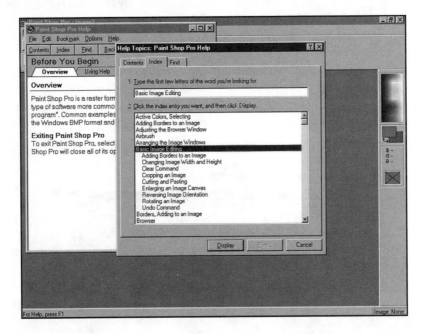

Part II

Making Great Images

3 Creating Simple Graphics

4 Working with Existing Images

5 Scanning and Enhancing Photos

6 Filters, Deformations, and Special Effects

CHAPTER 3

Creating Simple Graphics

Welcome to the second part of this book. In this chapter, you'll learn how to create actual images from scratch for your Web pages.

Paint Shop Pro is a robust graphics package that gives you all sorts of advanced flexibility when creating your own images. In this chapter, I introduce you to several of the basic Paint Shop Pro tools and show you how to draw and paint simple graphics. Using common shapes and a powerful paintbrush, you will have all the tools at your fingertips to create fantastic masterpieces of computer art. This chapter will teach you how to:

- **Create New Images**

    Making a new image isn't as easy as it seems. Understand how to decide image size and the number of necessary colors for your Web graphics.

- **Save Your Images**

    Making your images is useless unless you can save and recall them at a later date. I'll walk you through the entire process of saving a new graphic in the right format for the Web and familiarize you with all of your options for saving a graphic.

- **Understand Pixel Height and Width**

    Nothing is more critical to understanding graphics than how to control the size of your images. Learn what pixels are, how your computer measures them, and what to remember when making new images.

■ **Draw Multiple Shapes**

Ovals, lines, and rectangles are all readily available with built-in drawing tools. Understand how to draw these shapes when building an image.

■ **Use the Powerful PSP Paintbrush**

The most useful Paint Shop Pro Tool is the paintbrush. Become familiar with all of its options and nuances to choose your color, brush size, shape and texture.

Making a New Image

At this point, you've already installed Paint Shop Pro and have taken a tour of PSP using several icons and palettes that house the drawing and painting tools. Much of this book focuses on using those Paint Shop Pro tools to create and enhance the appearance of your Web graphics.

Although Paint Shop Pro has great resources and tools available, you cannot begin to draw an image with those tools and resources until you learn how to create and save a new image (graphic) as a file. Saving a new image with Paint Shop Pro is a straightforward process, but it is important to thoroughly understand your color and sizing options because they affect the amount of time it takes for visitors to download and see Web pages. In this section, I'll lead you through the process of making and saving a new image from scratch and describe your available file options.

Your first step in learning how to create and save a new graphics file is to start up Paint Shop Pro by double clicking inside the Paint Shop Pro icon that appears on your computer after installation. Alternatively, you can choose Start | Programs | Paint Shop Pro, Paint Shop Pro 4 from the Windows 95 menu bar at the bottom of your screen. Paint Shop Pro will begin with an empty desktop, ready to create cool graphics.

 Once Paint Shop Pro is loaded, choose File | New from the menu bar to bring up the New Image dialog box (see fig. 3.1). This dialog box enables you to select three important properties of your new image—size, number of colors used, and the default background color. Next, I describe each of these options and summarize the issues surrounding each of them.

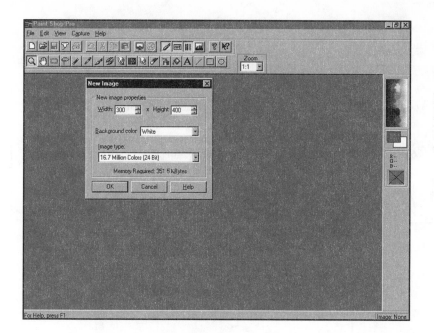

Fig. 3.1
All new images
start from this
dialog box.

Understanding Pixel Sizing

Before you can create a new image, you have to decide how large you want it
to appear on the computer screen. Deciding your image's height and width is
extremely important because it affects how Web browsers display your image,
and has direct correlation to your image's file size. Thus, your image's height
and width affect the time it takes for the image to download and be seen on
a Web page, an important metric in WWW usability. In general, you want
graphics to be as small as possible so Web browsers can see them immediately.

Your computer screen's height and width is measured in pixels—which
stands for *picture element*. For example, a standard VGA monitor can display
640 pixels across and 480 pixels vertically (640×480). Super VGA (SVGA)
resolution offers 800×600 pixel resolution, and Enhanced SVGA offers 1024
$\times$ 768 resolution and better. Pixels are little dots going across your screen that
make up the pictures and images you see.

The higher the resolution, the more information that can fit on one screen.
Thus, creating a new image that has 320×240 pixel coordinates takes up approximately half of a VGA screen, and about one-third of an Enhanced SVGA

screen. Figure 3.2 shows how these three resolutions compare with one another.

Note

In this section, I talk primarily about screen resolution characteristics for PC compatible computers. Remember that the WWW is universal in computer access and that all sorts of computers will have access to the graphics and images on your Web page. Some Macintoshes and high-powered Sun or Hewlett-Packard workstations might have significantly higher screen resolutions available at their disposal. In general, though, the PC pixel sizings are a good common denominator and should be used as a guideline when creating your Web images.

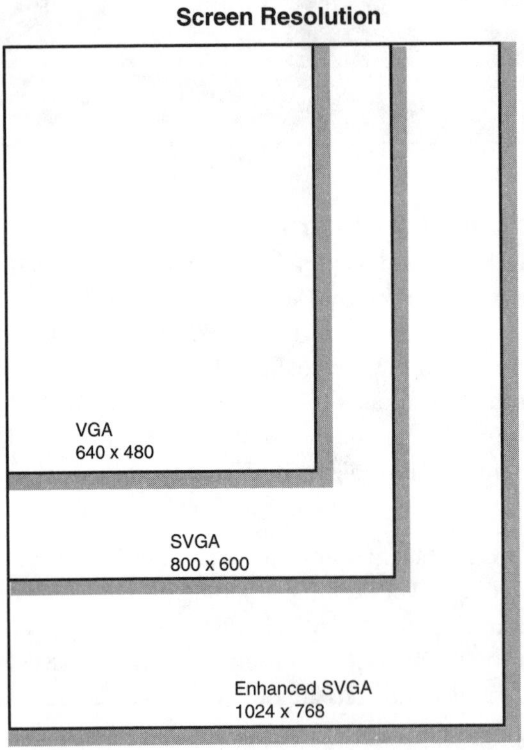

Fig. 3.2
Compare the three popular screen resolutions.

Screen Resolution

VGA
640 x 480

SVGA
800 x 600

Enhanced SVGA
1024 x 768

As a general rule, you always want to design your Web page (and, consequently, your Web images) for the lowest screen resolution. This ensures that your images can be seen by anyone who surfs the WWW without extra inconvenience or difficulty. This means you should always size your image within the 640 × 480 height and width category. In fact, to properly ensure that your images can always be seen on a Web page, no image should ever be more than 600 pixels wide and 440 pixels tall. I removed 40 pixels from each axis to ensure that the graphic can fit within Netscape's or Internet Explorer's borders.

Figures 3.3 and 3.4 show a sample headline image that is only 200 pixels tall but 750 pixels wide. Although the two images look similar, they are taken in two different screen resolutions. Figure 3.4 shows this image on a monitor that has resolution of 800 × 600. The image looks fine here. However, in figure 3.3, the image doesn't fit on my Web page with a 640 × 480 screen resolution. As a result, the image only looks good for people using higher screen resolutions. One solution is to re-size my image so that it fits on the smaller screen resolution, thus making it work for all visitors who stop by.

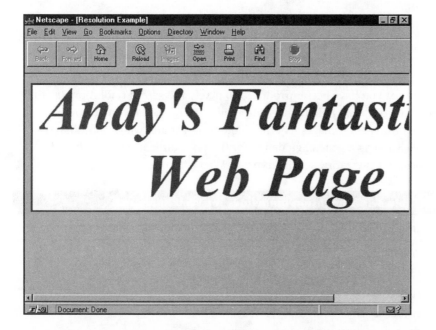

Fig. 3.3
My headline image at VGA resolution.

Tip

One strategy that many Web developers follow when using images that fit smaller screen resolutions is to center their image on the screen. By adding <CENTER> and </CENTER> around my HTML that displays the image, the Web graphic looks fine on higher screen resolution monitors because it is centered on the screen and the white space doesn't look like blank, wasted area on my Web site.

Fig. 3.4
The same image in
Netscape but at
SVGA resolution.

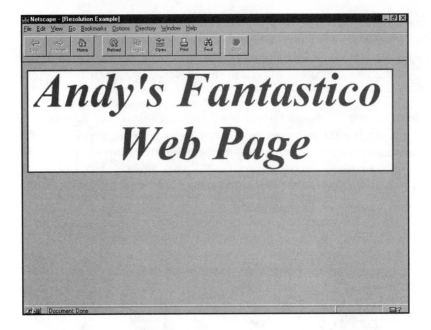

Now that you have been introduced to pixels and screen resolution, it's time
to figure out what height and width you want to use for your Web image.
Different types of images require different height and width coordinates.
Table 3.1 gives a general guideline for the pixel dimensions you should
choose when creating specific types of Web graphics.

Table 3.1 Dimension guidelines for Web Images	
Image Type	**Height and Width Coordinates (pixels)**
Small icon	25 x 25
Medium-sized icon	40 x 40
Large icon	60 x 60
Horizontal Bar	10 x 500
Headline Graphic	150 x 600
Common WWW Ad Size	300 x 72
Logo or Photograph	300 x 400

In the New Image dialog box that appears in Paint Shop Pro (refer to fig. 3.1),
choose the appropriate Width and Height in pixels for your particular image.

Don't worry, you can always re-size your image later by selecting Image |
Resize or Image | Enlarge Canvas from the menu bar.

It is important to note that the size of your image in pixel coordinates is
somewhat proportional to file size. Although not always true, images that
contain more pixels will be larger in file size than those which contain less
pixels. However, file size is much more dependent on the number of colors
used in the picture, the file type you choose (GIF or JPEG), and how busy, or
full of different shapes and designs, your image actually is.

Picking the Right Background Color

Now that you've decided how big your image should appear on screen, the
next choice in the New Image dialog box is Background color. This selection
simply refers to the default color your newly created image will appear. You
can choose from a handful of colors, depending on the type of image you
want to create.

Another method of choosing a background color allows you to select from
the 16.7 million drawing colors available (or 256 if creating a GIF). Before creating a new image, use your mouse to select the appropriate color from the
PSP Color Palette. Set the color to either the foreground with the left mouse
button or the background with the right mouse button. Now, when creating
a new image, the Background Color drop-down box enables you to select either *Foreground Color* or *Background Color* instead of the handful of standard
colors listed.

In general, most Web images start with a background color of white and add
more colors as necessary.

Choosing the Correct Number of Colors

The last choice available in the New Image dialog box is the Image type,
meaning the number of colors available for this graphic. From this drop-
down box, you have five options. Table 3.2 lists each option and explains
when you want to use each of them for your own graphics.

The number of available colors has a direct impact on how your image appears and its file size. You should choose an Image type with a lot of colors
only if you really need many colors because file size increases as the number
of colors increases, as shown in table 3.2.

Table 3.2 Image Type Explanation	
Image Type	**When you want to use this Option**
2 Colors (1-bit)	Allows only two colors—black and white. No shades of grey are permitted, but images in this format are extremely small and efficient. Ted Turner would hate this file type, but you should use it if you can.
16 Colors (4-bit)	Windows originally supported only 16 colors. These 16 colors covered most of the rainbow and became the defaults for many applications and graphics. Many impressive images can be created with this many colors. Only the GIF format supports the limited palette of only 16 colors. The JPEG image format automatically allows 16.7 million colors regardless of the number selected.
256 Greys (8-bit)	The maximum number of shades that GIFs can support, this option provides more flexibility than just black and white by offering 256 different shades of gray. There is no performance incentive to using 256 shades of gray instead of 256 various colors, so you'll find yourself using this format sparingly. Chapter 8, "The Black-and-White Alternative," delves into several situations where gray scale images come in handy.
256 Colors (8-bit)	The standard 256 colors that most GIFs use, you'll probably choose this selection most often when creating your own images from scratch. 256 colors is probably the maximum number you'll ever use unless you scan or digitize a photo (see Chapter 5, "Scanning and Enhancing Photos") or take advantage of Paint Shop Pro's advanced features. The default 256 colors used are the same ones you'll find at the default VGA setting for most monitors.
16.7 Million Colors (24-bit)	With 16.7 million colors available, you never have to use a single color twice. This option is used when you plan on saving your image in JPG form. Many of Paint Shop Pro's advanced features require you to have 16.7 million colors available because it mixes and matches thousands of colors for you automatically. For example, the button you created in the section titled "What Can You Do With Paint Shop Pro?" in Chapter 2, "Using and Installing Paint Shop Pro," required 16.7 million colors. GIF images cannot be saved in 16.7 million color (24-bit) format. Paint Shop Pro will reduce the number of colors used in an image to only 256 if you try to save a 24-bit image into the GIF file format.

Note

Here's how compucter programs such as Netscape and Paint Shop Pro know how many colors are available in an image. Computer files are saved in a format called binary, a bunch of ones and zeros concatenated onto one another. Large strings of binary numbers saved together are interpreted by a computer and then displayed as your image.

In table 3.1, each format parenthetically shows a value that depicts how many bits are needed for that format. You can figure out how many colors are available for a format by multiplying 2 to the nth power, where n is the number of bits listed. So, for 2 colors (1-bit), you multiple 2 to the 1st power, equaling a value of 2. For 256 colors (8-bits), multiply 2 to the 8th power, which is 256. And for 16.7 million colors (24-bits), multiply 2 to the 24th power—which equals 16,777,216 different colors available (Wow!).

In a 16.7 million color file, it takes 24-bits of computer memory to recognize which color you are referring to. However, when you use only 256 colors, it takes just 8-bits of memory to recognize a specified color. Therefore, three different colors can be defined in the 256 color file in the same amount of space it takes to define just one color in the 16.7 million color file. As you can imagine, the fewer number of colors you choose, the smaller your file size will be, because Paint Shop Pro doesn't have to waste 24-bits defining a single color. If your image is simply black and white, only one bit is needed to save each color, representing a savings of 95 percent in file size.

In general, when creating a GIF image choose *256 colors*, and when creating a JPEG image, choose *16.7 million colors*. JPEG images are optimized for 16.7 million colors and tend to offer better file sizes when you use many different colors in an image. Later, you can always decrease or increase the number of colors available in your image. Remember that the number of colors you use in a Web graphic is only as useful as the screen resolution of the people who stop by your site. Say you choose an image that uses 16.7 million colors, but a visitor who runs at VGA resolution—only 256 displayable colors—stops by. They'll see your 16.7 million color image displayed as a 256 color graphic. That's why most Web images, even JPEG graphics, often use a maximum of 256 different colors so that they will look fine to all Web visitors, regardless of their screen resolution.

Now, select an Image type and click the OK button. Paint Shop Pro makes your new image appear on the screen. Figure 3.5 shows a freshly created blank image.

II

Making Great Images

Fig. 3.5
So far, this 200 × 200 size image is pretty boring.

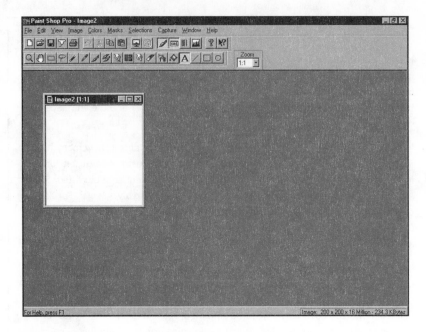

Saving Your Graphic

This section will show you how to save your newly made image so you can use it on your Web page or edit it again at a later date. You'll want to save often when creating Web graphics so your enhancements are permanently stored as a GIF or JPEG file.

Saving your images in Paint Shop Pro is rather easy. Choose File | Save As from the menu bar to bring up the Save As dialog box (see fig. 3.6).

Fig. 3.6
Name your file and tell Paint Shop Pro which image type to use.

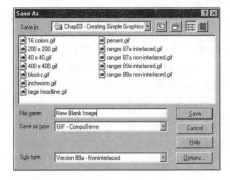

There are three steps required to save your file, which are explained in detail below. First, you choose a file name. Next, you select an Image Type. The last step is to set your image options.

Naming your Web graphic file is easy. Simply type in a short but descriptive name in the box labeled File name. Although Windows 95 enables a name to be any length and to contain spaces and punctuation, try to keep your name short and sweet. You may have to type in your file name when creating your HTML Web page and typing a long name is burdensome.

> **CAUTION**
>
> Some WWW servers and browsers have problems with file names that use spaces, commas, slashes, and the tilde (~) character. Avoid using these characters in your file name to ensure that you won't have any problems when adding Web graphics to your site—unless you are sure your Web Server can handle the extended characters in file names.

After naming your file, the next step is to select an Image type from the Save as type drop-down box. Although Paint Shop Pro enables you to pick from over two dozen different image types, you should stick with GIF or JPEG when making Web graphics.

GIF Format

To save your graphic in GIF format, choose GIF—CompuServe from the drop-down box. Paint Shop Pro enables you to pick from four different sublevels of the GIF file format. Although the four subtypes are all similar to each other, each subtype slightly affects the way an image appears on a Web page in a different manner. Below is a quick description of the four GIF subtypes you can choose from:

Version 87a NonInterlaced—The original GIF standard developed by CompuServe in 1987. Commonly known as the *CompuServe GIF Standard*, it is widely in use on CompuServe and across the Internet and was the first image type supported by WWW browsers. It is the default in which GIF images are stored as a simple file that is decoded and displayed normally by your Web browser.

Version 87a Interlaced—A small variation of the original format, interlacing images enables WWW browsers to display the image in several passes, each pass bringing the image into more detail. Displaying an interlaced image is similar to visiting an optometry office and having a few adjustments made to your glasses so that fuzzy letters become clear. Using interlaced images slightly increases your file size, but it is an excellent option for most Web developers. (See the section in Chapter 7 titled "Interlaced Images Work Best.")

Version 89a Noninterlaced—In 1989, two years after the original GIF standard was introduced, the standard was enhanced to provide increased flexibility, compression, and efficiency. Also new to Version 89a was the ability to create GIF animation (see Chapter 10, "Moving Graphics: GIF Animation").

Version 89a Interlaced—The same as Version 89a, but with built-in interlacing capabilities. This standard is the most popular option amongst Web developers today because it offers the best GIF functionality and flexibility.

For all of your graphics, choose Version 89a—Interlaced in the Sub type box. It is the best option for Web developers because interlaced images offer increased flexibility when used on Web pages. Interlaced images load in several steps, with each step becoming clearer and more detailed, enabling you to see a broad outline of your Web graphic almost immediately when downloading it. The 1989 standard is also slightly more advanced and offers better compression than the 1987 counterpart. Most WWW browsers (including Netscape and Internet Explorer) can recognize all four types of GIFs.

Note

Paint Shop Pro also allows you to set certain GIF transparency options by clicking the Options button in the Save As dialog box. See Chapter 9, "Creating Transparent GIFs," for an in-depth description of the options and when you should use them.

JPEG Format

The other available image type is JPEG. Save your graphic in JPEG format by choosing JPG—JPEG—JFIF Compliant from the Image type drop-down list box (refer to fig. 3.1) Remember that the JPEG image type uses 16.7 million colors but is often more efficient when compressing large images that use many colors—such as photographs.

Similar to GIF, the JPEG file type also has two subtypes available—Standard and Progressive. The Standard JPEG format uses excellent compression algorithms and displays graphics on a Web page like a noninterlaced GIF. As the image is downloaded, your WWW browser displays it from top to bottom.

Progressive JPEGs, on the other hand, are similar to the interlaced format. Progressive JPEGs are displayed in multiple passes, with each pass making the image slightly clearer. Unfortunately, Progressive JPEGs aren't as widely supported as the multiple GIF formats. Currently, only Netscape 2.0 and Internet Explorer 3.0 support the Progressive JPEG image format; other older WWW browsers cannot show the image when browsing Web pages. When saving an image as a JPEG, use only the Standard subtype. Progressive JPEGS also offer a 5 percent savings in file size from the original JPEG standard.

Once you've selected an image type and subtype, click the Save button and Paint Shop Pro will write your graphic onto your computer's hard drive.

Drawing Shapes

Making and saving Web images is only the first part of creating Web graphics. Once you have these two fundamentals down, it's time to start adding some shapes, text, and color to your actual graphics. Thus far, you've been working with boring graphics that are only a rectangular block of a single color.

Although Paint Shop Pro offers tremendous flexibility in saving and converting graphics of all types and formats, PSP originally got its start as a robust drawing and paint package. Whether you are a graphics artist or a new user, anyone can create great looking Web graphics with PSP's built-in tools.

This section shows you how to draw several different types of shapes and objects when building your graphics from scratch. Most Web graphics are simple combinations of these basic shapes and objects.

Choosing Colors

Before you can draw an object, you must choose the color of the object. In Paint Shop Pro, you use the Color Palette on the right-hand side of the screen to select and choose the different colors for your image.

Notice the overlapping squares in the color palette. These two squares represent your current foreground and background colors. These two overlapping colors are shown in more detail in figure 3.7.

The foreground color corresponds to drawing something with your *left* mouse button and the background color corresponds with the *right* mouse button. Whenever you draw or add an object to your Web graphic, it appears in the color selected, depending on which mouse button you choose to draw with. Foreground and background colors have several additional and different uses. They can be used to create special effects such as buttonizing an image, or to select the original color of a new Web graphic.

Fig. 3.7
These two squares
are used to decide
which color you
are painting in.

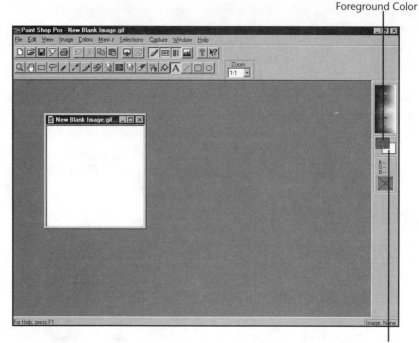

Foreground Color

Background Color

You can change the current foreground or background colors in two ways.
The easiest way is to click your left or right mouse button in the rainbow of
colors directly above the overlapping color squares. Your color is set according to whichever color you click in the rainbow. Clicking your left mouse
button sets the foreground color and clicking the right mouse button sets the
background color.

The other way to set your current colors is to click your left mouse button on
either the foreground or background square, depending on which one you
want to set. If you are using 256 colors, the Edit Palette dialog box (see
fig. 3.8) will appear. If you are using 16.7 million colors, the Color dialog box
will appear (see fig. 3.9).

You can select a particular color just by clicking it and then clicking the OK
button.

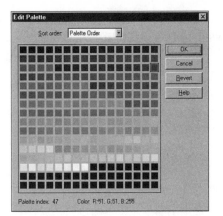

Fig. 3.8
Lots of default colors are available to select from.

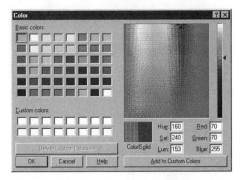

Fig. 3.9
A choice of 16.7 million colors enables for any combination of the three primary colors.

II

Making Great Images

Tip

Many people keep the background color white and only change the foreground color when creating their graphics. This enables them to easily draw over mistakes or cover something up with white when necessary. Also, changing the background color has additional benefits when making transparent GIFs. See Chapter 9, "Creating Transparent GIFs," for more information on how to use the background color for these situations.

Drawing Lines

A line is the most basic object you can create on an image. Paint Shop Pro allows you to create a line by simply clicking the Line icon from the Tool Palette at the top of the screen and then drawing a simple line on your image. Use your left mouse button to draw your line in the foreground color and the right mouse button to use the color defined as the background.

Once you click the Line icon, the Paint Shop Pro Style Bar will present a <u>W</u>idth box, which enables you to specify the thickness (in pixels) of the lines you want to draw. You can specify any whole number between 1 and 100 as the line thickness you want to draw with.

When drawing, make sure you use a thickness that isn't too thin and difficult to see. Figure 3.10 shows a simple drawing I created that uses only three lines (of the same color) with a thickness of 5 pixels.

Fig. 3.10
Although only three lines, all baseball fans should recognize this image.

Drawing Rectangles

Similar to using a line, Paint Shop Pro also enables you to create rectangular shapes in any size and color. Simply click the Shapes icon in the Tool Palette and tell Paint Shop Pro which shape you want to draw. Then use your mouse to click and draw the shape on your Web image.

In the Style Bar, you have three options. First, you can select the thickness of the outside border of the rectangle (in pixels). Next, you can select whether to draw only the border of the rectangle with your chosen color or fill-in the entire rectangle with that color. Finally, under the Shape heading, you can decide whether you are drawing a rectangle, square, circle, or oval. For this example I chose a square.

Figure 3.11 shows a handmade drawing created only with filled in rectangles. For each part of the pyramid, I chose a different color.

Fig. 3.11
Rectangles are the building blocks of most images.

Drawing Ovals

The same general procedure that is used for creating rectangles is used to create ovals—another important shape you should be aware of as a Web Graphic developer. Ovals and rectangles have the same available style options discussed above and you can draw any kind of oval, ellipse, circle, or round shape with the Shapes tool in Paint Shop Pro.

First click the Shapes icon, then decide the line thickness of your oval or circle and whether you want it to be filled in or drawn as an outline shape. Then, from the Shape option in the Style Bar, decide whether you want to create an Oval or Circle. Once you have selected your options, use your mouse to draw as many ovals as possible. Of course, you can also change colors for each new oval you draw. Figure 3.12 shows an inchworm made completely of ovals. Sixteen ovals filled with different colors combine to make this terrific Web graphic.

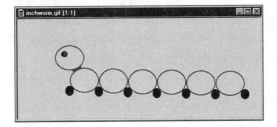

Fig. 3.12
Using circular and oval shapes, any shape imaginable is at your fingertips.

> **Tip**
>
> If you accidentally draw a shape or line of the wrong size, shape, or color, you can always choose Edit | Undo from the menu bar (or hit Ctrl-Z from the keyboard) and Paint Shop Pro will retract the last shape drawn or change made to your Web graphic.

Using the Paint Brush

Now that you are familiar with drawing shapes and lines for new Web graphics, it's time to look at some other important tools available with Paint Shop Pro. Leading that list of tools is the Paintbrush, a virtual marker that lets you draw freehand any shape, color, or pattern on your Web graphic.

With the use of your mouse and the PSP Paintbrush, you can draw literally any shape or design imaginable. It's just like drawing on a piece of paper with a marker but using your mouse and screen instead. You can draw a line, erase a smudge, change colors, accentuate a shape, save your changes, and choose different types of materials to paint with (chalk, marker, pen, etc.).

 Out of all the available PSP tools, you'll probably use the Paintbrush most often. It can be used to add small touch-up details to a Web graphic, to create colorful and interesting patterns and backgrounds, and to paint shapes of all sorts on your screen. In fact, unless you are creating a specific line, oval, or rectangle, the Paintbrush is likely to be your tool of choice when making your Web graphics.

Click the Paintbrush icon from the Paint Shop Pro Tool Palette. Immediately, several options are available in the Style Palette at the top of the screen. These options give you control over how your paintbrush performs when you draw on the screen. They are tremendously useful and effective when designing your own graphics from scratch.

Brush Type

The easiest style change for you to select is probably the Brush Type that you want to use. Normally, you can use a standard paintbrush that paints as you might expect it to.

Additionally, Paint Shop Pro lets you select from among seven different brush types that each emulate a different type of drawing utensil. Instead of a standard paintbrush, you can choose from charcoal, crayon, pen, pencil, marker, or chalk.

Each of these brush types have their own unique flavor and style, which allow you to add different appearances and textures to drawings by simply working with multiple brush types. For example, if you are creating a graphic for a Web page about children, you can choose to draw your image using the Crayon brush type, because that type of appearance is commonly associated with kids. Figure 3.13 shows a listing of all seven brush types and an example of how each appears when used.

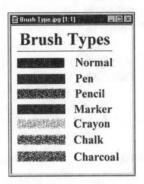

Fig. 3.13
Customizing your brush type lets you add unique personality to your images.

> **NOTE**
>
> In case you're interested, creating this graphic required me to select each different brush size and manually draw a straight line across the screen with a steady hand.
>
> Creating images like this for your reference are often useful. This allows you to refer back to this picture and select the brush type you want without trying each one individually. You'll find this strategy useful when testing different colors, brush shapes, and paper textures. I've included all of these reference images for your use on the CD-ROM that came with this book.

Brush Size

This selection in the style box decides the thickness of the brush you paint with. Measured in pixels, you can use any Brush size ranging from 1 to 99.

Brush Shape

When you paint your graphics, sometimes you may want to use a paintbrush that has a slightly different or unique shape to it. With the Paintbrush tool, Paint Shop Pro provides six different shapes that you can choose to paint with.

By default, your paintbrush is square. But this can be changed, as shown in figure 3.14, which lists six different paintbrush shapes you can select from and an example of each shape.

Fig. 3.14
Different brush shapes often fit the mood and style of your Web graphics better.

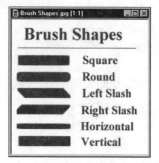

Paper Texture

The final and most impressive option of the Paintbrush tool is the ability to select a particular Paper Texture. This option works similar to the Brush Type option described above but offers significantly more flexibility and usefulness when painting. Normally your paintbrush paints with a single color in the size and shape you specify.

Paint Shop Pro gives you nearly 30 different options other than painting with a single solid color. Each paper texture has it's own unique style that creates a different effect when used. You can choose any of these Paper Textures to paint your own Web Graphics on. Figure 3.15 lists each Paper Texture and shows a small sample of how each of them appear when painted.

> **CAUTION**
>
> To paint with Paper Textures, you must be in an image that has 16.7 million colors available. That means you cannot create GIF images that use paper textures, only JPEG images.

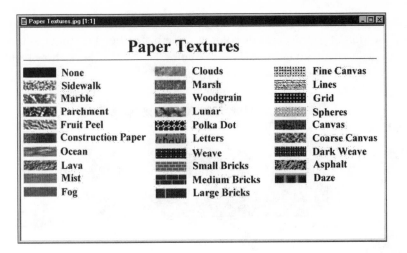

Fig. 3.15
With 29 different textures available, you'll never run out of stylistic options when painting and making a new image.

Other Drawing Options

Paint Shop Pro is a truly robust graphics package. Artists and amateurs alike can create their own customized images from scratch using the tools provided. In this chapter, you learned how to use Paint Shop Pro's general image drawing tools such as drawing Shapes and working with the Paintbrush. Drawing shapes and using the paintbrush tool are the two basic and critical functions that you will use consistently when creating your graphics with PSP.

In addition, there are several other tools which may prove useful when creating new graphics from scratch. Several popular Paint Shop Pro options are listed below with a detailed explanation of when to use them.

- **Airbrush**—This tool draws like you are using spray paint. Instead of drawing a crisp, solid line across the screen, the airbrush enables you to draw more general patterns that aren't solid. You can use the airbrush tool when you paint the background of your Web graphics or when you want to add some texture and personality to an otherwise boring image. Some people refer to the airbrush as the "graffiti" tool because the resulting graphics often look like they were spray painted on an image.

II

Making Great Images

■ **Flood Fill**—Another useful tool, flood fill allows you to paint an entire section of your image one color or pattern. The flood fill tool is often used to paint an entire canvas one color. Figure 3.16 shows how I added a gradient flood fill to my inchworm image.

Fig. 3.16
This background texture looks difficult to create, but it only took a single flood fill.

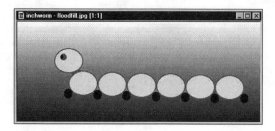

 ■ **Eraser**—Everyone makes mistakes. Even if you are a master artisan, eventually you'll color a square the wrong color or make some graphical equivalent to a typo. That's why you'll quickly want to get familiar with the built-in eraser. When used, Paint Shop Pro erases the section you mark and replaces it with the current background color, according to the Color Palette.

 ■ **Retouch**—One of my favorite tools, it lets you add neat special effects to your image, such as smudging, embossing, or softening the lines of your image. These tools are great for blending images together or making modifications to existing ones. ❖

CHAPTER 4

Working With Existing Images

Even when you want to create a unique Web page with original graphics, it may not be necessary to start completely from scratch. There are thousands of excellent images freely available on the Internet—and many on the CD-ROM that comes with this book. You will often find it easier and faster to modify, add to, or borrow from an existing image than it is to start with a completely blank slate.

This chapter will show you how to find and work with images that someone else has already created. You'll learn how to adjust the colors and details for your own applications, and discover a number of handy techniques for customizing Web graphics. This chapter will teach you about:

- **Finding Graphics on the Internet**

  A world of graphics is waiting for you to explore—and exploit, as long as you get permission from the original artists.

- **Using the Graphics on the CD-ROM**

  The CD-ROM that comes with this book is packed with reusable graphics. Learn how to quickly browse through them—and any other graphics collection—to find what you need.

- **Capturing Screen Shots**

  Sometimes the graphics you need are right in front of you. Paint Shop Pro makes grabbing and using them super-efficient.

- **Modifying Graphics for Your Pages**

  Learn the four basic steps needed to adapt any graphic for use on a Web page.

Finding Graphics on the Internet

One of the best ways to save time creating graphics files is, of course, to avoid creating them altogether. With the entire World Wide Web at your fingertips, you have access to thousands upon thousands of images.

Any graphic you see on any site is instantly reusable, as soon as the copyright holder grants (or sells) you the right to copy it. Because almost all Web pages include the e-mail address of their creators, it's usually quick and easy to ask permission to download and adopt a piece of artwork.

The familiar Web search engines and directories such as Yahoo! (**http://www.yahoo.com/**), Lycos (**http://lycos.cs.cmu.edu**), and InfoSeek (**http://www.infoseek.com/**) can be a gold mine of graphics images, just by leading you to sites related to your own theme. They can also help you discover the oodles of sites specifically dedicated to providing free and cheap access to reusable media collections.

A Lycos search for "background textures" turns up, among many other sites, the Texture and Background Wonderland, located at **http://netletter.com/cameo/hotlist/hotlist.htm** and pictured in figure 4.1. This is one of my favorite hotlists, with links to consistent high-quality sites for finding great background tiles and graphic accents for Web pages. (Gini Schmitz is also the artist who created many of the graphics on the CD-ROM that comes with this book, which are discussed later in this chapter.)

Fig. 4.1

Gini Schmitz's Textures and Backgrounds Wonderland is one of the best places to find lively graphics for your own Web pages.

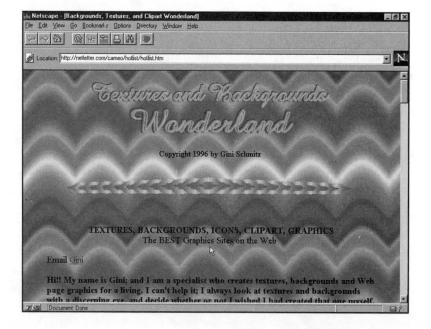

On the CD-ROM that comes with this book, you'll find live links to many other graphics and multimedia hotlists and hot sites. Links to all the major search engines are on there, too, just in case you don't already have them all on your own bookmark list.

Grabbing the Graphics You Find

As you probably know, grabbing a graphic from a Web page is as simple as clicking it with the right-mouse button, then picking Save this image as... in Netscape Navigator or Save Picture as... in Microsoft Explorer.

With Microsoft Explorer, extracting a background image from a page is just as easy: right-click it and pick Save Background As. However, the procedure for grabbing a background tile isn't quite so obvious in Netscape Navigator and most other Web browsers:

1. View the source code (select <u>V</u>iew | Document <u>S</u>ource in Netscape; see fig. 4.2).

2. Select the filename in the BACKGROUND= attribute in the BODY tag, and copy it to the Clipboard. (In Windows, hold down the Control key and press the Insert key.) Do not include the quote marks around the address.

> ### Tip
>
> In Netscape Navigator, you can also find the full address of the background image by selecting <u>V</u>iew | Document I<u>n</u>fo. In other browsers, however, your only option is to view the source code as described in the two steps above.

3. Close the source window.

4. Paste the filename by clicking the location and pressing Shift-Insert, and then press Enter to go to that address. If the address doesn't begin with http://, it is relative to the original page address and you'll need to paste it onto the end of that original address.

5. The background file should appear, as shown in figure 4.3. You can now use Save this image as... or the right-click menu to save the file.

Fig. 4.2
To find out the address of a background graphic in Netscape Navigator, view the source code for the HTML file.

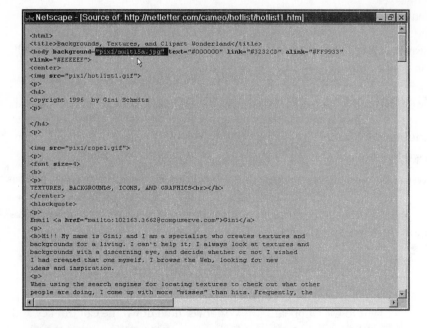

Fig. 4.3
When you load the background tile by itself, you can save it as you would any other image.

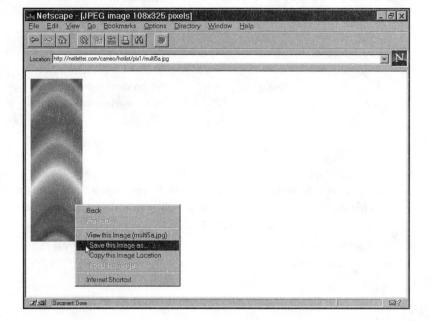

Archie and Veronica Go to the Pictures

If you're looking for something so specific that you can guess part of the file name or title, you can use two Internet indexing systems called Archie and

Veronica to find graphics files that may not be accessible through the World
Wide Web.

Even some experienced Webmasters have never used Archie and Veronica, so
I'll explain the basics of using them to find graphics. I'll also let you in on the
secret codes that enable you to limit your search to only graphics files.

> **Note**
>
> In the old days, you had to have special programs to access Archie and Veronica, but
> nowadays you can access them easily through the same browser program you use for
> the World Wide Web. Some advanced users still prefer the old-style search programs,
> but I'll explain how to do it without them.

Archie

Archie is a comprehensive, freely accessible, and automatically searchable index of every file accessible through public File Transfer Protocol (FTP). The
bad news is that Archie only knows the names of the files and the disk directories they're stored in, neither of which have any text description attached,
so a picture of five elephants juggling on bicycles might be called ejob5.jpg.
You could search Archie for the text "elephant," "juggle," and "bicycle" all
day and not find the picture.

The good news is that people are generally nice and often give files descriptive names. There very well might be a picture file named elephants-
juggling.gif stored right next to ejob5.jpg. And even better news is that many
images have such specific content that you can easily guess what somebody
would name the image file. If you were looking for an image of *The Three
Stooges* TV show, an Archie search for the word "stooges" would be a pretty
good bet. Archie indexes directory names, too—so you may discover a whole
directory folder full of files related to your search topic.

To search Archie, start by pointing your browser to the list of all Archie servers at:

http://pubweb.nexor.co.uk/public/archie/servers.html

Choose the Archie server nearest you, or one located in a time zone where it
is night and few local people will be using it.

To run a search, click the search box and type the letters you want to search
for. For the search type, you'll almost always want Case Insensitive Substring
Match unless you know the exact name of the file you're looking for. Click
the Submit button, and in a few seconds (sometimes longer at busy times),

you will have a list of clickable links to every publicly archived file in the world containing the letters you searched for in its name.

Veronica

The image files that Archie finds are almost always hiding in a long list of other types of files with similar names. Of course, you can tell Archie to look for images containing the letters GIF or JPG if you want to increase the chances of hitting a graphics file. But wouldn't it be nice if you could just say, "Just find me image files, nothing else"? And while we're making out a wish list, it would also be handy if the files had short descriptions attached to them so we could search the descriptions for keywords, too.

Veronica is another master search index of public files. Like Archie, all Veronica needs from you is a few letters or words to search for, and away she goes to fetch every file she can find that matches your query. Most of the files Archie has access to are also accessible through Veronica.

Often, however, Veronica has access to longer descriptions of the files than Archie does. And, more importantly, Veronica knows what type of file she's looking at and tells you by displaying the appropriate icon on the search result menu; you can go straight to the graphics and ignore the rest.

> ### Tip
>
> You may notice that the search list Veronica comes up with is titled Gopher menu. The file system that Veronica indexes is called Gopher, or sometimes GopherSpace. Gopher itself has been largely superseded by the World Wide Web, so you probably won't have much reason to access Gopher menus directly unless you're doing a Veronica search.

"Straight to the graphics and ignore the rest," I say. But the rest may still be a heck of a lot of files! Veronica searches often turn up thousands upon thousands of matching files, only 200 or so of which are shown, unless you request to see more. Even with handy icons to guide you, weeding through 200 files or more for the desired graphics images is no fun.

But not to worry. You can tell Veronica to find just graphics files and ignore everything else: Simply enter -tIg (that's hyphen, small t, capital I, small g) as one of the words to search for. This will command Veronica to show you only graphics.

Let's walk through a Veronica search so you can get an idea of how it works. First, pick a Veronica server from the list at:

http://www.scs.unr.edu/veronica.html

The Veronica search form (see fig. 4.4) is pretty basic: just type the keywords and hit the enter key. Along with the words to search for (which can be entered in any order), you can also give special commands to Veronica. For more information on the command language, choose the How to Compose Veronica Queries link from the Veronica server list page. As mentioned previously, if you enter -tIg as if it were one of your search words, Veronica will return only graphics images and ignore all other file types. You may also include menus and Web pages with the command -tIgh1 (a dash followed by the letters tIgh and the number 1) instead of just -tIg.

Figure 4.4 shows a Veronica query for graphics images whose names or descriptions include the word "wizard." Veronica responds by building the Gopher menu shown in figure 4.5, which leads to several images along the lines of figure 4.6.

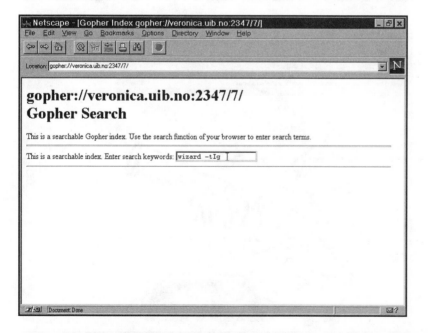

Fig. 4.4
Veronica offers an express lane down the yellow brick road.

Fig. 4.5
In a flash of shimmering light, 24 wizards appear. Clicking each menu item will display or download the associated image.

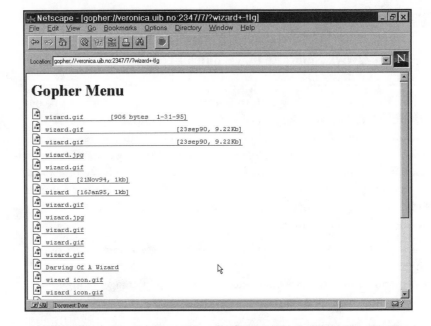

Fig. 4.6
This image could be really handy if, for example, you want to illustrate the wizardry of searching the Internet for graphics.

Using the Graphics on the CD-ROM

To get you started creating your own Web graphics, we have placed several collections of images on the CD-ROM that comes with this book. These collections were chosen especially for their wide-ranging applicability and adaptability.

The best way to explore the graphics collections on the CD-ROM is by using Paint Shop Pro's File | Browse command. It will display a standard file open dialog box. Navigate to the directory folder you want to explore and then click the Select button. Small "thumbnails" of every image in the folder will be displayed; you can double-click any thumbnail to open the full-sized image (see fig. 4.7).

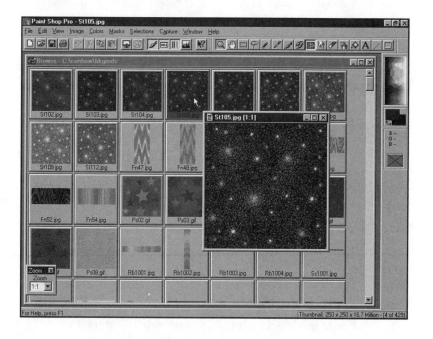

Fig. 4.7
These background tiles are just a few of the hundreds of images included on the CD-ROM with this book.

II

Making Great Images

The first time you browse a directory, it may take some time for Paint Shop Pro to scan all the image files and make the thumbnails. However, you will only have to wait for this long process once because a special file named pspbrwse.jbf, containing all the thumbnails, is saved in the folder. Thereafter, every time you browse that folder, the thumbnails will display very quickly.

If you change the contents of a folder, you can choose File | Update when the browse window is open to update the pspbrwse.jbf file (and the thumbnails you see on the screen).

Tip

Pre-made pspbrwse.jbf files have been included on the CD-ROM, so you won't need to wait for the images to be scanned, even the first time you browse them.

And it's a good thing we did this for you, because the pspbrwse.jbf files obviously can't be written to a "Read-Only Memory" CD after it is created. If you use Paint Shop Pro to browse other CD-ROM-based collections of images, you will notice that the images must be rescanned every time you browse a folder. This doesn't prevent anything from working correctly with any folder of images on any CD-ROM—it just might slow you down a little.

You'll see how to make changes to images like the one in figure 4.7 a bit later in this chapter, under "Modifying Graphics for Your Pages."

Capturing Screen Shots

It's quite likely that you use your computer for other things besides building Web pages. You may even use it to build old-fashioned paper pages with a word processor or page layout program. Or perhaps you've created or bought some other programs that display interesting graphics or type. In any of these situations—and many others—it often comes in handy to transfer part of an image you see on your computer screen to a Web page.

Just as one example, figure 4.8 shows a carefully laid out page that I created in Adobe PageMaker for a paper publication. Suppose I wanted to post this page on the Internet. How would I do it?

Even though PageMaker has a built-in Web page export feature, I would lose all the fancy typography and borders at the top of the page if I used it. Unfortunately, there is no command in PageMaker to export this entire title as a graphic that I could load into Paint Shop Pro.

The answer to my quandary, as you have probably already surmised, is to capture an image of the title straight from my computer screen while the PageMaker program is running. There are two easy ways to do this:

- Use Window's built-in screen capture capabilities by pressing PRINT SCREEN to capture the entire screen or ALT+PRINT SCREEN to capture the active window. Then select Edit | Paste | As New Image in Paint Shop Pro to paste the image from the clipboard.

- Use Paint Shop Pro's Capture menu to grab the image directly. This is usually faster, and gives you a number of options that Windows' built-in screen capture doesn't provide (see fig. 4.9).

Fig. 4.8
Adobe PageMaker doesn't offer any command to export the title and layout of this page to a Web page without mangling it beyond recognition.

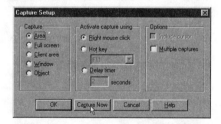

Fig. 4.9
Paint Shop Pro offers a number of time-saving options for screen captures that the PRINT SCREEN key doesn't provide.

In this case, I opened both PageMaker and Paint Shop Pro at the same time, and hid all page layout guidelines in PageMaker. Then I selected Capture

II

Making Great Images

Setup in Paint Shop Pro, made sure that Capture | Area was selected, and clicked the Capture Now button. Paint Shop Pro automatically minimized its own window so PageMaker's window became visible.

I clicked with the right-mouse button inside the PageMaker window, and the mouse cursor turned to a crosshair. This indicates that Paint Shop Pro is ready for an area to be specified. One left-button click to the top left of the title and one click to the lower right corner is all it takes for the image to be cropped and captured directly into Paint Shop Pro. (If I had selected Full Screen, Client Area, Window, or Object instead of Area in the Capture Setup dialog box, only the single right-mouse click would have been needed to capture the image.)

Once the title graphic has been captured, it's easy to use any of Paint Shop Pro's tools and commands to modify the image. Generally, I recommend saving one copy of the image as captured (top image in fig. 4.10) and using Edit | Copy followed by Edit | Paste | As new image to create a working copy before you make any modifications (bottom image in fig. 4.10). That way, if you don't like your changes, you won't have to set up the screen capture again to get the original file back.

Fig. 4.10

A screen capture brought this title into Paint Shop Pro from Page-Maker at just the right resolution for a Web page.

Tip

If you have other graphics software, such as CorelDraw!, Adobe Illustrator, or a 3D rendering program, it is probably capable of exporting some file format that Paint Shop Pro can open.

However, the graphics files that your applications save may be at a resolution that is better for paper printing or video production than Web pages, and there can often be a significant difference between the colors you see on the screen and the colors you'll see when you open the resulting graphics file.

You may often find it faster and more reliable to simply capture images straight from the screen while a graphics application is running. That way you know the image will appear on your Web page exactly as you see it when you do the capture.

Don't forget that you can also use screen captures to grab still shots from moving video clips or animations as they play.

Modifying Graphics for Your Pages

Imagine for a moment that you are me, the person who wants to put *New Scientific's* "World Records" page on the Web. You've captured the fancy title shown in figure 4.10. You've selected a suitable background graphic, perhaps the one back in figure 4.7 from the *Create Your Own Web Graphics* CD-ROM. And you have all the graphics files that were used to print the paper version of the page.

Print Graphics vs. Web Graphics

So you toss all those graphics together with a little HTML and you should be all set, right?

Wrong. Unfortunately, the requirements for Web graphics are radically different than the requirements for printed graphics. In fact, almost all the rules are reversed:

- For paper, you want giant, high-resolution graphics files. For the Web, you want small graphics that load fast and look good on a relatively low-resolution computer screen.

- Printing color isn't cheap, and preparing color graphics for printing is a complex and often agonizing endeavor. On the Web, color is easy to work with and almost free.

- Once a document is on paper, it doesn't change until the next print run. Web documents often need to be instantly and constantly updated.

- On paper, dark colors will bleed into the light colors and it's a struggle to make bright colors shine. On a computer screen, it's the lighter colors that leap out and overwhelm nearby dark areas.

The bottom line is that graphics created for print publications seldom work, unmodified, for Internet publication. Since most clip-art and stock photography was originally designed for print publications, you will need to be aware of these differences, even if you've never printed a paper page in your life.

Resizing Graphics

Figure 4.11 shows two fairly typical images from a clip-art collection, which were used to illustrate the paper version of the article on scientific world records. Notice that the files are very large—the lower right corner of the Paint Shop Pro window indicates that the image of the Earth is 1,656 by 1,131 pixels. You'll also notice that the one-third-sized rendition shown doesn't look very interesting, since much detail is lost.

Fig. 4.11

These clip-art images would print well on paper, but are too big and too intricate for Web pages.

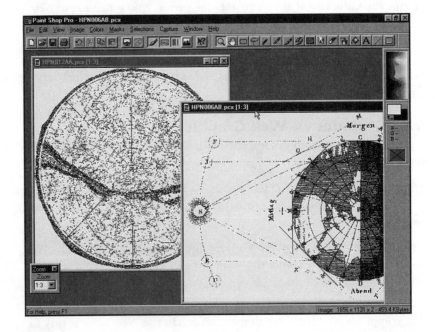

To make these images smaller, while losing as little detail as possible, I converted them to greyscale with Colors | Decrease Color Depth | 256 Colors, then selected Image | Resample. The Resample command uses sophisticated image processing math to maintain the best quality when shrinking an image. If I had used Image | Resize instead, the results would have been dramatically less detailed.

Tip

Here's another trick you should know to squeeze the absolute best out of images when you reduce their size. Always try to resample to exactly one half, one quarter, or one eighth the original size, if possible. The mathematical reasons why this works better are beyond what I could explain in this little tip, but trust me: it works.

For example, a 1200×800 pixel image will usually look better when resampled down to exactly 300×200 pixels than it would if you resampled it to 312×208 pixels—even though the 312×208 image is slightly bigger.

If the requirements of your page don't allow a division in size by exactly 2, 4, or 8, try to stick to other simple division factors like 3, 5 or 6.

Another technique for bringing out detail in graphics that will be viewed mostly on a computer screen is to make sure that any thin lines are in a lighter color than the background around them (the opposite of what you'd do on paper). In this case, simply negating the image colors with Colors | Negative Image works well to portray stars and a planet in space—better, in fact, than the original black-on-white. Figure 4.12 shows the final images—reduced, recolored, and ready for the Web.

Once the overall size of the image is reduced, you may still need to crop it and reduce the number of colors to get the file size down. The images in figure 4.12 were reduced to 16 colors with Colors | Decrease Color Depth after some color adjustments with Colors | Adjust | Gamma Correction and Colors | Adjust | Brightness/Contrast.

All these techniques combined reduced the star map image file from 180K to 23K in size, and the Earth image from 90K to 18K. These are still a bit large for Web pages, but they couldn't be reduced much more without losing so much detail that they'd be difficult to recognize. Because of the relatively large file sizes, I chose to save them as interlaced GIFs, which will display a

▶ The most important color adjustments are highlighted briefly under "Customizing Backgrounds," next in this chapter.

▶ You'll find a complete rundown on Paint Shop Pro's color adjustment controls in Chapter 5, "Scanning and Enhancing Photos."

II

Making Great Images

blurred version of the file long before it is completely done downloading. Since these graphics aren't essential in understanding the text content of the page, visitors won't need to wait for the images to finish downloading before they start reading the page.

Fig. 4.12
White-on-black shows details better on computer screens than black-on-white. It also works well with the cosmic theme of these illustrations.

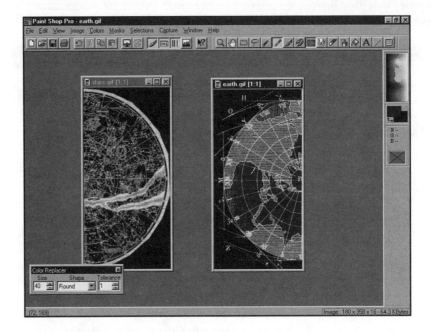

Customizing Backgrounds

Such cosmic graphics deserve a suitably celestial background. Fortunately, the starry background tile selected earlier (in fig. 4.7) will do the trick nicely. However, like most of the backgrounds on the CD-ROM included with this book, this background was intentionally provided at a larger size than would be appropriate for most Web pages. (Gini Schmitz, the background guru who contributed them, knew that it's easier to reduce the size of an image than to increase it.)

As with the greyscale graphics discussed earlier, Image | Resample is also the command of choice for reducing the size of full color graphics. In figure 4.13, the image is resampled to exactly half its original size in each dimension (to 125×125 pixels from 250×250 pixels).

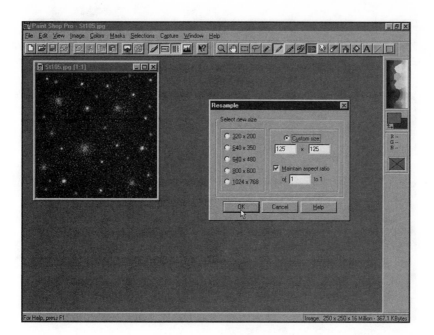

Fig. 4.13
The Resample command will almost always work better than Resize when reducing the size of a full-color or greyscale image.

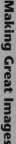

The backgrounds on the CD-ROM are also intentionally provided with too much contrast and too wide a color range for most Web pages. As with size adjustment, it's easier to decrease contrast and get rid of too much color than the other way around.

The most useful command for adjusting background colors is <u>C</u>olors I <u>A</u>djust I <u>G</u>amma Correction. This changes the bright/dark balance in an image without losing any color information. I'll leave a discussion of why this command is usually better than the Brightness/Contrast adjustment to Chapter 5, "Scanning and Enhancing Photos." All you really need to know for now is that a correction factor between 0 and 1 will darken an image, while a number between 1 and 4 will lighten it.

A correction of 0.81 is applied in figure 4.14. I came up with 0.81 just by twiddling the setting up and down until it looked like white text would show up clearly over it, but the stars were still easily visible.

Making Great Images

Fig. 4.14
Gamma correction
is the best way to
fade background
images without
losing detail.

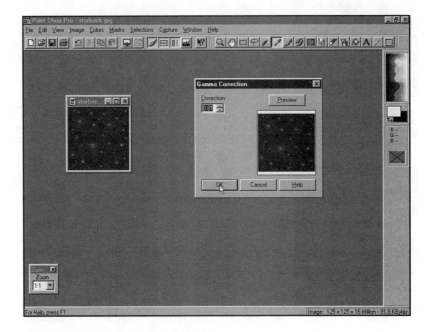

Finishing Touches

You've seen three of the four key steps involved in adapting almost any image for use on a Web page:

1. Find or capture a promising image

2. Adjust the colors to match the other elements of the page

3. Resize the image and reduce the color depth

4. Touch up any colors or details that don't quite work

Alas, number four on the list is often the most time consuming by far. The others will become pretty much automatic once you've created a few pages. But, the more you explore Paint Shop Pro's powerful capabilities, the more tempted you'll be to spend half an hour with Colors | Edit Palette to get that title color "just right," or to play around with Image | Special Effects | Add Drop Shadow for the precise 3D-look you're after.

But take my advice: discipline yourself to spend only a few minutes "perfecting" the graphics on each page. I did indulge in a couple of worthwhile improvements to the completed pages pictured in figures 4.15 and 4.16. For example, the gradient fill of "World Records" and filling in the words "NEW SCIENTIFIC" with white were well worth the minimal effort they involved. Likewise, using the color replacer tool to fill the continents of the Earth with a non-transparent shade of black definitely made the graphic more easily recognizable.

But will my picky adjustments and readjustments of the palette of colors in the title really make any difference to the people who visit this site? Probably not. And that "glow effect" experiment I tried when you weren't looking was a nice idea, but it increased the file size of the title image from 4K to 23K. (Oops. Never mind.)

So, do like I say, not like I do; Stop having so much fun playing around with your pages and focus on "productivity" and serious stuff like that. And hey, I don't want to see anybody fooling around with that Image | Deformation Browser command any more, got it? Good.

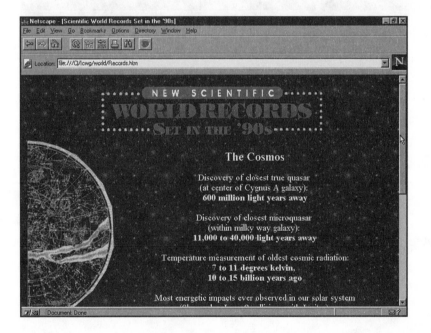

Fig. 4.15
The completed masterpiece is less detailed but far more colorful than the original two-color printed version.

Fig. 4.16
As a final touch, I had to touch up the Earth so you couldn't see the stars through the continents.

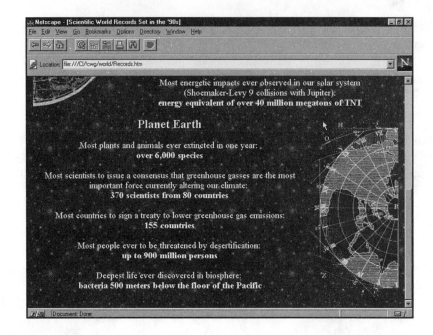

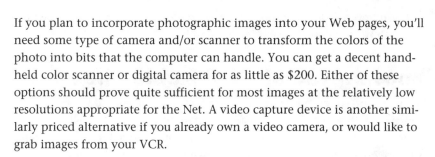

CHAPTER 5

Scanning and Enhancing Photos

If you plan to incorporate photographic images into your Web pages, you'll need some type of camera and/or scanner to transform the colors of the photo into bits that the computer can handle. You can get a decent hand-held color scanner or digital camera for as little as $200. Either of these options should prove quite sufficient for most images at the relatively low resolutions appropriate for the Net. A video capture device is another similarly priced alternative if you already own a video camera, or would like to grab images from your VCR.

Though you will usually get better image quality by scanning conventional photographs, using a digital video camera or video capture device also gives you the option of incorporating moving images into your Web pages. This isn't particularly practical for general Internet use quite yet because even short, compressed video files are still a bit too fat to fit comfortably through the average modem. Of course, the near future of the Internet will certainly involve more and more multimedia as bandwidth and compression technologies improve.

However you choose to digitize your images, this chapter will take you through the process of capturing, correcting, and enhancing a photo for placement on your Web pages. In this chapter, you will learn how to:

■ **Choose the Most Suitable Photos**

Learn to pick the photo that will look best online—not the one that looks best on photographic paper.

- **Scan from Paint Shop Pro**

  Paint Shop Pro makes scanning with any TWAIN-compatible scanner a one-button operation.

- **Use Other Scanning Options**

  Even if you don't own a scanner, you can easily get your own photos into electronic form.

- **Correct and Retouch Images**

  Take a crash course in Paint Shop Pro's professional-level image correction and enhancement features—and you don't have to be a pro to put them to work.

- **Isolate a Subject from the Background**

  Learn how to place a great picture of your dog on your home page without those ugly humans standing behind him.

Choosing the Most Suitable Photos

Before you scan—or even before you take a picture—you should remember that many details will be lost when a photograph is converted to 640×480 or lower resolution. Does your subject still look as you intended if you blur your eyes when looking at it? If not, it probably won't survive the journey into cyberspace very well.

Figures 5.1 and 5.2 demonstrate the fact that the best looking photo isn't always the one that will respond the best to scanning and electronic enhancement. As a color print, figure 5.1 looked remarkably more vibrant than figure 5.2. However, when scanned and printed or viewed on the screen, the more vibrant color print contained too much contrast to retain all of its details (see fig. 5.1). No amount of retouching can bring back information that simply doesn't make it through the scan. The flatter color print, when scanned, needed some contrast enhancement and gamma correction (covered later in the section entitled "Correcting and Retouching Images") but held up well during the process because almost all the image details survived the scan (see fig. 5.2).

Fig. 5.1
This was a great photo—until a low-cost scanner destroyed its best features. (Dandy's lovely white whiskers, for instance, were lost.)

Fig. 5.2
The same scanner that killed figure 5.1 did little damage to this rather flat image. Electronic retouching fixed the color problems and Dandy's looks actually improved in the whole process.

Making Great Images

Scanning from Paint Shop Pro

To properly prepare photographic images for online display, you need some photo retouching software—like Paint Shop Pro. It handles almost any image correction and enhancement task needed for the Net, and Paint Shop Pro even includes the standard TWAIN interface for scanners, so you can scan without leaving the program. To scan an image, select File I Acquire, and the scanning controls for your particular scanner will appear (see fig. 5.3).

The dialog box that you see when you select File I Acquire will probably look different than the one shown in figure 5.3. The exact interface will depend on which scanner you use and the software drivers that you installed when you connected the scanner to your computer.

Figure 5.3 shows the interface for my Logitech Color ScanMan. The basic elements shown in figure 5.3 will undoubtedly be present in the dialog box for your scanner (or digital camera), too. These include settings for resolution and color depth, a rough preview of what the image will look like, and some buttons to accept or cancel the image aquisition.

For Web page images, you will generally want to choose the lowest resolution and the highest color depth (72 to 100 dpi, with 24-bit color).

Note

If you get an error message or nothing happens when you select File I Acquire, then your scanner (or digital camera) is not compatible with the TWAIN standard. If your scanner isn't compatible with the TWAIN standard, you will need to use the software that came with your scanner to scan and save images. You can then open them in Paint Shop Pro.

You will want to add the Acquire Image button to your toolbar if you plan to scan images often. To do so, select File I Preferences I Customize Toolbar, highlight the Acquire Image icon as shown in figure 5.4, and click the Add button. While you're at it, you also might want to add the Brightness/Contrast, Adjust RGB, and Gamma Correction buttons to your toolbar (see fig. 5.4). These functions are frequently used to enhance scanned images, as I explain later in this chapter.

Fig. 5.3
Pressing the
Acquire Image
button brings up
the dialog box
for your specific
TWAIN-
compatible
scanner driver.

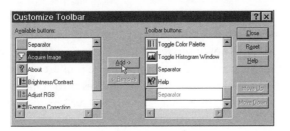

Fig. 5.4
If you scan and
correct images
frequently, you'll
want to add the
Aquire Image and
Color Adjustment
buttons to Paint
Shop Pro's toolbar.

Making Great Images

Other Scanning Options

If you find yourself in the unlikely situation of needing more capabilities than Paint Shop Pro provides, there are any number of commercial photo editing programs available to meet your needs—from the Corel Photo-Paint module (included free with the CorelDraw art program), to the ultimate photophile's dream, Adobe PhotoShop. (I've tried most of them and PhotoShop does deserve its reputation as the most powerful and most difficult to use.)

If you have some non-electronic artwork that you'd like to post on the Net, you can take a good photo of it (preferably with a copy stand or some other carefully controlled lighting setup) and make a matte print for scanning. Or, if the art is small and flat, you may be able to scan it directly.

Tip

Another alternative you should consider is Kodak's PhotoCD service. You can take any 35mm film into an authorized Kodak photo lab and they'll do a professional-quality scan of your images and put them on a CD at several resolutions, all for a relatively modest fee. (Prices are currently in flux—check your local Kodak lab for current rates. Due to policy changes at Kodak, soon more "unauthorized" labs will be able to use the technology, too.) Paint Shop Pro and most other photo retouch programs can read PCD files, so handling these files is as easy as opening them. If you know that you plan to use photos for posting on the Net before you get your film developed, PhotoCD will definitely give you far better results than a cheap hand-held scanner—or even a more expensive desktop scanner.

Some other companies such as America Online and Seattle Filmworks also offer free or inexpensive scanning services for their customers.

You may hear desktop publishing pros say that nothing can beat the quality you get by hiring a top-notch service bureau to scan and correct your most important images. Be warned, though, that those pros are skilled at working with images destined for printing on offset presses with standard CMYK inks. They may not understand that images to be displayed on a computer screen really should be treated differently—from the scanner setup, on down the line. And, given the low resolution of most images you're likely to put on the Net, hiring a pre-press team to prepare them is kind of like trying to swat flies with a steam roller.

Correcting and Retouching Images

Many of the snapshots you scan are likely to be in need of some repair work. However, you don't have to be a highly trained professional to learn the basics of correcting and enhancing images. The quick-and-dirty run down that follows isn't going to qualify you for a degree in graphic arts, but it will show you how to use Paint Shop Pro (or a comparable graphics program) to polish almost any image you plan to put on a Web page.

Color Correction

Almost all photographs, and many computer-generated pictures, will benefit from color correction. An image designed to be printed on paper will almost always look bleak and washed-out when viewed on a monitor.

There are also plenty of poorly scanned snapshots on the Net that need color correction to look good on display devices or printers. Let's use the worst-case scenario and pretend you found a poorly scanned snapshot on the Net that you really want to use for your Web page. For example, figure 5.5 is a rather flat image of a rather flat-coated retriever that I retrieved from the **alt.binaries.pictures.animals** newsgroup. Pictures of flat-coated retrievers are hard to come by, so if someone wanted a masthead for the fictitious *Flat-Coated Retriever Breeder's Journal*, they might just have to make-do with this rather poor shot.

Fig. 5.5
A bad picture of a good dog.

I don't know this dog's name and "the flat-coated retriever" may get a bit stale after a while, so I'll refer to it by the nickname of a similar looking dog I once knew: "Fry-Brain." (He liked to keep his head under the woodstove, but ended-up singeing some of the hair off the top of his head, ergo "Fry-Brain.") There wasn't much they could do to fix Fry-Brain's fur, but we can bring this version of Fry-Brain into Paint Shop Pro for some graphical grooming.

Brightness and Contrast Enhancement

Fry-Brain's primary problem is that he's too dark. In Paint Shop Pro, the Colors menu and the Colors | Adjust submenu give several options for correcting this problem. You might be tempted to rush right in and select Brightness/Contrast, which certainly could do Fry-Brain some good, but there are a few other choices you should consider as well. To consider them intelligently, you should carefully take note of the range of tones in the image rather than simply glancing at it and pronouncing it "dark."

> ### Tip
>
> For simplicity, I'll treat this as if it were a greyscale picture. However, it is generally a good idea to correct a color image *before* you turn it into a greyscale image, even if you plan to place it on your Web page as a black-and-white image. Converting to grey before you balance the image can result in some degradation of an image due to the combining of similar-valued colors into a single shade of grey. By optimizing the color image first, you can often bring out distinctions between subtle shades that will then be retained when you eventually convert to grey.

When you look closely, you'll notice that Fry-Brain appears too dark for these specific reasons:

- His coat lacks highlights.
- He doesn't have a very wide tonal range. That is, his darkest color is too similar to his lightest color.

These distinctions may seem like "hair-splitting," but they are actually essential in adapting an image for successful display, especially on a low-resolution output device like a computer monitor. To see the range of tonal values in an image, you can select View | Histogram Window. The *Histogram* is a graph of the relative amount of each brightness level in the image, as shown in figure 5.6.

> ### Tip
>
> When you first display the Histogram Window, you will see four separate colored graphs, all displayed at once. These represent the amount of red, green, and blue light in the image and the sum of all these colors, called the *luminance*. It will be easier to correct the brightness and contrast of the image if you display only the luminance graph, and turn off the others by clicking in the Red, Green, and Blue checkboxes at the bottom of the Histogram Window. Figure 5.6 shows the Histogram Window with only the luminance displayed.

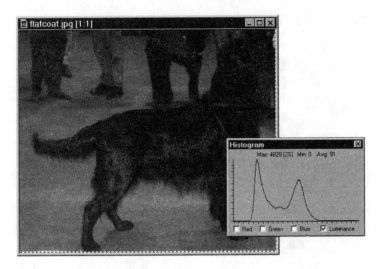

Fig. 5.6
Opening the
Histogram
Window gives you
a graph of the
relative brightness
of an image.

The histogram of a good image almost always covers the entire range of
tones, from the far left of the graph to the far right. You can see from figure
5.6 that Fry-Brain's histogram is bunched in two very small areas. In the next
few figures, you'll see how each of the available color adjustment controls effect the image and its histogram.

Note

From this point forward, the figures show the images (and the histogram) after I
press OK for the corresponding color adjustment. You won't see this change until
you click OK or Preview. (To make these illustrations easier to follow, I just opened
the same control a second time and specified the same adjustment.)

Also note that I went back to the original unmodified image before each adjustment
shown. Therefore, this series of images represent different alternatives for correcting
the image, rather than subsequent corrections applied one after the other.

Adjusting the brightness and contrast are intuitively the easiest corrections to
apply and are quite effective for many images. As you might expect, increasing the brightness simply moves the entire histogram to the right, and increasing the contrast spreads the histogram out horizontally. Figure 5.7 shows
the Brightness/Contrast control from Paint Shop Pro's Colors | Adjust menu,
along with the results on the image and its histogram. Compare this and the
subsequent figures with figure 5.6 to see how each adjustment changes the
original image and histogram.

Fig. 5.7
A small preview image lets you see what you're doing when you make color adjustments in Paint Shop Pro.

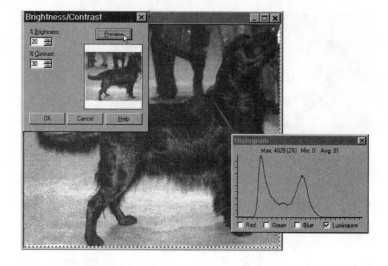

Gamma Correction

Another common tool for adjusting the balance of light and dark in an image is gamma correction. If you choose Gamma Correction from Paint Shop Pro's Colors | Adjust menu, you are asked to specify a single number between 0 and 5 as a correction factor. Numbers greater than 1 will brighten the image, while numbers less than 1 will darken it. The difference between this and direct brightness control is that gamma correction achieves its results by changing the "shape" of the histogram rather than simply shifting it to the left or right. For example, notice that the gamma correction of 2.0 shown in figure 5.8 increases the relative amount of light tones, rather than simply making all the tones lighter. This can be important since simply shifting a dark image too far to the right can cause loss of information by turning a range of light colors all pure white. Gamma correction keeps all the tones distinct, but changes their values.

Don't worry too much if this distinction still seems a bit elusive to you. Try gamma correcting a few images and you'll start to get the feel of which images benefit from it. Generally, gamma correction alone will leave an image too "flat," as figure 5.8 demonstrates. Gamma correction is usually most helpful when used in conjunction with contrast enhancement. The pros will often use the combination of gamma correction and contrast enhancement instead of the more obvious combination of brightness and contrast.

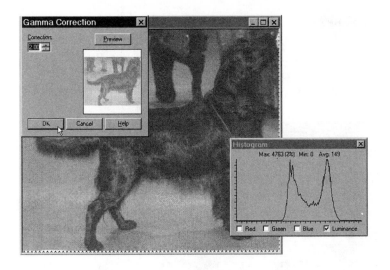

Fig. 5.8
Although gamma correction is more subtle than simple brightness adjustment, it is generally more useful when combined with other corrective measures.

Tonal Corrections

As you get used to looking at histograms and correcting the tonal range for images, you may start to think in terms of the specific regions of the histogram, and the role each region plays in the overall image. The brighter tones (or highlights) tend to add spark and character to the image, while the darker tones (or shadows) provide the visual anchor and underlying mood. In between are the mid-tones, which give an image a pleasing range of tonal variety. With the Highlight/Midtone/Shadow control on the Colors I Adjust menu, you can manipulate each of these regions independently or in conjunction with one another. Although this takes a bit of practice to get used to, it's the most powerful way to really improve most images, and therefore worth the time and effort.

Essentially, these controls let you horizontally stretch the histogram any way you like. When the control box pops up, Highlight will be set at 100%, Midtone at 50%, and Shadow at 0%. If you leave them at those values, the image will not change at all. But if you set Highlight to, say 80%, then the rightmost part of the histogram will be "pulled" to the right, making the bright tones brighter and turning any tones in the far right 20% of the graph to pure white. Similarly, if you set Shadow to 20%, the bottom part of the histogram will stretch to the left and the dark tones will get darker. Changing the Midtone setting pulls the center of the histogram to the left or right, making the middle range of tones either darker (for settings below 50%) or brighter (for settings above 50%).

If I were going to prepare Fry-Brain's inclusion on a Web page, I would start with Highlight/Midtone/Shadow adjustments and then apply slight contrast enhancement and gamma correction. Figure 5.9 shows Highlight, Midtone, and Shadow values that significantly improve the image by spreading the histogram out nicely.

Fig. 5.9
Adjusting the highlights, midtones, and shadows gives you more flexibility than simple brightness and contrast controls can provide.

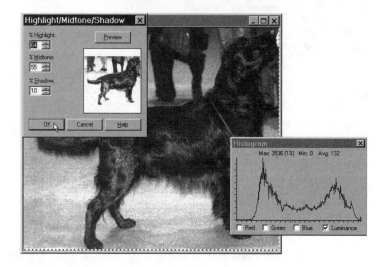

Correcting Color Images Using HSL and RGB Controls

There are two more color correction tools available in Paint Shop Pro (and most other photo editing programs), but they are primarily for full-color images rather than greyscale images. These color correction tools are the Hue/Saturation/Luminance (HSL) Controls and the Red/Green/Blue (RGB) Controls. Although the figures in this book are not printed in color, we can still meaningfully discuss these two controls. Most images on the Web are in color, so you will probably need to use color corrections as often as tonal corrections.

Select Hue/Saturation/Luminance from the Colors | Adjust menu in Paint Shop Pro and you get a control box like the one shown in figure 5.11. By adjusting the settings for % Hue, % Saturation, and % Luminance, you can move your whole image through "color space" to a more desirable location. Increasing the luminance is essentially the same thing as brightening the image. Saturation controls the richness of color and you will often find that photographic images greatly benefit from increased saturation. By adjusting the hue, you can eliminate a "color cast" caused by the film or lighting conditions where a photo was taken. You can also adjust the hue to deliberately give the image an artificial or surreal coloring.

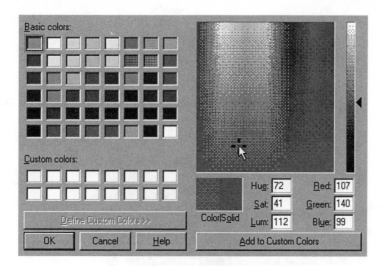

Fig. 5.10
The standard Windows color selector uses hue, saturation, and luminance to navigate through color space.

Since Fry-Brain is predominantly black, his image didn't need much color correction, other than bumping the luminance way up. I also pulled the hue over a little bit to make the ground brown instead of pale green, and I enriched the colors slightly by increasing the saturation.

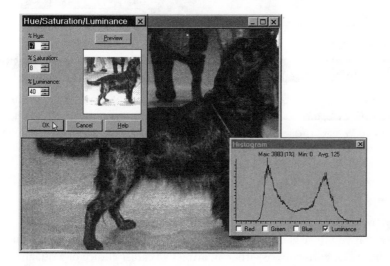

Fig. 5.11
By adjusting hue, saturation, and luminance, you can eliminate color problems in an image.

Hue, saturation, and luminance aren't the only ways to describe color. Any image can be represented on a computer screen or TV by combining the three primary colors: red, green, and blue (RGB).

Making Great Images

In fact, since RGB is what your computer monitor uses, you may prefer (as I usually do) to adjust the RGB values of a photo rather than the HSL values. Figure 5.12 shows the Red/Green/Blue controls from the Colors | Adjust menu.

When doing RGB color adjustments, you may find it helpful to turn the red, green, and blue graphs back on in the Histogram window.

Fig. 5.12
Red, green, blue adjustments are theoretically equivalent to hue, saturation, luminance adjustments, but require a different intuitive way of seeing images.

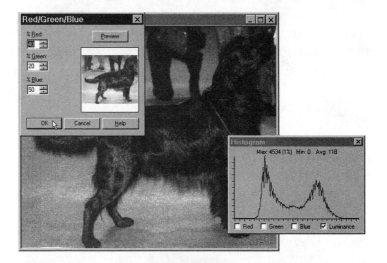

Tip

Using red, green, and blue to "make" colors is actually a trick, based on the physiology of the red, green, and blue receptors in our eyes. An image which appears yellow on TV may actually emit no light in the "yellow" region of the physical spectrum; it just fools your eye by stimulating the same receptors that real yellow light would stimulate. As you can see, there's more to color than meets the eye!

Equalization

Now that you have graduated from my crash course in color theory, you may feel like color correction is either an attractive career choice or a quagmire to be avoided. You might also wonder if some of this could be automated somehow. If the basic procedure for most images is merely to spread out the histogram to use the full range of tonal values, why can't the computer just figure it out and do it for you? Well, it can—quite often with spectacular results. But alas, at other times the results are disastrous and some hand-correction is almost always necessary.

To automatically redistribute the tones in your image over the entire histogram, select Colors | Histogram Functions | Equalize. Fry-Brain's response to this is typical: the range of tones is dramatically improved, but there aren't enough colors in the image to fill all the "gaps" that stretching the histogram opened up (see fig. 5.13). Therefore, the transitions between colors becomes too abrupt.

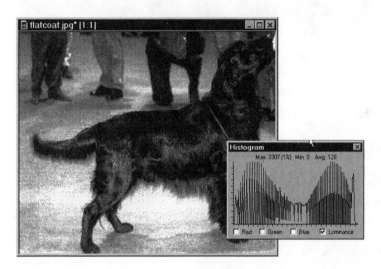

Fig. 5.13
Equalizing the histogram dramatically improves some images and destroys others. For this one, the result was a mixed blessing.

Selecting Colors | Histogram Functions | Stretch also stretches the histogram, but much more gently. Occasionally, this is enough to correct an image completely, but it's usually more of a place to start, before further massaging with the other tools we've discussed. Figure 5.14 shows the result of stretching Fry-Brain's histogram twice. Even after two times, the difference between this and the original in figure 5.5 is not very dramatic.

Making Great Images

Fig. 5.14
Stretching the histogram is gentler than equalizing it.

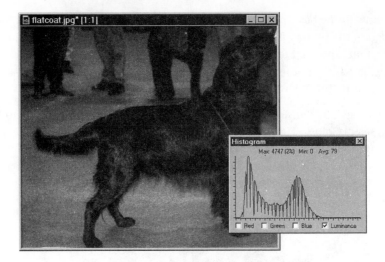

When used with the tone and color correction tools, equalization and histogram stretching are essential tools that can save you a lot of fussing and fiddling.

Isolating Subjects from the Background

You will often want to isolate the main subject of an image from its original background before you place it on your Web page. (Isolating a subject from its background becomes especially useful when you use transparent images. More on this in Chapter 9, "Creating Transparent GIFs.")

The difficult way to isolate Fry-Brain would be to outline him with the "lasso" hand-selection tool. Given the irregular boundaries of a flat-coated retriever, it would be impossible to "lasso" him with a mouse, and tiresome with a drawing tablet.

An easier way to isolate the main subject from its background is to use the "magic wand" tool to automatically select a similarly colored area. In this image, Fry-Brain is fairly well contrasted with the background, so this approach has promise. By double-clicking the magic wand, I can even adjust the tolerance to best capture the range of colors that distinguishes Fry-Brain from the ground. Selecting a region this way generally takes some trial-and-error to find the best tolerance, but in high-contrast images it can save a lot of work. Figure 5.15 shows the Magic Wand control box and tool, ready to make a selection.

Fig. 5.15
The "Magic Wand" tool automatically selects a region based on color similarity.

After highlighting Fry-Brain (and some unwanted but similarly colored background details) with the magic wand, I can then select Edit | Copy and Edit | Paste | As New Image to produce a cut-out picture as shown in figure 5.16. By carefully tweaking the tolerance and using the other painting tools to smooth the edges, I can get a better outline than this. Figure 5.17 shows where I started this approach but didn't bother finishing because it required a lot of picky work, which I knew could be done in a better way for this particular image.

Fig. 5.16
By pasting a magic wand selection onto a new image, you can cut a subject away from the background—sort of.

II

Making Great Images

Fig. 5.17
Careful tuning of
the magic wand
tolerance and
meticulous hand
editing (shown
here in progress)
can liberate even
the most complex
object from any
background.

The better choice, in this case, was to use the brightness and contrast controls
to fade-out most of the background to pure white. Figure 5.18 shows the result, which has much cleaner edges than any magic wand selection could
achieve on a low-resolution image.

Fig. 5.18
Using brightness
and contrast
controls to "wash
out" a light
background
sometimes works
wonders the magic
wand can't match.

> **Note**
>
> All the tools mentioned in the following paragraph are on the select toolbar in Paint Shop Pro. Similar tools are also found in almost every major image processing or photo editing program. For more details on how they work, consult the online help for Paint Shop Pro or your favorite comparable software.

To remove the rest of the background, I first eliminated the people's legs and shadows with the rectangular selection tool, the lasso selection tool, and the Edit | Clear menu command. Then I went in by hand with the paintbrush and "pushbrush" tools to clear away the background around Fry-Brain's head. Finally, I touched-up a bit with the softening tool to eliminate any jaggy edges. I chose to leave the small shadows under his feet, but I did use the image clone tool to get rid of that pesky leash. In figure 5.19, Fry-Brain is finally free!

▶ You'll discover more tools and techniques to improve your online photos in Chapter 6, "Filters, Deformations, and Special Effects."

Fig. 5.19
A bit of touching-up with the painting tools and he's a free dog!

Filters, Deformations, and Special Effects

Whether you are painting your Web page graphics "by hand," modifying existing artwork, or scanning your favorite photos, graphics software like Paint Shop Pro can do some of the hardest work for you. This chapter introduces a host of automatic tools that are used to create, modify, and enhance images at the push of a button. Then it explains how to use a number of seemingly magical effects to create snazzy buttons, 3D titles, and backgrounds as quick as you can click. Here is a brief overview of the subjects covered in this chapter:

- **Image Filters**

  Find out how Paint Shop Pro's automatic image processing features can improve your images and inspire your creativity.

- **Deforming Images**

  Warp, twist, pinch, punch, and otherwise mangle your photos and artwork to add flair or create the illusion of 3D perspective.

- **Combining and Layering Images**

  Here's a quick lesson in "image arithmetic." Create dramatic fades, partial transparencies, and many more professional-looking image effects.

- **Color Effects**

  Knowing how to manipulate color is crucial if you want to produce eye-catching Web graphics. Explore some odd-sounding but easy-to-use controls for color.

- **Special Effects**

  Learn to create "3D-look" buttons, drop shadows, glow effects, and seamless background titles almost instantly.

Image Filters

A good photographer or publishing professional can do very impressive color correction in a traditional dark room. Other forms of image enhancement, however, are difficult or impossible to do without a computer. Image filters based on a mathematical technique called "convolution" may seem especially magical in their ability to bring out detail, sharpen or soften edges, and automatically produce complex-looking special effects like embossing. But you don't have to understand the math or the magic to use filters. In fact, Paint Shop Pro's Image/Filter Browser control (see fig. 6.1) makes choosing and applying filters an almost brainless task (see fig. 6.2).

Fig. 6.1

Use the filter browser to preview any of Paint Shop Pro's image filters.

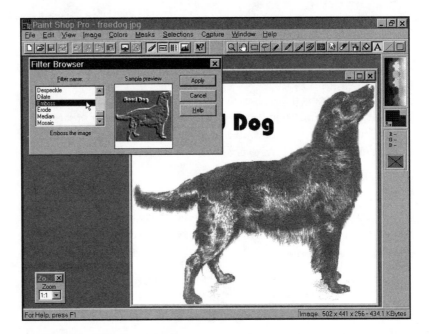

The Emboss filter (demonstrated in fig. 6.2) is especially popular with Web page builders for creating backgrounds and other graphics that appear to be embossed onto the page. By making the predominant color in an embossed image transparent (refer to Chapter 9, "Creating Transparent GIFs"), you can combine embossing with a background title for sophisticated effects like the one depicted in figure 6.3.

Fig. 6.2
The Emboss filter
is automatically
applied to the
entire image at the
push of a button.

Fig. 6.3
You can use
transparency with
filters for effects
that would be
nearly impossible
to create "by
hand."

II

Making Great Images

Because filters are easy to use once you see what they do, Table 6.1 gives you
an example of each type of filter. You should be able to tell from these examples and the filter browser which filter might help improve your image.
When in doubt, try it! You can always select Edit | Undo afterward if you
don't like the results.

Table 6.1   Fry-Brain Gets Filtered.

The Original Image

Edge Enhance

Find Edges

Find Horizontal Edges

Find Vertical Edges

Trace Contour

Blur

Soften

Sharpen

Unsharpen

Add Uniform Noise

Dilate

Emboss

Erode

Median

Mosaic

> **Tip**
>
> Note that the edge and emboss filters give better results on images that aren't scanned with a hand scanner (as the dog appears to have been). The extra "noisy edges" are by-products of the scanning process.
>
> I corrected this problem somewhat in figure 6.3 by reducing the contrast in the image before embossing it. Selecting Colors | Posterize can also help "tidy up" messy images before you use an edge-oriented filter on them.

Deforming Images

Retouching images can be a lot of work. However, it can also be a lot of fun—image deformation tools might be the most fun you can legally have with a computer (with all the new censor-the-Net craze!). As with filters, Paint Shop Pro gives you an interactive preview browser for deformations (see fig. 6.4). When you pick a deformation in the browser and click the Apply button, you get a dialog box that enables you to adjust the effect settings for that particular deformation and preview the results on the entire image before committing to it (see fig. 6.5).

Fig. 6.4
The deformation browser is your own computer-controlled funhouse mirror.

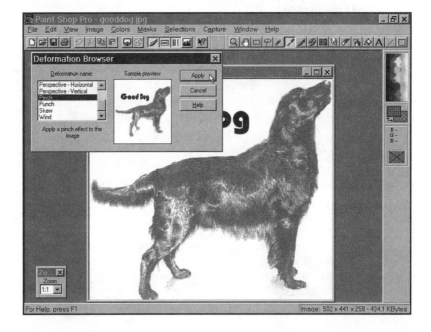

Since the results of these effects are almost always completely obvious, even in the small preview window, using deformations is pretty much a no-brainer. Since the process of using deformations is fairly simple, I have provided table 6.2 as a quick reference guide rather than go into a lengthy explanation of deformations.

Combining and Layering Images

Some of the most dramatic and useful graphics effects can be achieved by combining two images with "image arithmetic." To combine images in a variety of ways, use the Image | Image Arithmetic menu choice in Paint Shop Pro. For example, you can "add" two images together, making one appear superimposed over the other with partial transparency, as shown in figures 6.6 and 6.7.

Here's a quick tour of the Image Arithmetic dialog box shown in figure 6.6:

- Choose the images you want to combine from the Source image #1 and Source image #2 drop-down pick lists. For best results, make sure the two images are the same size.

- Select an "arithmetic" operation such as Add or Multiply from the Function selections. (Table 6.3 shows each of the choices in action.)

Making Great Images

Table 6.2   Fry-Brain Gets Deformed.

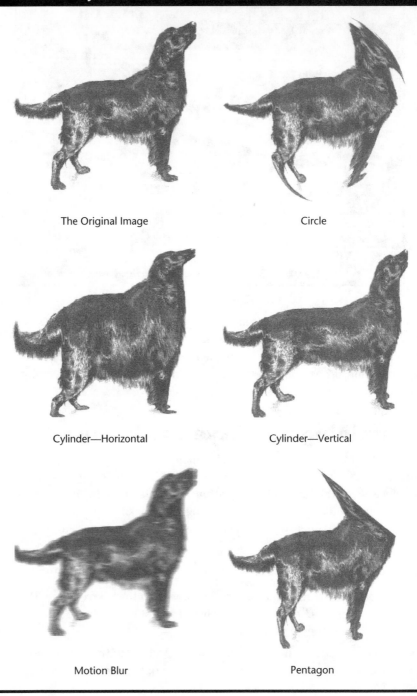

The Original Image

Circle

Cylinder—Horizontal

Cylinder—Vertical

Motion Blur

Pentagon

Perspective—Horizontal

Perspective—Vertical

Pinch

Punch

Skew

Wind Blur

- For color images, you can choose to work with the red, green, and/or blue color channels only. Normally, however, you would select All channels to work with all the colors in the image at once.

- Under Modifiers, enter a Divisor and Bias suitable for the operation you have in mind. (How to choose these values is discussed later.)

- You will almost always want to select Clip color values. If it isn't selected, super-bright whites turn to black or gray, and super-dark blacks turn to white or gray. This can create interesting effects, but it is difficult to predict and control.

When you click OK, Paint Shop Pro goes through each pixel in the first image and adds (or multiplies, subtracts, etc.) its value to the corresponding pixel color value in the second image. The result is divided by the number entered in the Divisor box, and then the Bias is added to that number.

For example, in figure 6.6, I selected Add and entered a divisor of 2. This adds each pair of pixel color values together and then divides by 2, effectively "averaging" the two images together, as shown in figure 6.7. I know all this may seem a bit complicated, but you don't need a mathematics degree to use these functions—really! Read the following sections to make sense of it all.

Fig. 6.6
The Image Arithmetic dialog box enables you to combine two images mathematically.

Combine these two images...

— to get this one.

Fig. 6.7
The settings shown in figure 6.6 create a third image by adding together the source images and then dividing by two to take the "average."

Image addition is relatively easy to describe, but the other Image Arithmetic Functions offer creative possibilities that words could never begin to convey. Therefore, instead of words, I offer you table 6.3, which shows each of the mathematical operations in action. For the second image, I used a gradation from black to white, which makes it easier to see how the operations work.

For all the examples in table 6.3, the divisor was 1 and the bias was 0, except for the Multiply example which used a divisor of 128 (a divisor of 1 would have produced a solid white image). You can generate many other effects by varying the divisor and bias to control the overall brightness of the resulting images—and, of course, by using different images. Simple gradations created with the paint bucket tool are especially useful for creating special effects with Image Arithmetic.

> **Note**
>
> Note that the Subtract example in table 6.3 shows the "bad dog" image subtracted from the "good dog" image. Since subtraction isn't symmetrical, subtracting them vice versa would give a significantly different result. All the other operations are symmetrical.

Color Effects

Paint Shop Pro, like most other serious graphics programs, offers a number of automatic color manipulation commands. These are easy to use once you understand what they do. But, if you aren't a trained graphics artist, simply reading their names on the Color menu may not give you much of an idea what they are used for.

The following quick run-down should give you enough information to start working (and playing) with these automated color commands. It also gives you some pointers on when these commands are useful for creating Web pages.

II

Making Great Images

Table 6.3   Image Arithmetic: The Good, the Bad, and...

Source Image #1

Source Image #2

Add: #1 + #2

Subtract: #1 – #2

Multiply: (#1 x #2) / 128

Difference: absolute value of (#1 ÷ #2)

Darkest pixel from #1 or #2

Lightest pixel from #1 or #2

Grey Scale and Colorize

Colors | Grey Scale simply turns an image into shades of gray, which is useful for the old black-and-white TV or '50s retro look. Colors | Colorize tints a greyscale or color image with a single color, while maintaining the relative brightness throughout the image (see fig. 6.8). You specify the Hue as a number between 0 (red) and 255 (violet), which are in rainbow order as displayed on the color picker at the right-hand side of the Paint Shop Pro window. You also specify the Saturation between 0 (greyscale) and 255 (brilliant color).

Fig. 6.8
Colorize lets you tint an entire image with the hue of your choice.

▶ Some of the most basic commands on Paint Shop Pro's Colors menu are not discussed in this chapter. For a basic introduction to the Colors | Adjust options and the Histogram functions, refer to Chapter 5, "Scanning and Enhancing Photos." The palette editing and color depth controls are discussed in Chapter 7, "Making Your Graphics Lean," and Chapter 8, "The Black-and-White Alternative."

The Colors | Colorize function is very handy for matching photos, background titles, and existing graphics with the color scheme you've chosen for your Web page. You can also create an "old-fashioned photograph" effect by first selecting Color | Grey Scale and then using Colorize to tint the image slightly brown or blue. Open the **maple/makeit.htm** page on the CD-ROM for an example of an old-fashioned photograph (shown—alas, without the color tint—in fig. 6.9).

Negative and Solarize

Colors | Negative Image replaces each color in an image with its opposite, just as the familiar negative in traditional photography. Compare the original image with that in figure 6.10.

Fig. 6.9
On your computer screen, these photos will appear tinted brown for an old-fashioned country look.

Fig. 6.10
There's no need to wait for developing negatives in your digital darkroom.

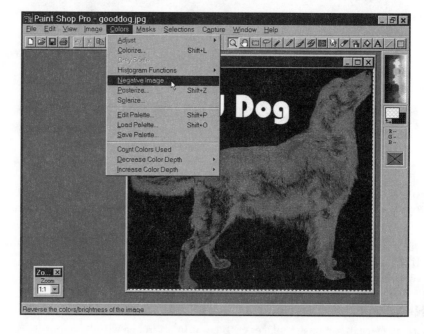

Colors | Solarize is also an effect borrowed from chemical photography. In photography, this process involved taking a print or film frame and intentionally exposing it to sunlight for a controlled, brief period of time. Some mid-twentieth century photographers became very fond of "solarizing" their images for the resulting half-negative, half-positive look. You can now experiment with this effect without so much as a whiff of developer fluid, and you can exert perfect control over the solarization threshold, as demonstrated in figure 6.11.

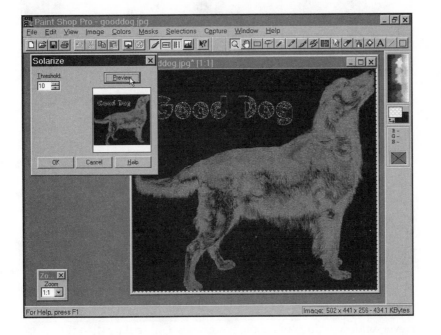

Fig. 6.11
By adjusting the Solarize Threshold, you can create some strange and dramatic effects.

On Web pages, Negative Image and Solarize should be used sparingly unless you want a dark, dramatic, and bizarre look. The photo in figure 6.12 uses a colorized negative along with deformation to create a scary looking site indeed.

Fig. 6.12
Negative images
are most useful
when you want a
macabre and/or
humorous look.

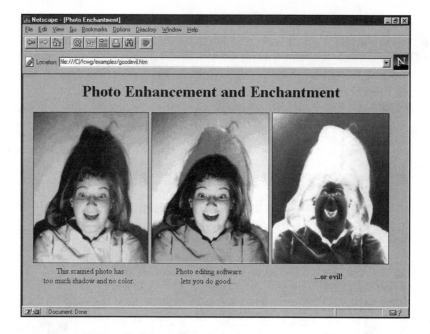

Posterize and Decrease Color Depth

The Colors | Posterize command borrows its name from an old technique used to reduce the number of colors in an image so that it could be printed inexpensively on a poster, in the days before four-color process inks were commonplace. Essentially, you indicate the number of colors you want to use in your image and Posterize picks the best colors to match the dominant colors in your image. (see fig. 6.13).

However, understanding and using Posterize is a bit trickier than this simplified explanation because you must specify the *number of bits* used to describe each color channel in the image, rather than simply specifying the actual number of colors. (see fig. 6.13).

Specifying the number of bits per color channel may be confusing if you're not up on color theory and computer math, so table 6.4 lists the correspondence between the Bits Per Channel and the total number of colors.

Fig. 6.13
Posterize reduces
the number of
colors in your
image, which can
give photos an
artistic look.

Table 6.4   How bits per channel controls the number of possible colors in an image

Bits per Channel	Number of colors per channel	Total number of distinct colors
1	2	8
2	4	64
3	8	256
4	16	4,096
5	32	32,768
6	64	262,144
7	128	2,097,152
8 (full color)	256	16,777,216

For greyscale images there is only one channel so the number of possible greyscales will correspond to the middle column in table 6.4. For color images, the rightmost column in table 6.4 tells you how many possible colors will be used to select the best colors for your image.

As an example, suppose you have a full-color image that you want to Posterize. If you enter 2 Bits Per Channel, Paint Shop Pro will pick the closest matching colors for each pixel in your image out of a "rainbow" of 64 distinct colors. The resulting image will usually not contain all 64 colors of the rainbow—it may contain only the six or eight colors that most closely match the image's color scheme.

If all this sounds complex, my advice is to simply experiment with Posterize and not worry about the theory behind it. The bottom line is that Posterize will reduce the number of colors in your image. Besides, you can easily use the Preview button to see the results for various settings without understanding exactly how it works.

You can also decrease the number of colors in your image by selecting Colors | Decrease Color Depth. This uses more sophisticated color mapping and dithering techniques than Posterize to get a better approximation of the original image's appearance. It can also be used for unique dramatic effects such as the dithered dog in figure 6.14.

Fig. 6.14
The Decrease Color Depth command can be used for special effects as well as reducing the size of image files.

You'll find out more about using Decrease Color Depth and other related commands to reduce file size in Chapters 7 and 8. However, as you read these practical chapters, keep in mind that the same commands can be used for the interesting special effects seen in the transparent, dithered and colorized "LOOK" title (see fig. 6.15).

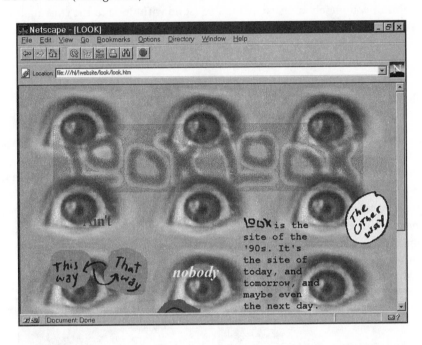

Fig. 6.15
This transparent title was created by dithering an image with the Decrease Color Depth command.

▶ One of the most magical and practical items on the Image | Special Effects menu is Create Seamless Pattern. Because this is specifically for making background titles, you'll find coverage of it in Chapter 13, "Backgrounds and Creative Layouts," instead of in this chapter. All the other items on the Special Effects menu are discussed here.

Special Effects

I've saved the best tricks in this chapter for last. Paint Shop Pro's Image | Special Effects menu is a treasure chest of time-saving gems to make your Web pages richer. (Note that you won't find most of these tricks in many other graphics programs.)

Drop Shadows and Highlights

One of the most popular and coveted effects used by every graphics pro is the "drop shadow"—a subtle darkening of the area directly behind a graphic or text to make it look like it's floating above the page. And, unlike many automatic computer effects, shadowing is in no danger of becoming an overused visual cliché. Shadows are just too prevalent in the physical world—in fact, *not* knowing how to use shadows is more likely to make your pages look mundane than overusing them.

II

Making Great Images

Fortunately, Paint Shop Pro makes drop shadows incredibly easy. You can add a shadow behind any selected text or region with the Image | Special Effects | Add Drop Shadow command. The Drop Shadow dialog box lets you pick the color of the shadow and gives you several other controls as well (see fig. 6.16). You can set the Opacity setting of the shadow to any number from 1 (almost completely transparent) to 255 (solid with none of the existing image showing through). The Blur setting controls how many pixels across the fuzzy edge of the shadow will be—a setting of 1 will make the edges crisp with no fuzziness and the maximum setting of 36 will make a hazy shadow or a "glowing" effect if you use a bright color. In figure 6.16 I chose a medium-bright shadow color around the light text, which gives both a shadow and a glow effect to the letters.

To control how far your object "leaps out" of the page, use the Vertical and Horizontal slider controls in the bottom part of the Drop Shadow dialog box. These set the vertical and horizontal offset of the shadow from the selection in pixels. Larger values make the selection look further from the page, and negative values put the shadow on the upper left of the selection instead of the lower right. For a glow effect, set both offsets close to zero and use a high blur setting, or select Add Drop Shadow twice and put one shadow below and the other above, as I did in figure 6.16.

Fig. 6.16

You can use the Add Drop Shadow command to create glow effects and fuzzy outlines as well as shadows.

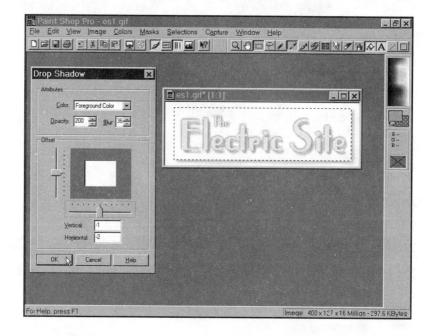

> **Note**
>
> To select Add Drop Shadow, you must have a full-color or greyscale image open and an active selection (with moving dotted lines around it). This is also required in order to use most other Special Effects commands; Paint Shop Pro can't add an effect if you haven't selected anything to add the effect to!

Creating 3D Buttons

Once you have an impressive title with a drop shadow behind it, you'll naturally want to create some 3D buttons for the links between your Web pages. Once again, Paint Shop Pro makes it a snap. Select a rectangular area with the selection tool and choose Image | Special Effects | Buttonize to turn it into a shaded 3D button in an instant.

Well, almost an instant. First you have to choose the exact button effect you want from the Buttonize dialog box shown in figure 6.17.

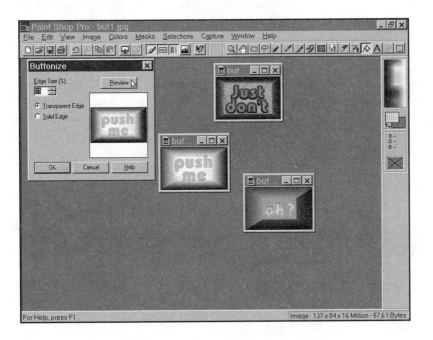

Fig. 6.17
The "ok?" button has solid edges, while the other two have transparent edges. Chiseling and Hot Wax Coating highlight the button labels.

The height of the button is set with <u>E</u>dge Size as a percent of the total button width. You can also choose between a button with transparent edges (like the "push me" button in fig. 6.17) or solid edges (like the "ok?" button in fig. 6.17). In either case, the button will be shaded with a combination of the current foreground color, the existing image, and shades of gray to create the 3D look.

Figure 6.17 also uses two of the three remaining options on the Paint Shop Pro Special Effects sub-menu: C<u>h</u>isel outlines the current selection for a chiseled effect, and <u>H</u>ot Wax Coating tints and chisels at the same time (more on Hot Wax below). The final option, C<u>u</u>tout, creates a beveled effect at the edges of the selection so it appears to be dropped slightly into the page. This is the same idea as the 3D-look borders of most inset controls in Windows 95 programs.

Hot Wax and Tinting

The last item on Paint Shop Pro's Special Effects list is a bit different than the rest. "Hot Wax Coating" doesn't sound like something you'd do with your computer, let alone a graphics program. Nonetheless, it is a very useful tool for Web pages because it combines a number of common tasks into a single, one-click operation.

The math behind Hot Wax is tricky and the effect is too. Basically, it tints the current selection with the foreground color while it also enhances the edges, improves the contrast, and darkens the highlights in a way that would be difficult to achieve without applying a number of other tools, one after the other. This makes Hot Wax an excellent choice for any part of a page or image where you want a button or illustration to look like it is layered over something else.

Of course, you could simply tint the area you want to highlight using the <u>C</u>olors | <u>A</u>djust tools, but then you wouldn't get such a cool looking effect. And hey, isn't that what it's all about?

Figure 6.18 compares a Hot Wax Coating region (the large rectangle on the left) with a region that was simply tinted (the smaller rectangle on the right). Gotta like that Hot Wax!

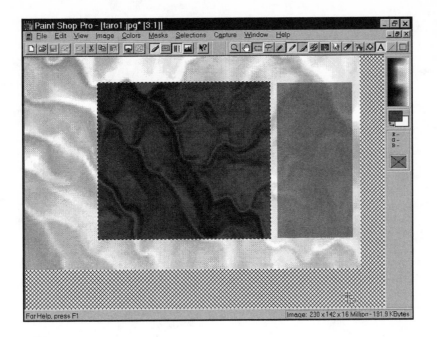

Fig. 6.18
Hot Wax Coating
(left rectangle)
provides a trans-
parent region with
more richness and
contrast than
simple tinting
(right rectangle).

Plug-in Filters

Though this chapter has covered just about every special effects tool that
Paint Shop Pro offers, I would be remiss in my duties if I didn't remind you
that Paint Shop Pro also supports standard graphics plug-in filters created by
many, many third-party developers. These plug-ins, from serious graphics gurus such as the makers of Kai's Power Tools, Alien Skin Black Box and Adobe
Photoshop, can give you even more creative power to make your Web pages
fly! ❖

Making Great Images

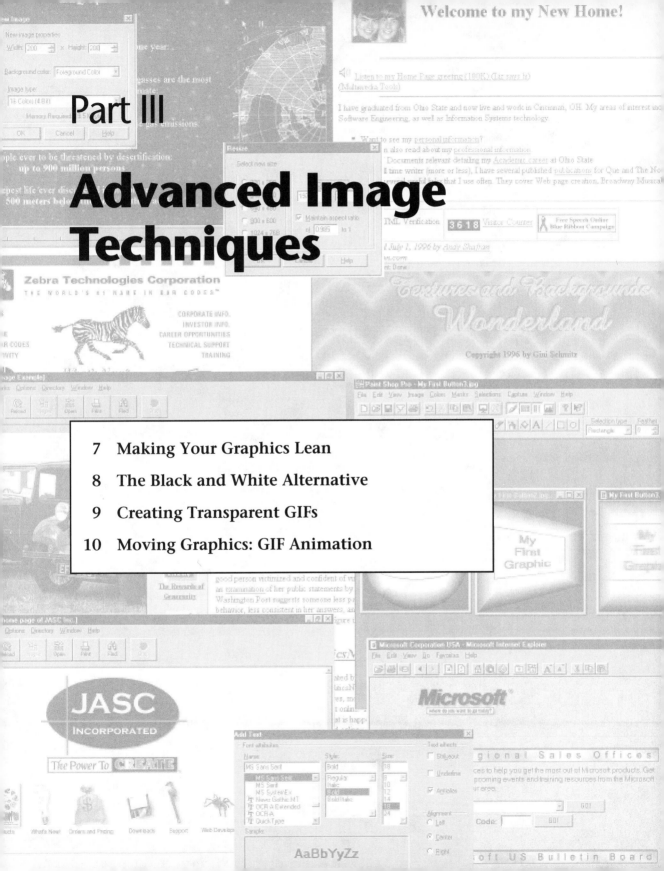

Part III

Advanced Image Techniques

7 Making Your Graphics Lean

8 The Black and White Alternative

9 Creating Transparent GIFs

10 Moving Graphics: GIF Animation

CHAPTER 7

Making Your Graphics Lean

In the first two parts of this book, you learned how to make and manipulate all sorts of images for your Web pages. Whether you created a new image from scratch, used Paint Shop Pro's advanced graphics capabilities, or scanned a photograph or logo, the chapters focused on creating and saving your images in electronic format. Learning how to create good images is the important first step in adding graphics to your Web pages.

This part of the book takes a decidedly different spin on working with Web graphics. Starting with this chapter, you'll learn several important techniques for making sure your images are small, efficient, and take advantage of important file compression possibilities. Since each image file must be downloaded before a Web page can be seen in its entirety, keeping your Web graphics small and efficient will make your Web site much quicker to explore and, consequently, more entertaining. Nobody wants to wait forever when visiting a Web site.

This chapter introduces you to several effective strategies that enable you to keep your image file size small, while maintaining reasonable detail and quality. Unfortunately, these additional performance benefits often come at the expense of image color and resolution. I'll show you how to balance these sacrifices to achieve the best quality and the most efficient Web images. This chapter will help you:

■ **Understand How File Size Equates to Performance**

In general, size, quality, and image format directly affect how long it takes for a GIF to download from the WWW and display on your computer. Learn how these different features correlate with one another.

- **Change Image Pixel Sizing to Save Time**

  By resizing, thumbnailing, and cropping your Web graphics, you can achieve a significant savings in Web page download time. See how these three strategies can be employed to make your graphics more effective and efficient.

- **Count the Number of Colors Used**

  GIF images are highly dependent on the number of different colors used in the particular image. Learn how to control the number of colors used in your GIFs to see a large difference in file size.

- **Understand JPEG Compression**

  Like GIFs, the JPEG file format offers special techniques to control the overall file size. Using JPEG compression, you can change the final file size of an image significantly without loosing much image detail.

- **Understand Interlaced and Progressive Images**

  One popular way to make images appear on Web pages quicker is to create interlaced GIFs or Progressive JPEGs. Learn how these special file options allow visitors to explore Web pages immediately.

Why Use Lean Files?

One of the largest obstacles facing Web users today is the amount of time it takes to browse through WWW pages across the Internet. When you visit a Web page, you must wait for all of the text and images to be electronically transferred, or *downloaded*, from the Internet onto your personal computer. The time it takes for this downloading process to occur depends upon the type and speed of Internet connection you maintain for your personal computer. The majority of individuals use a modem to browse through the WWW, while many businesses have faster, direct connections to the Internet.

Modem speed governs the rate at which graphics can be downloaded. Popular modem speeds range from 14.4 to 28.8 thousand bits-per-second (baud), but some people use faster—and slower—modems. In fact, new compression techniques can drastically increase your modem throughput and speed. The higher the baud, the faster the graphics can be downloaded for viewing by visitors browsing the Web. Table 7.1 below shows a comparison between several common modem speeds and the amount of data that can be downloaded at each speed.

Table 7.1 Download time comparison	
Baud	**Amount of data per minute**
9600	60 K
14,400	90 K
28,800	180 K
33,200	210 K

As you can see, even at the fastest baud rate it can take several seconds to download and see images on a large Web page. Therefore, one of the most critical tasks when creating Web graphics is to minimize the overall file size of each image on your Web page. By reducing the download time for visitors who stop by your Web site, you'll have better response to your site and people will be more likely to return for another visit.

Everyone expects to wait a few moments when visiting a Web site, but nobody wants to wait 30 seconds for each page to load, just to click on a hypertext link to move to another page. They want to quickly see a particular page, read through it, and decide where to go next. The longer people have to wait to observe a particular page, the more likely they will click the Stop or Back button in the WWW browser and never even see your site.

For example, let's say your home page takes about sixty seconds to download and view. If ninety people visit your Web site every day, one and a half hours are spent downloading your single Web page. By finding some way to reduce the download time to twenty seconds—maybe reducing the size or quality of an image—you can save visitors a lot of time, both individually and collectively.

Keeping your graphics small and efficient is imperative but extremely challenging. There are several methods you can use on Paint Shop Pro to help make your graphics small and lean.

Cropping, Resizing, and Thumbnailing Images

One of the most popular ways to reduce the total download time of a Web page is to reduce the actual area in pixels of the image being downloaded. You can save a significant amount of time by cropping or resizing an image so that a much smaller image is sent instead of the larger original one. Visitors can then click a hypertext link if they want to see the larger, full-size version of the image.

This section outlines two excellent ways to reduce the size of images on your Web page. You will use these methods primarily when dealing with photographs and pictures on your Web site. Not only do these methods make the Web site quicker to download, they also make it easier to design your Web page because it's often easier to design pages that use smaller graphics.

Resizing an Image

Perhaps the biggest mistake made by Web developers is to use an image that is just too large and unwieldy. In figure 7.1, I created a Web page for a dog named Ranger. This picture perfect GIF is over 55K in file size. Visitors who stop by have to wait over 30 seconds just to see this single picture if they are using a 14.4 baud modem (the most common speed).

Note

Another method of controlling an image's size is with special HTML tags—HEIGHT and WIDTH. See "Height and Width HTML tags" in Chapter 14, "HTML Tips for Web Images," for more information on the possibilities and drawbacks of using these two tags to control image size and appearance.

Although the image looks fine on this Web page, it just takes too long to download. One way to overcome this problem is to resize the image using Paint Shop Pro. By resizing the image, the GIF file size is made smaller because there aren't as many pixel coordinates in the file.

Originally, this image was 288 pixels wide and 230 pixels tall. I'm going to resize it to half its original size on the screen. At its original size, the image was 55K—pretty large!

The first step in resizing an image is loading the original in Paint Shop Pro. Choose File | Open from the menu bar and select the image you want to work with. To resize images in Paint Shop Pro, choose Image | Resize from the menu bar to bring up the PSP Resize dialog box (see fig. 7.2).

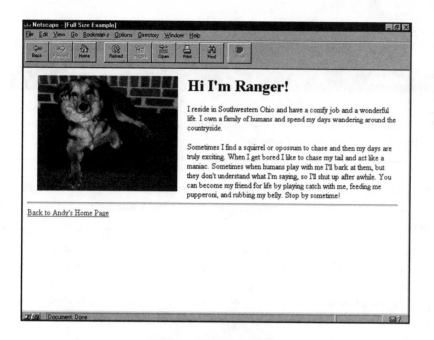

Fig. 7.1
Ranger is no
ordinary canine,
he owns a family
of five.

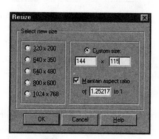

Fig. 7.2
Your new image
can be nearly any
rectangular shape
or size.

You can now choose from several default sizes or you can enter your own custom sizing. For this example, I am going to cut the pixel height and width in half and resize my image to 144×115 pixels by typing these numbers in the Custom size box. The Maintain aspect ratio checkbox allows you to control your image size relatively. You can tell PSP to make your image's height a relative size in comparison to its width. Selecting this checkbox allows you to specify an aspect ratio to maintain for height to width. So, typing in 2 to 1 as the ratio means that the width of the new image is twice what its height is. Paint Shop Pro takes care of the calculations for you. Once you've selected a

III

Advanced Techniques

new size, click the OK button and your image is instantly resized. Now save your newly sized image.

Caution

Make sure you don't overwrite your original image by mistake. Instead, save to a new file using the File I Save As command. Rename your image with a similar but descriptive name so you can easily tell the difference between the two files.

You can resize your graphics to nearly any size imaginable. Don't be afraid to evaluate several different sizes until you find the right one for your Web page.

As you can imagine, the newly resized image has a significantly smaller file size. At 144×115 pixels, the new file size is only 17K, quite a difference from the original size! At 17K, this image can be used comfortably on your Web page because visitors will see it in just about one third of the time it took to see the original 55K image.

Note

You can resize JPEG images just as easily as GIF images. The original photograph saved in JPEG format was only 17K, already quite a savings over the GIF file size. The smaller, resized image is only about 7K. At that rate, you could add a whole gallery of photographs to your page and visitors will happily download your image!

Remember that the JPEG format doesn't recognize special GIF features such as transparency and interlacing. Although you may decrease your overall file size, some features of your Web graphic might be lost.

Use of the smaller image on your Web page requires a bit more creativity. It's a good idea to learn several HTML text formatting tags to change your page's appearance to make up for the loss of your larger image. Chapter 14, "HTML Tips for Web Images," describes many different methods and strategies for integrating graphics onto Web pages in a logical and creative manner.

Figure 7.3 shows the newly redesigned Web page. I added an additional Horizontal Line (the <HR> tag), and increased the standard size of the text so that it takes up more of the screen (<FONT=+1> and </FONT> tags).

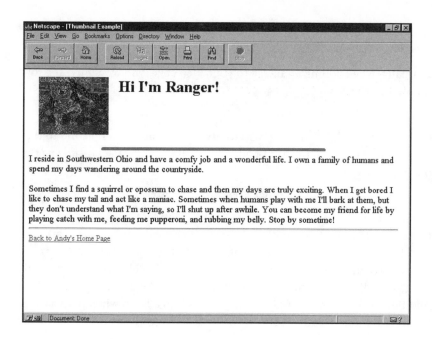

Fig. 7.3
Creative use of
HTML tags make
up for the smaller
photo of Ranger.

Making Thumbnails

When you resize the Web graphics on your Web page, you significantly reduce the amount of time it takes for visitors to browse your site. Unfortunately, resizing to a smaller image sometimes makes your graphic more difficult to see and less enjoyable for people who really want to see the full size image. Since it is physically smaller, you have to look with increased scrutiny to notice smaller, obscure details on your photograph.

To compensate for this potential problem, most Web sites use a process called *thumbnailing*, which gives visitors the opportunity to see both the large and small versions of a photograph, if they so choose. Thumbnailing is a process in which you display the smaller, resized image on your Web page but add a hypertext link to the larger, full size graphic. This enables visitors to see the photograph in its original, larger size and form—but only if they choose to do so.

Thumbnailing is easy. First create the full-sized image. Then, according to the steps outlined in the previous section, make and save a resized version. For this example, I have two files—BIGDOG.GIF and SMALLDOG.GIF. Notice how I named the files accordingly. There is no doubt about which file represents the full size image of the dog and which is the smaller, or thumbnail size, version.

Normally, when adding an image to your Web page, you would use the following line of HTML:

```
<IMG SRC="SMALLDOG.GIF">
```

However, when thumbnailing, you want to link your smaller picture to the full size one. To accomplish this, add the <A HREF> and </A> tags *around* the original image tag:

```
<A HREF="BIGDOG.GIF"><IMG SRC="SMALLDOG.GIF"></A>
```

This line of HTML not only tells your WWW browser to display SMALLDOG.GIF as part of the Web page, but it also tells visitors they can click on that image. When the visitor clicks on the image, BIGDOG.GIF is downloaded and displayed. Your Web browser adds a blue border around the image to indicate that the smaller image links to an additional photograph. Additionally, your mouse pointer transforms into a hand when placed over the linked image. Figure 7.4 shows the linked image in Netscape.

Fig. 7.4

The small dog image is now linked to the larger dog.

The mouse pointer ⎯

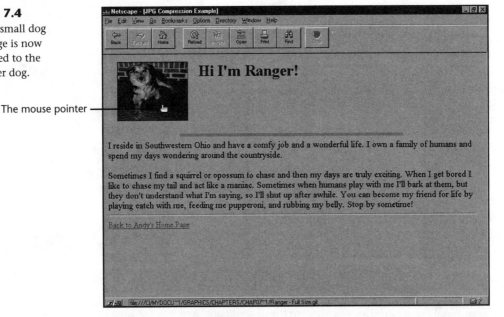

Cropping

Another way to reduce the size of your Web graphic is to crop it and display a small section of the original image. Image cropping has long been a tool of desktop publishers, newspaper editors, and graphic designers. Often, there are extra, unnecessary parts of an image that can be cropped away. The resulting image is smaller and contains only the entertaining and useful material.

Continuing with the same canine example, we might not need to display the entire picture of the dog to give visitors an idea of what Ranger looks like. By cropping to just his head, you end up with a significantly smaller image in both appearance and file size.

Paint Shop Pro has built-in cropping capabilities. Using your mouse, you can simply indicate which part of the image should be saved and the extraneous parts will be discarded. To crop an image, follow these steps:

1. Load your original image in Paint Shop Pro using the File | Open command.

2. Click the Selection icon from the Paint Shop Pro Tool Palette. This permits you to select a rectangular area of your image to crop and save. You can also select a square, circular, or elliptical shaped area by specifying the shape in the PSP style palette.

3. Using your mouse, select the part of the image you want to crop. Figure 7.5 shows an area being selected within Paint Shop Pro.

Fig. 7.5
I only need Ranger's head for this Web page.

The selected area

4. Choose Image | Crop from the menu bar. Paint Shop Pro will keep the selected area and discard the rest of the original image. Figure 7.6 shows the newly cropped area.

Fig. 7.6
Where'd the rest
of the image go?

The cropped image

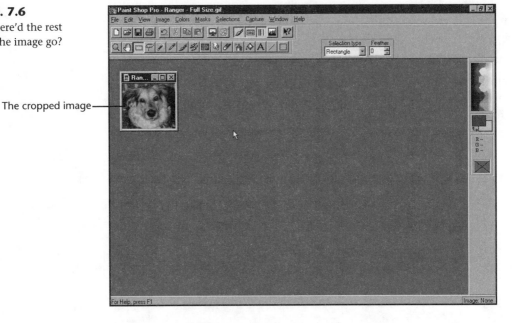

5. Save your newly cropped image with the File | Save As command so you don't overwrite the original graphic.

For this example, the resultant cropped GIF is only 7K, significantly smaller than both the original and even the resized graphic. Since we cropped the picture instead of resizing it, visitors won't have to squint to see the image because it is the original size and detail of the photograph.

As with resized images, many Web developers also link the cropped image to the full size one. This enables your cropped image to serve as a thumbnail so that visitors have the option of seeing the entire photo.

Make sure you consider cropping an image when using it on your Web page. If I decided not to make such a drastic crop of my dog picture, I could still crop the original full-size photograph to remove just the background and still save a significant amount of file size.

How Many Colors are Right for a GIF Image?

The number one way to decrease your GIF image's file size is to reduce the number of colors being used in the image. In GIF files, the number of different colors used has a direct correlation with the size of the file. The fewer number of colors used, the smaller the file size. This is different than the file structure that JPEG images use, where the file format depends less on the amount of colors used, but more on the compression level chosen. You'll learn how to shrink your JPEG images in "JPEG Compression," later in this chapter.

In this section, you'll learn how changing the number of colors can affect the appearance and file size of your image. Reducing the number of colors in a Web graphic offers the highest level of file compression for enhancing performance, but you can loose significant detail from your original full color image.

How Colors Affect GIF File Size

Actually, the file size isn't as completely dependent on the number of colors used as you might think. The placement of colors in an image also affects the GIF file size, as I explain below.

According to the specifications of the GIF format, an image is saved as a series of horizontal lines that go across the screen from left to right. Starting with the first pixel on the left hand side of the screen, the image records the specifications for that particular color—let's say blue. Continuing to the right, one pixel at a time, the GIF assumes that it should keep using the exact same color until a different one is specified. So, if the whole line is a single shade of blue, only one color definition is needed for the whole line of that image. Often there are several different colors in a single line of an image. Each time a different color needs to be displayed, that information is saved into the GIF file. Once the right hand side of the image is reached, the GIF starts over, like a typewriter, and starts defining the next line (pixel by pixel) of colors in the image.

It's easy to see that if only one color is required for the whole image, the file is likely to be small because there aren't any color changes. Therefore, a single-color Web graphic that is 300 × 300 pixels is only 1K. However, an image of the same pixel size will have a dramatic increase in file size if it has a bunch of different color changes on each line.

Figure 7.7 shows two 300 × 300 images with strikingly different file sizes due to the number of colors and color changes in each one. The image on the left is only 1K, while the image on the right is around 14K. Only 14 different colors are used in the second example, but there are a lot of different switches back and forth from one color to another.

Fig. 7.7
Same size,
different amount
of colors used.

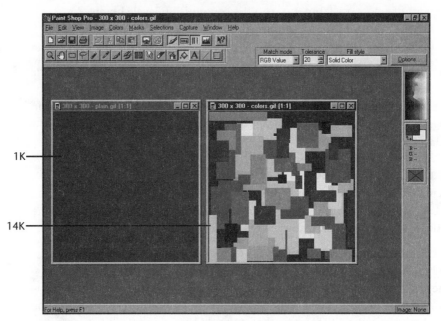

Unfortunately, this strategy only works for GIF images. JPEG files always have 16.7 million colors available and use a file structure and compression scheme that is different than GIFs. Additionally, a large GIF file that uses lots of colors will often significantly improve when converted into the JPEG file type. You'll notice this benefit particularly when working with scanned photographs for your Web page, which always use lots of colors and have a significant amount of color changes in them.

JPEG Compression is not dependent on the number of colors. Instead, JPEG files use a different form of compression that can sometimes lose detail. See Chapter 3, "Creating Simple Graphics," for an in-depth look at the GIF and JPEG file formats.

Usually, you'll want to save your Web graphics in both GIF and JPEG format and see which represents the best file size. Remember that file size isn't the only metric in creating Web graphics. Special features such as transparency, interlacing, and animation all have bearing over what file format you choose on your Web page.

Reducing Colors

Now that you understand the correlation between the number of colors used and the resulting GIF file size, let me give you an important strategy lesson on how and when colors can be manipulated to reduce your file size. By reducing the number of colors and color changes in an image, you can shrink your image's file size by as much as 75 percent!

The most popular color reduction strategy is to take an existing 256 color GIF and transform it into a 16 color image. Paint Shop Pro does all the color mapping and switching for you. This strategy must be used carefully. Sometimes, reducing the number of colors used degrades your image's appearance to the point where it is not usable on a Web page. You'll have to transform each GIF image individually and evaluate the results yourself.

When you reduce the number of colors, you instruct Paint Shop Pro to transform your 256 color image into one that uses only 16 separate and unique colors. Paint Shop Pro tries to match each of the original 256 colors with one of the 16 remaining ones. By reducing the number of colors used, your image loses some detail, but you get a tremendous file savings.

The first step is to get an idea of how many colors are currently being used in your GIF image. Load your GIF in Paint Shop Pro and choose <u>C</u>olors | Co<u>u</u>nt Colors Used from the menu bar. A small dialog box will appear (see fig. 7.8) and show you the unique number of colors in this image. For this example, my image has 244 different colors. Click the OK button to remove this dialog box.

Fig. 7.8
244 colors of the 256 maximum allowed are in use.

To reduce the number of colors in your GIF, choose <u>C</u>olors | <u>D</u>ecrease color Depth | <u>1</u>6 Colors (4 bit). Not only do you have fewer colors to choose from, but each color is defined in only 4 computer bits, half the amount required when 256 colors are used. The Decrease Color Depth–16 Colors dialog box appears (see fig. 7.9).

Click OK to continue. Paint Shop Pro automatically interpolates your current image and displays the resulting new one to you.

Fig. 7.9
PSP does the color reduction for you.

By reducing the number of colors from 256 to 16, you get a wide variety of results, depending on what your original image looked like. For example, figure 7.10 shows an example of a great transformation from a 256 color GIF to a 16 color GIF—you simply cannot tell the difference between the two images. The file results are excellent. The original GIF was 67K, which is too large for most Web pages. After the transformation with Paint Shop Pro, the new GIF is only 29K.

Fig. 7.10
For a substantial savings, you might as well use only 16 colors here.

256-Color GIF —

16-Color GIF —

Tip

This is an excellent example of when resizing the image would help. By shrinking the image down to half the original size, you don't loose any of the original image's affect—but you still see a hand of cards. By shrinking the image and reducing the number of colors to 16, my new image is now only 11K.

Caution

After reducing the number of colors used, be sure to give your new image a different file name from the original. Otherwise you might overwrite the original 256 color image permanently. Use the File | Save As command to save your 16 color GIF with a different file name.

Reducing the number of colors used in an image isn't always a perfect solution. Sometimes you lose significant detail and precision from the original image. This happens primarily when a vast range of different colors is used within a single image. Matching 256 colors to a 16 color set becomes a difficult task. Paint Shop Pro does the best job it can, but as figure 7.11 shows, sometimes image deformations occur.

In this example, though, we reduced a 150K GIF down to a manageable 40K—just by reducing the number of colors. Although we lose some quality, the performance gains may be worth it for your particular Web site.

Sometimes, of course, reducing the number of colors deforms your original image so much that the results aren't even worth the reduction in file size. Although the card example shown in figure 7.11 lost some detail, the resulting image was still usable. Figure 7.12, below, shows an example where reducing the number of colors just doesn't work.

This picture of an apple branch offers 75 percent compression when reduced from 243 colors to only 16 colors (101K down to 26K) but nobody would recognize the newly created image if added to a Web site.

III

Advanced Techniques

Fig. 7.11
Both sets of cars look fine, but there's a noticeable difference between them.

256-Color GIF

16-Color GIF

Fig. 7.12
You'll never want this 16 color GIF on your Web site—stick with the one on the next page.

256-Color GIF

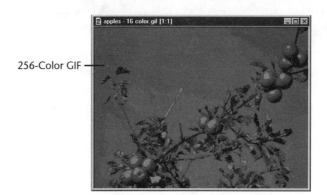

16-Color GIF —

As you can observe, reducing the number of colors used in a GIF image yields wildly different results, depending on what the original image looked like. The performance results are fantastic but often at a price of quality and detail. Test out your Web images by reducing the number of colors and checking out the results.

JPEG Compression

For GIF images, the best way to reduce file size is to reduce the number of colors in the graphic. As you observed, in some situations you received a huge file savings.

Similarly, the JPEG file format allows you to tweak performance and file size metrics, but in a different manner. The JPEG file format enables you to specify how much detail/compression should be used when saving a file. The higher the compression setting, the smaller the overall file size. Of course, there's no such thing as a free lunch. Compressed JPEGs take slightly longer for WWW browsers to process and display on a Web page because the image must first be decompressed before it is displayed. Additionally, by compressing JPEG images, you can lose some image quality. This loss isn't usually noticeable unless you have an extremely high resolution image with lots of details.

In Paint Shop Pro, JPEG image compression is set when you are saving your graphics. Open any JPEG image and choose File | Save As to bring up the PSP Save As dialog box. Then click the button labeled Options to bring up the File Preferences dialog box (see fig. 7.13).

Fig. 7.13

JPEG Compression is controlled here.

In the box labeled Compression Level, you can type a number ranging from 1 to 99. The higher the number, the better compression your JPEG will use and, consequently, the smaller the resulting file size. The default setting in Paint Shop Pro is 20. This offers little loss of quality for even detailed images and results in a reasonable file size. The other setting in this dialog box, DPI to be saved, is used by desktop publishers and word processors to control how an image appears and prints, and isn't useful to Web developers.

When the image is saved, the compression level is also saved with the image. Click OK to return to the Save As dialog box. From here you can specify a file name for your JPEG image.

Caution

In your Save As dialog box, make sure that the file type specified is JPEG.

Let's look at an example of how JPEG compression affects the way images appear on a Web page. Although it takes a few moments longer to process and display a compressed JPEG on-screen, the time is generally negligible.

Figure 7.14 shows the exact same JPG image displayed in six different compression levels ranging from 01 to 99. Each image is labeled with the compression level used and the file size of the image when saved at that level. Unless you have tremendous eyes, you probably can't tell much of a difference between the images, except for the one at 99 compression.

In general, compression levels above 90 provide so much interference that your image becomes unusable. Since my original image was 19K at a compression level of 15, and only 7K at compression level 80, it's easy to see how effective JPEG compression can be.

01 Compression, 43K   15 Compression, 19K   40 Compression, 10K

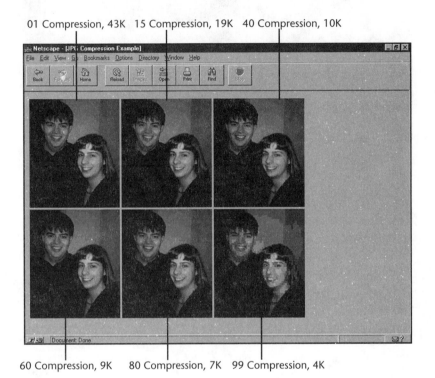

Fig. 7.14
Five out of these six images are virtually inter-changeable.

60 Compression, 9K   80 Compression, 7K   99 Compression, 4K

Much like reducing the number of colors used in GIF images, it's a great idea to save your JPEG at several different compression levels. Then you can compare each one and choose the level that has the smallest file size. This example provided a 50 percent reduction in file size with no significant reduction in image quality.

To emphasize how effective JPEG compression is, look at figure 7.15. This image of a jungle is shown at four compression levels. The file savings is amazing and even with this detailed picture, your image quality is great.

Fig. 7.15
I can't tell the difference between them, can you?

Using Interlaced and Progressive Images

Back in Chapter 3, "Creating Simple Graphics," you learned all about interlaced and progressive GIFs and JPEG graphics. You learned that interlaced GIFs display themselves in several passes, with each pass becoming more detailed and more clear.

Interlaced GIFs are nice, even when downloading a gigantic GIF, because you are able to get a general idea of what the image looks like as it is being downloaded—a nice feature for those people using a slower modem.

The JPEG file format allows similar functionality when saving an image in the Progressive JPEG format.

Saving an image in an interlaced or progressive format is simple. After creating your image, choose File | Save As to bring up the Save As dialog box (fig. 7.16). After deciding between JPEG and GIF format, look at your options in the Sub type drop-down list box.

Fig. 7.16
Interlaced images are the way to go for larger Web graphics

When saving a GIF, you can choose between Interlaced and Noninterlaced image formats. With JPEGs, you can use Standard or Progressive Encoding. As a general rule, saving your images in Interlaced or Progressive format is only useful when dealing with an image that is 10K or larger. For smaller icons, buttons, and bars, don't worry about Interlaced or Progressive formats because they are so small they download almost instantaneously.

Saving in Interlaced or Progressive format makes your image file around 10 percent larger than the original file, but the benefit is well worth the larger file size when saving larger images. Allowing visitors to see a rough outline of an image as it is downloaded increases usability for a Web page because visitors can start reading information on that page before the whole image is completely downloaded. Figures 7.17 and 7.18 show an interlaced image being downloaded from the WWW.

For more information on how Interlaced and Progressive images work, see the section titled "Saving Your Graphics" in Chapter 3.

III

Advanced Techniques

Fig. 7.17
This Interlaced image has just finished its first pass.

Fig. 7.18
Now the image is becoming clearer.

CHAPTER 8

The Black-and-White Alternative

Back in 1994, when *Schindler's List* was released, all the pundits believed that it wouldn't be successful, no matter how well it was done, because it was a black-and-white movie. For years, Technicolor had colorized the glamour and glitz of Hollywood and nobody could dream of filming and releasing a big screen picture that lacked color through nearly all the movie. Even the all time movie classic *Casablanca*, originally shot in black and white, has been colorized by Ted Turner and his creative production companies. Fortunately, Spielberg demonstrated that B&W movies aren't hopeless when well planned, produced, and filmed.

On the WWW, you'll notice a very similar philosophy. Color images are the defacto standard, with black-and-white Web graphics few and far between. But, as you'll learn in this chapter, colorless graphics aren't necessarily yesterday's news. Black-and-white pictures are often used on Web pages around the world for a variety of reasons.

In this chapter, you'll learn all about using black-and-white graphics on your Web pages. You'll learn to decide when to consider black and white, how to create these colorless images, and what interesting tips Web browsers use when working with B&W images. Most importantly, you'll realize that black-and-white images have an important place on the WWW for artistic impression and have significantly smaller file sizes than their color counterparts. In this chapter, I'll discuss these topics:

- **Know When to Use Black and White**

  Black-and-white images often evoke a unique feeling and setting when used on a Web page. Learn why many people use B&W pictures to offer artistic or thematic Web pages.

■ **Create New B&W Images**

Paint Shop Pro lets you draw new graphics using 256 shades of grey instead of the full color spectrum. See how to make new colorless images and how to use a grey color palette.

■ **Convert Color Images into Shades of Grey**

Saving full color pictures in the black-and-white format means that each unique color is matched up to a different shade of grey. Learn how PSP manages this conversion process so you don't lose any details in your image.

■ **Use Only 16 Colors Without Distortion**

Unlike color images, black-and-white graphics can easily reduce the number of grey shades colors used in an image from 256 to 16. Learn how to take advantage of this tremendous file savings bonus geared for B&W images.

■ **Overlay Images on Top of One Another**

Recently introduced, overlaying two images allows users to quickly get a feeling for how Web graphics look, without waiting for extremely large files to download. Learn to use the LOWSRC keyword as a valuable graphics tool on the Web.

Finding a Place for Black and White

In general, most images and graphics available on the Web use lots of different colors. Green, red, purple, yellow, orange, and blue are all a part of most people's everyday life when exploring with a Web browser. That's because colorful and vibrant graphics tend to catch the visitor's eyes, and make them come back again and again to a colorful Web page. When you visit the Walt Disney Web site shown in figure 8.1 (**http://www.disney.com**), you expect to see information about new movies and animated films, and you'd be sorely disappointed if you had to look at Quasimodo in only shades of grey.

Much of this book is dedicated to instructing you how to create these colorful images. You've learned that working with the Paint Shop Pro color palette to manage and match colors is critical when designing good Web graphics.

Since most people can see full color images without a problem, designing color graphics tends to only enhance a Web site. However, just like other art forms, there is a smaller (yet important) place for black-and-white images within Web pages. For example, visit the on-line Black-and-White Photo

Gallery at **http://world.std.com/~sjh/**, where you won't see even a hint of color (see fig. 8.2).

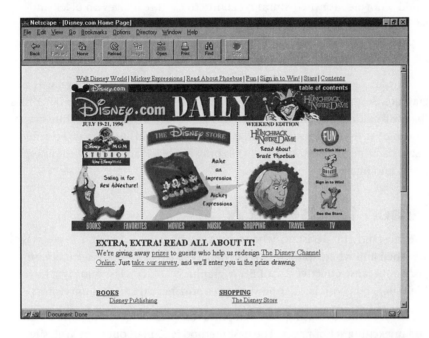

Fig. 8.1
We've come to expect brilliant displays of color imagery from the Disney Web site; too bad this book is in black and white!

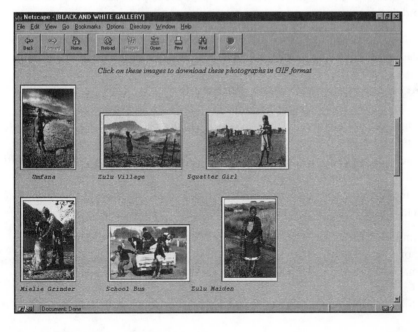

Fig. 8.2
Black and White photos are the way things work at this Web site.

III

Advanced Techniques

Black-and-white photography has its own distinct place in the art world. Famous photographers such as Ansel Adams and Robert Mapplethorpe are world renowned for their stunning ability to capture images on black-and-white film, knowing that color photographs would detract from the image. The overall effect of these B&W photos speaks for itself, letting viewers imagine how the colors might actually appear.

On-line art galleries aren't the only sites that use black-and-white images and graphics. Several sites also include them because they are usually smaller files than full color Web graphics. When properly created, black-and-white graphics can offer tremendous file savings over their color counterparts. To reduce download time for visitors, these sites only use black-and-white headlines, icons, and images.

When to Use B&W

The most difficult decisions when working with black-and-white Web images are when and where to use them on your Web site. These decisions are important because effective use of B&W graphics can add class and style to your Web site, and possibly offer powerful performance advantages for visitors.

On the flip side, overusing B&W graphics runs the danger of making a boring and unexciting set of pages. The best method is to plan out your Web site and decide why, where, and how many black-and-white images to use.

This section explores several reasons why you may want to consider creating black-and-white images for your site.

Artistic Emphasis and Value

When Steven Spielberg put together *Schindler's List*, he realized he was tackling a difficult and emotional topic—the Holocaust. Instead of filming a colorful and bright movie, he chose to produce a movie shot almost entirely in black-and-white film. The overall effect was tremendous. The black-and-white nature of the movie incorporated a dignified thoughtfulness that helped make the movie an Academy Award winner. He simply couldn't have achieved the same effect with a color movie.

Similarly, there may be situations where your Web pages relate to a specific topic that enables, or even requires, you to consider using black-and-white images. For example, if you were to create a memorial Web page for victims of a plane crash, a set of black-and-white photographs might better fit the mood of such a solemn topic.

There are other artistic and practical reasons to consider black-and-white pictures. A botanist might create a Web site that depicts several different tree leaves, emphasizing the shape of a leaf instead of its color and hue. Or, a movie purist might create a Web page for their favorite old cinema stars—Clark Gable, Ingrid Bergman, and Humphrey Bogart. You can find these actors mainly in black-and-white movies, so using B&W images at this particular Web site would fit the theme and artistry of this specific topic. Figure 8.3 shows a Black & White Web site dedicated to The Jazz Singer (**http://www.cwrl.utexas.edu/~nick/e309k/texts/jazzsinger/jazzsinger.html**), the first movie that used sound.

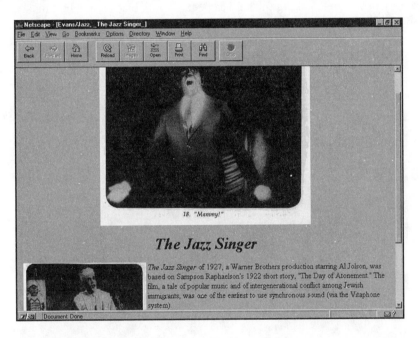

Fig. 8.3
This site thought ahead and integrated black-and-white images.

Theme Coordination

Another popular reason for keeping color out of your Web graphics is to follow a particular theme or topic for your site. There are many common ideas and themes that make you think solely of black and white. When creating a Web page about one of these topics, it may be creative to play on these colorless euphemisms.

For example, a zoo might have a page dedicated to zebras, albino monkeys, or even have a photo of a white tiger. There's simply no purpose for a full color photo of an animal that exists only in shades of grey. Similarly, imagine creating a wedding Web page. Often a wedding's colors are simply black and white. Nothing could be more appropriate for a Web page than matching that particular theme with black-and-white images.

Be careful not to overload your Web page with only black-and-white images. Even an appropriate topic can get boring when everything is colorless. Choosing black and white for theme-based Web pages can quickly lose its novelty. It may leave too many visitors with a desire for colorful images.

One example of a Web page that uses black and white to follow a theme is found at the Santa Ana Zoo Web site (**http://santaanazoo.org**). With lots of animals on-line, making the bald eagle page only black and white makes sense (see fig. 8.4).

Fig. 8.4
You'd expect this web page to be only in black and white (or red, white, and blue).

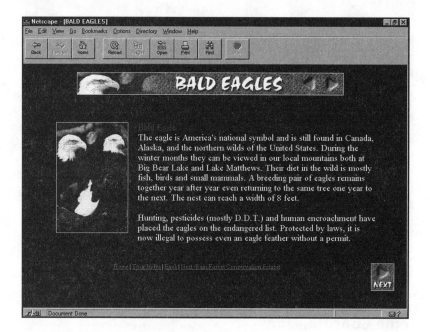

Performance Considerations

The third popular reason for using black-and-white graphics on a Web page, instead of color pictures, is for increased performance through reduced image file size. Often, black-and-white pictures are smaller in file size than their color counterparts. As you learned in Chapter 7, "Making Your Graphics Lean," file size is highly dependent on the number of colors used in an image, and converting a color image into B&W can significantly reduce the number of colors in an image.

Additionally, many Web sites take advantage of a new HTML tag that allows you to integrate high resolution and low resolution graphics on a Web page. These Web sites create lower resolution black-and-white images that load quickly on a Web page. Then, your WWW browser goes back and reloads a color, higher resolution picture, which replaces the original B&W image. You'll learn more about this performance enhancing technique in "Overlaying Images," later in this chapter.

Creating B&W Graphics

Now that you are familiar with when to use black-and-white Web graphics, it's time to see how you can create some for yourself. In this section, you'll see how Paint Shop Pro allows you to build new images from scratch and convert color pictures into shades of grey.

You'll see that making black-and-white graphics is very similar to creating Web graphics that use a full set of colors. Converting existing color images into black and white is an important part of building Web graphics because many images you'll want to use will originally come in full color.

Making New Images

Creating a black-and-white image in Paint Shop Pro is easy. Simply choose File | New from the menu bar to bring up the New Image dialog box (see fig. 8.5).

Fig. 8.5
Creating color and B&W images starts here.

In the Image Type drop down list box, choose 256 Greys (8 bit) and then click the OK button. Paint Shop Pro sets the image size depending on your selection. This example is sized at 300 × 300 pixels. You now have 256 colors—all different shades of grey, ranging from black to white, available to draw and design with. Set your drawing color by clicking either the foreground color box or the background color box, which are the overlapping boxes found in the Color Palette. The Edit Palette dialog box appears, letting you choose from a plethora of different intensities of grey (see fig. 8.6).

Fig. 8.6
Every shade of grey under the "rainbow" is available here.

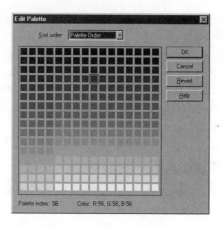

> **Note**
>
> When you click anywhere in the rainbow of colors available in the Color Palette, Paint Shop Pro translates the color you clicked into an appropriate shade of grey.

Now you can create a black-and-white image just as you would any other Web graphic. All of the techniques you learned in Chapters 3 and 4 for drawing and using Paint Shop Pro work identically using B&W, as if you had a full color palette available to you.

It's important to point out that when you create black-and-white images in this fashion, your file size will be identical to the file size you would have if using color graphics. That's because file size is dependent on the number of colors available and the number being used in the image. Reduced file size comes from using fewer unique colors, a process usually much easier to accomplish when only working with black-and-white graphics. One popular technique used to reduce file size is to choose Colors | Decrease Color Depth | 16 Colors from the menu bar to reduce the available color palette to only 16 shades of grey instead of the default number of 256. Don't reduce the number of colors on a blank image. Paint Shop Pro will provide you with a blank palette (all white). Instead, only reduce the number of colors on a Web graphic that has some text or drawing in it.

For all practical purposes, when creating Web graphics from scratch, you'll find 16 shades of grey plenty of variety for making buttons, bars, headlines, and other types of Web graphics.

When you are finished making your image, choose File | Save to store your new graphic on your computer. Remember that only the GIF file format allows you to save in the 256 color mode. The JPEG file type uses 16.7 million colors and incorporates all of the shades of grey. Black-and-white images tend to be saved in GIF format.

Converting Color Graphics To B&W

Although you'll occasionally create new B&W graphics from scratch, many useful black-and-white images come from pictures that were originally in full color. Using Paint Shop Pro, you can convert color images into grey scale format quickly, and vice versa.

Converting a color graphic into black and white doesn't change how the picture appears. You'll still be able to detect subtle shadows, brighter and darker colors, and different lighting effects. It's really just like watching a color television show on a black-and-white TV. You're watching the same program but seeing the scenes slightly different.

To convert a full color image into black and white, load your color graphic into Paint Shop Pro. Then choose Colors | Grey Scale from the menu bar. Paint Shop Pro will perform a special algorithm to match up each color to a particular shade of grey. Once Paint Shop Pro is finished, you can save your newly converted graphic. Be sure to give it a different file name so you don't overwrite your original full color graphic.

Caution

This can be a memory intensive operation. Converting a large color graphic into a black and white image can take several moments for PSP to calculate.

When converting color images to the B&W format, you'll reduce file size by 5-25% from the original size. In general, you can expect your new file to be around 10% smaller than the original color image. That's because the conversion most often reduces the number of colors used in the newer image.

Using 16 Shades of Grey

In Chapter 7, "Making Your Graphics Lean," I talked about reducing the number of colors in your graphics from 256 to 16 to realize a significant savings in the overall file size. Unfortunately, a drawback to using only 16 colors in a graphic is that it produces a lower quality image. Often, you lose detail when you reduce the number of available colors, which makes your Web graphics less enjoyable to look at and less suitable for inclusion on your Web pages.

When working with black-and-white images, you can likewise reduce the number of grey shades from 256 to 16 and get quite a savings in the original file size—often with little to no loss in image detail and quality, unlike color images. That's because the human eye has more difficulty separating different shades of grey when looking at a computer graphic. With color images, it's easy to discern different colors, even between individual pixels, because our eyes easily notice the differences. Black-and-white images work slightly different because all shades of grey are so similar in nature. Therefore, grey scale differences between pixels are less pronounced and less noticeable.

Additionally, Paint Shop Pro is slightly more optimized when working with grey scale because it doesn't have to do the work of mixing different values of red, green, and blue when interpolating a color; it only has to decide upon a single shade of black, a much easier task, which results in higher quality and better resolution images in the black-and-white format.

You'll find that the problems you encountered when reducing color images to 16 colors simply don't exist with B&W graphics (as you'll see momentarily in an example). To reduce the amount of colors used in your Web graphic, choose <u>C</u>olors | <u>D</u>ecrease Color Depth | <u>1</u>6 Colors from the menu bar to bring up the Decrease Color Depth dialog box shown in figure 8.7.

Fig. 8.7
Converting 256 shades of grey to 16 is a piece of cake.

This dialog box enables you to make an important decision on how Paint Shop Pro should convert each of the original 256 colors into the remaining 16. You have two options in the Reduction method section of this dialog box:

Nearest Color—Paint Shop Pro does a strict conversion color by color. Each pixel is evaluated dot by dot and transformed into one of the remaining 16 shades. It's simply a rote transformation. This method is often preferred when using color images because it's the best type of color reduction available when working with reds, greens, and blues.

Error Diffusion—This method involves using slightly more advanced logic and is geared for working with black-and-white images, or graphics that use a smaller variety of colors. Paint Shop Pro looks at each image, section by section, and decides how best to reduce the number of colors/shades in that particular section.

Using a process called *dithering*, PSP doesn't bother transforming each pixel individually. Dithering reconstructs a small section of your Web graphic so that it uses fewer shades of colors. By mixing and matching new shades to replace the old section, all of the colors run together and trick your eyes. You end up looking at a group of pixels whose colors have been rearranged to emulate the original 256 color pattern.

Here's how dithering works: We all know that yellow and blue mixed together make green. What actually happens when you see green on the computer screen is that you are seeing a bunch of very tiny yellow dots interspersed with a bunch of very tiny blue dots. However, your eye can't distinguish between the separate colors because the dots are so small. Therefore, your brain interpolates the collected pattern of yellow and blue as green. If more yellow dots are in the pattern, you end up seeing a lighter green. Consequently, more blue dots in a pattern make up a darker green in your eye's detection capacity. Dithering is that process of mixing lots of tiny dots together to fool your eye into thinking it is observing something else. So, it changes a section of pixels and mixes all different shades of grey together so that you think you are looking at the same picture.

With black-and-white images, the results of the error diffusion, or dithering, are astounding. You'll lose virtually no detail in your image but will get tremendous file savings. I recommend always choosing this setting when reducing the number of shades of grey in your image.

Once you've selected a reduction method, click the OK button to continue and PSP runs the color/shade reduction algorithm through your Web graphic. Often, this process will take longer than converting it from a color image into one that is black and white.

Below, in figures 8.8, 8.9, and 8.10, I've shown three different black-and-white versions of the same image. Figure 8.8 is the image that has 256 shades of grey.

Fig. 8.8
256 shades of grey image—92K.

Figure 8.9 is a 16 shade image that uses the Nearest Color Reduction Method, which yields a 60% savings in original file size from the 256 grey scale image.

Fig. 8.9
16 shades of grey image using Nearest Color— 38K.

Figure 8.10 uses the Error Diffusion Reduction Method and yields a slightly worse file size reduction at only 50% from the 256 grey scale image, but also has slightly better detail and quality.

Fig. 8.10
16 shades of grey image using Error Diffusion—44K but great quality.

Just for a fair comparison, figure 8.11 shows how the color image looks when we reduce it to only 16 colors from 256. Even though this book is in black and white, you can easily notice a tremendous difference in resolution and quality. Check out this set of images on the CD-ROM included with this book to see these examples in color.

Fig. 8.11
Reduced to only 16 colors, this image stinks, but has the smallest file size at 26K.

Overlaying Images

As you can see, creating and working with black-and-white images often has significant performance enhancement opportunities for Web developers. It's easy to take a detailed color image and convert it into one that is black and white. This saves up to 75% from the original file size without losing much detail from the original picture. That's even before you consider resizing, cropping, or thumbnailing your image to save even more in file size.

However, many Web developers still prefer using bright and colorful images on their Web pages, even when given the performance options of B&W pictures. Visitors tend to enjoy colorful images more and will come back to visit more often when they remember and like a particular Web site. Web developers are often in the juxtaposition of choosing between brilliant colors and great file performance.

To solve this dilemma, a new HTML keyword was added to the <IMG> tag, which enables Web developers and visitors to experience the benefits of both worlds. Called the Low Resolution keyword (LOWSRC=), this new bit of HTML lets you instruct your WWW browser to first load and display a smaller, low resolution image file and then, when the whole page is finished loading, begin displaying a normal, high resolution image.

III

Advanced Techniques

In practice, Web developers often have a large, color image that is simply too big to use on a Web page. Instead, they follow the steps outlined in this chapter and create a significantly smaller black-and-white image that can load and be displayed for visitors immediately. Once the whole page is loaded, the Web browser overlays the original black-and-white image with the higher resolution color image. This enables the visitor to read and explore the Web site while the colorful pictures are being downloaded.

For example, let's say I have two images. One is called LOWCAR.GIF which is a 16 color, less detailed, black-and-white picture of two automobiles. My colorful, high resolution image that uses all 256 colors is named HIGHCAR.GIF. To use the new LOWSRC keyword, I add the following line of HTML:

```
<IMG SRC="HIGHCAR.GIF" LOWSRC="LOWCAR.GIF">
```

That's it! Figure 8.12 below shows this process in action. Netscape first loaded LOWCAR.GIF and then HIGHCAR.GIF, which figure 8.12 shows in the middle of being displayed on top of the B&W image.

Fig. 8.12
Although difficult to tell, half of this image is in color and half is in black and white.

The color line —

Many professionally designed Web sites use this method to achieve a great effect. Try visiting the Cover Girl Web site (**http://www.covergirl.com**) to see how the color and non-color images overlay one another (see fig. 8.13).

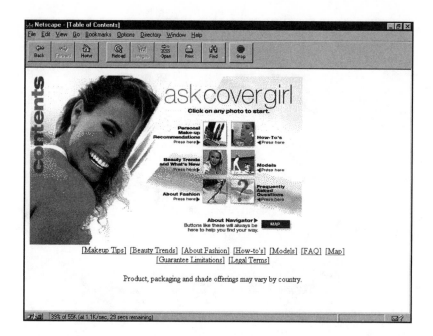

Fig. 8.13
Cover Girl really
knows how to
speed up perfor-
mance.

Spot Color and B&W

Another popular way of using black-and-white images on the WWW is to
mix them with limited use of spot color. By mixing a primarily black and
white set of graphics with complimentary color graphics, you achieve the file
savings and theme-based desire of black and white images.

One example of a site that uses mostly black and white, with just a hint of
color, is found at **http://www.zebra.com** (see fig. 8.14). This high quality
site represents a company that makes bar coding machines. All of the images
on its home page are appropriate in black and white, but it uses a hint of bur-
gundy in its larger headlines to attract subtle attention to important information and to break up simple monotony.

Using mostly black-and-white images with slight color is very useful. You can
add simple color to your existing images, integrate multiple images on a
single Web page, or simply change the color of your text to something creative. For more information, see the section titled "Color Coordination" in
Chapter 14, "HTML Tips for Web Images."

III

Advanced Techniques

Fig. 8.14
This Web site knew when to add a splash of color to keep visitors interested.

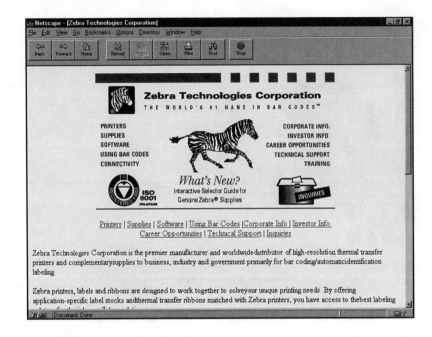

CHAPTER 9

Creating Transparent GIFs

Throughout much of this book, you've focused on the two primary image types—GIF and JPEG. Both offer different advantages over one another in various situations and part of the process of creating high quality Web graphics is choosing the correct image format.

In general, GIF and JPEG images have many of the same features and much of the same flexibility. The main difference is the way each of them handles image compression and large amounts of colors. In this chapter, I change gears and show you how to take advantage of a powerful GIF-only feature for your Web images called *transparency*.

GIF images enable you to specify one color within the file that WWW browsers will ignore and treat as transparent. The end result is that your WWW browser displays the normal GIF image but ignores the designated transparent color and, instead of the designated color, shows the Web page's background color or pattern. Much like an overhead machine displays transparencies with its projector, Netscape and Internet Explorer display transparent GIFs on Web pages as more natural looking images.

Transparent GIFs are a powerful tool in a Web developer's toolbox. Creating effective images for the World Wide Web requires that you understand and use transparent GIFs to enhance your entire Web page experience. This chapter covers these important transparent GIF topics:

- **What are Transparent GIFs**

  Learn the technical specifications for how transparent GIFs work, are saved, and displayed by WWW browsers.

■ **When to Use Transparent GIFs?**

   Like all new features, transparent GIFs are ideal only for certain situations. Decide when creating transparent GIFs is worth the time and
   effort.

■ **How WWW Browsers Treat Transparent Characteristics**

   Netscape and Internet Explorer both recognize transparent GIFs and
   know how to correctly display these images on a Web page. Understand
   the mechanics of how browsers treat these new images.

■ **Specify a Color to be Transparent**

   Only one color in a GIF file can be designated as transparent. Learn
   how to identify and indicate that a particular color be transparent using
   built-in Paint Shop Pro tools.

■ **Create Floating Photographs**

   Once you understand how to make simple transparent GIFs, learn how
   to add odd shaped "floating" photographs to your Web page instead of
   always having rectangular shaped photos.

What are Transparent GIFs?

It's easy to understand what transparent GIFs are and how they work. Just
think of how an overhead projector works. An overhead projector takes
pieces of clear plastic with writing on it and displays only the writing on a
screen. Since the plastic is transparent, it isn't projected onto the screen.
Transparent GIFs work in a similar fashion. The GIF file format enables you
to specify that a particular color (of the 256 available colors) appear transparent when shown within a WWW browser.

So, instead of appearing normal, the specified color appears transparent—
whatever is on the Web page's background is displayed instead of that color.
You can choose only one color to appear transparent on a graphic. Using
Paint Shop Pro, it is easy to identify and save the color that you want to appear transparent.

Often, transparent GIFs are used in images which use the color white in the
background of the image. The white part of the image represents area not being used in the image and is saved as a section of blank white area. By setting
white to be transparent, Netscape ignores this color in the image and makes
the image appear to "float," or fit in with the actual Web page better. The
white that is part of the image becomes transparent, or see-through.

Figure 9.1 shows an example of this phenomenon. On this Web page, I have created a simple Tic-Tac-Toe board using two images—an *X* and an *O*. For this example, the background color of the Web page is set to gray.

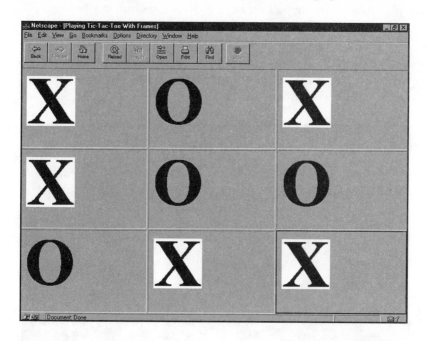

Fig. 9.1
The Os fit in much more nicely with the screen than the Xs do because the background of the Os is transparent.

Both images are nearly identical. They are the same size in pixel height and width and use only two colors—black and white. I used Paint Shop Pro to create both of them. The only difference is that I instructed Paint Shop Pro to make the white on the *O*s transparent—so we can see right through the center of the *O*s when added to the Web page. For the *X*s, I did not instruct PSP to make the white transparent. As a result, Netscape ignores the white for the *O*s, but not for the *X*s, and you can easily recognize which image looks better when used on a Web page.

Transparent GIFs improve the way images appear on your Web page. Non-transparent images sometimes look awkward and out of place because they display the Web page background graphic, or color behind your image, and interfere with the overall result of using images on Web pages. In general, you want to explore using transparent GIFs when you define any background color or use a background image on your Web page. This allows your Web browser to ignore parts of an image on your page that are not necessary.

III

Advanced Techniques

The creation and use of icons on Web pages is another example where transparent GIFs are extremely practical. Many people like to create their own colorful bullets and lines instead of the standard ones available through HTML. Web page bullets often appear round, but GIF images can only be saved in rectangular format. The end result is that the round bullet might not fit in with the design of the rest of the page. To compensate for this difficulty, icon designers make the background of their round bullets transparent. Figure 9.2 shows an example of a Web page using transparent and non-transparent bullets. Which would you rather use?

Fig. 9.2
Transparency functionality is why most icons and bullets are saved in the GIF format instead of JPEG.

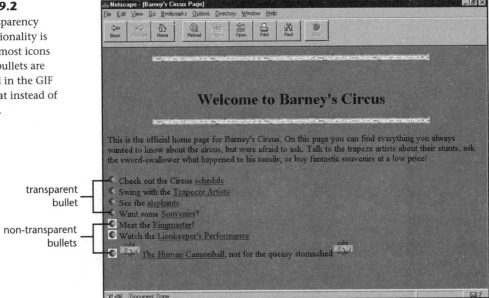

transparent bullet

non-transparent bullets

How Web Browsers Treat Transparent GIFs

When you select a color to be transparent, Paint Shop Pro saves that information into the actual GIF file. Since it is part of the file downloaded and displayed on your Web page, WWW browsers can easily recognize and ignore that particular color.

When you design GIFs, you have literally millions of colors to choose from to colorize your image; 16.7 million shades and hues of reds, greens, and blues can be used. Although you have millions of options, only 256 different colors can be present at any one time in a GIF file.

Tip

To see how many different colors are currently being used in your image, choose Colors | Count Colors Used, from the Paint Shop Pro menu bar. A Paint Shop Pro dialog box appears and answers your query (see fig. 9.3).

Fig. 9.3
Counting the number of colors being used is easy.

For more information on color specifics and limitations, see the section titled "Color Quantification" in Chapter 3, "Creating Simple Graphics."

Each color is assigned a number from 1 to 256. That's how Paint Shop Pro recognizes a color. It doesn't recognize "blue," instead it knows a color number such as color 175.

When your WWW browser displays an image, it divides the image into quadrants and displays each quadrant in a different color. It's just like painting by number as a kid, where the image is broken into many different numbered sections, with each number corresponding to a color of paint for that section. Although WWW browsers have 256 colors to choose from, the concept is still the same. Each part of the Web image is painted according to the number of the color specified.

Here's where the transparency issue comes into play. With transparent images, you can instruct your WWW browser *not* to paint one particular color of an image—leaving it blank instead. Because nothing gets painted in that particular part of the image, it is transparent and you can see right through it. Web browsers enable you to place colors and images in the background of your page, behind all the images and text. With a transparent color you see the background designs, if any, instead of the particular color assigned to that section of the Web image.

As you can see, Web browsers aren't very complicated pieces of software when it comes to displaying images and graphics. Understanding how Web browsers display transparent GIFs provides insight into how Web graphics can be designed to take advantage of a Web browser's simplicity and flexibility.

III

Advanced Techniques

Making Transparent GIFs

Now that you know what transparent GIFs are and how WWW browsers such as Netscape display them, it's time to learn how to create your own transparent GIFs.

Making transparent GIFs doesn't have to be tricky, but there are some steps in the process which can be misleading if you aren't certain how to proceed. In this section, I'll lead you through a step-by-step process for making a transparent GIF for your own Web page. You'll learn how to make transparent GIFs from scratch, how to convert existing images into transparent ones, and how to identify which color to make transparent.

Creating a Transparent GIF from Scratch

I'll first show you an example of how to make a simple transparent image from scratch. We'll look at how to create a transparent X to mate with the O used earlier in this chapter. I'll walk you through how to create the graphic from start to finish.

1. First, start up Paint Shop Pro and choose File | New from the menu bar to bring up the New Image dialog box (see fig. 9.4).

Fig. 9.4
Creating transparent images is just as easy as working with any other type of GIF file.

2. In the Image type drop-down list box, choose 256 Colors (8-bit) because the GIF filetype limits us to a maximum of 256 colors. Don't choose 16.7 Million Colors (24-bit). Even though Paint Shop Pro will automatically reduce the number of colors to 256 when you save the image as a GIF, you create extra work for yourself when you try to manage all of those extra colors while creating transparent images.

3. Choose the appropriate Height and Width for your new image. I'll choose 100×100 for this example, but transparency features work on GIFs of any size. Then click the OK button to continue. A new blank image is created.

4. Click the Text icon at the top of the screen so you can add an X to your image.

5. Click your mouse cursor in the image to bring up the Add Text dialog
box (see fig. 9.5).

Fig. 9.5
Text can be added
in any font, style,
and size.

6. Choose the Font attributes you want your text to appear in by selecting
the Name of the font, the Style of font, and the Size. Now type your
desired text in the Enter text here window. I am adding an *X* that is in
Times New Roman, that is Bold, and at 100 points in size. Use your left
mouse button to click OK after making your selections.

7. Your text appears on top of your Web graphic. Move your mouse over
the graphic until the pointer becomes a cross with arrows on each end.
Click your left mouse button and drag the text to the spot on the image
where you want the text placed. Then click your right mouse button to
permanently add the text to your image in that spot. Figure 9.6 shows
my newly created *X* image.

Fig. 9.6
Making this simple
image has been
cake so far.

III

Advanced Techniques

8. The next step is to set your transparent color. Paint Shop Pro assigns whatever color is currently in the background Color Palette to be the default transparent color. You need to instruct Paint Shop Pro which color should be deemed transparent. To do this, click the eyedropper icon from the rows of icons at the top of the screen.

9. Now move your mouse to anywhere in the background of your image and click the *right* mouse button. The eyedropper lets you select colors by pointing and clicking them. The left mouse button controls the foreground; the right mouse button controls the background.

   Notice how in the Color Palette on the right hand side of the screen, the background color switches and becomes whichever color you click. For this example, my background color is white, but it would work the same if my color was blue, red, or green—any color.

10. Finally, you are ready to save your newly minted transparent GIF. Choose File | Save from the Paint Shop Pro menu bar to bring up the Save As dialog box (see fig. 9.7). Although you are saving your image as a transparent GIF, be aware that the image will only display transparent characteristics in a Web browser that supports transparency, such as Netscape or Internet Explorer.

Fig. 9.7
Your image is
about to be saved.

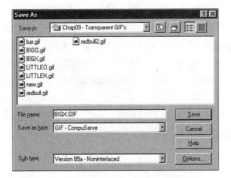

11. Click the button labeled Options to bring up the File Preferences dialog box (see fig. 9.8). From here, you can indicate exactly how you want Paint Shop Pro to save the color you indicated as transparent.

12. Select the option button labeled: **Set the transparency value to the background color**. This tells Paint Shop Pro to make a special note that the current background color (as defined in the Color Palette) is now the one that should appear transparent on a Web page. For more information on the other choices in this dialog box, see "Setting the

GIF Options" in the next section. Click OK to return to your Save As dialog box. Paint Shop Pro automatically remembers your GIF transparency options and sets your selection as the default when creating and saving future images.

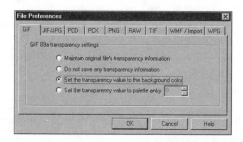

Fig. 9.8
Four GIF transparency options from which to select.

13. Give your image a file name and save it. Now your image is ready to be used on a Web page with the correct color marked as transparent. Figure 9.9 shows my newly created transparent *X* on a Web page.

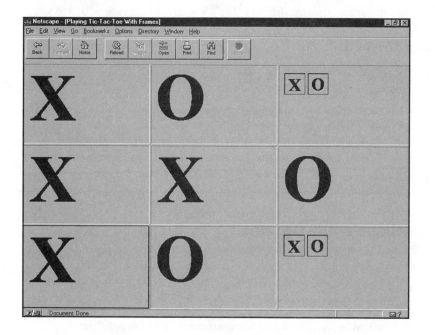

Fig. 9.9
Making that X wasn't too hard, was it?

Working With Existing Images

Creating new transparent GIF images from scratch is relatively easy. All you do is make your new image, draw or add a design to the graphic, and indicate the transparent color. Then save your image as a transparent GIF and voila, you are done.

You will often want to modify an existing image lacking indicated transparent values by converting it to fit better on your Web page. You may find that you want to incorporate an existing image onto your Web page from a graphics collection, the CD-ROM that came with this book, or from elsewhere on the Web.

In general, converting a GIF into transparent GIF format follows the exact same process outlined previously. First, you load the existing image into Paint Shop Pro. Then, using the eyedropper icon, click your *right* mouse button on the color you want to make transparent. Finally, save your new GIF and make sure you set the transparency option as you did in step 12. To set the transparency options on your existing GIF, you need to choose File | Save As from the menu bar to bring up the Save As dialog box. Make sure you give your new file a different name if you don't want to overwrite the original, non-transparent GIF.

> **Note**
>
> If an existing image has many intricate details, the eyedropper tool can sometimes be difficult to use without a little extra help. If you have trouble selecting the correct background color, try zooming in on the picture to get additional detail. Choose View | Zoom In from the menu bar and choose a magnification from the available list. When you are finished you can also View | Zoom Out.

Setting the GIF Options

When you save your transparency options, Paint Shop Pro gives you four selections to indicate which color should appear transparent on your Web pages. I described one of the options earlier. Here's a brief summary of the other three options in the File Preferences dialog box:

■ **Maintain original file's transparency information**

When a GIF is created, a color can be specified as the default transparent color for that file. You can set this value after choosing File | New from the menu bar. Often, the default transparent color is unknown. Therefore, unless you remember setting it when you created the image, it's best to stay away from this selection. See Chapter 3, "Creating

Simple Graphics," for a quick rundown on your options when setting the default transparent color. This option is useful when you don't want to have to worry about finding the color to mark as transparent. PSP automatically identifies the color that starts as the image's background.

■ **Do not save any transparency information**

As the name of this selection suggests, this option tells the GIF not to make a color transparent for Web browsers. This selection is often used for photographs and images with lots of colors that are saved in the GIF file format. You don't affect your image file size by ignoring transparency settings, just its appearance.

■ **Set the transparency value to palette entry**

This selection enables you to designate any one of the 256 colors (including the default background color) as the transparent color by specifying its corresponding number rather than the name of the color. As I discussed earlier, using the paint-by-numbers analogy, each color in a GIF is assigned a corresponding number. You can see a color's corresponding number in the Color Palette by double-clicking either the foreground or background color.

A Floating Photograph

Transparent GIFs are commonly used when making your own buttons, icons, drawings, and bars for your Web page. When you set the background color to be transparent, your images correctly display on your Web pages. You don't actually change the way an image appears in a paint program like Paint Shop Pro, you merely redefine how a WWW browser interprets and displays the GIF.

Another popular way to use the transparency feature in GIFs is to create a "floating" photograph. Like JPEG files, GIF images can only be saved in rectangular squares. Each file has a defined height and width, regardless of whether you use the whole space of an image. Therefore, with an image of a circle, your GIF file is actually still saved in a rectangular shape, but part of the image is left blank—as unused white space.

As you've seen with other icons and images, the GIF transparency feature is commonly used because it makes the icon appear to fit directly into the Web page. A "floating" photograph expands upon that approach. Often, you will not want to use the whole photograph for your Web page. One useful technique is to first crop the photograph to the smallest possible rectangular area needed and then erase the unnecessary part of the remaining picture. You can then set the background of the photograph to be transparent. Now, when added to a Web page, the resulting effect is a floating photograph that appears irregularly shaped and uniquely placed on a Web page.

Let's look at an example of this phenomenon at work. In this example, I only want to crop out the head of a particular photograph and add it to my home page.

Scanning the Picture

The first step is to select and scan a photograph. I'll use the scanning program that installed itself with my Logitech PageScan Color Scanner. Of course, you can use any scanner and software to digitize a picture onto your computer.

> **Tip**
>
> Don't forget that you do not have to own a scanner to get digitized pictures. America Online subscribers are permitted to mail several photographs that AOL will scan automatically for them. Additionally, your local Kinkos and other copy stores allow you to use scanners for a nominal fee.

I talk about scanning pictures in more detail in Chapter 5 "Scanning and Enhancing Photos." In that chapter you'll learn more about using Paint Shop Pro to acquire images from a scanner directly.

Cropping the Picture

Once your image is properly scanned, open it up in Paint Shop Pro. Figure 9.10 shows my scanned photograph ready for manipulation. Remember that you can only set transparent values for images saved in the GIF file type. JPEG images tend to have smaller file sizes for photographs and use more colors, but JPEGs do not have as much flexibility and don't use the transparent options described in this chapter.

Once loaded in Paint Shop Pro, the first step is to crop your photograph into the smallest rectangular area. Since GIF images must be saved as rectangles, use the Paint Shop Pro selection tool and choose Rectangle (or Square) from the Style Palette. Click the selection tool icon and draw a box around the portion of your image you want to keep. To draw a selection box, click and hold your left mouse button in the upper left corner of the image part you want to save and draw a box to the bottom right-hand corner of the desired area. Let up on your mouse button and a dotted line around the selected area appears.

Fig. 9.10
I'm ready to "float" my photograph.

Figure 9.11 shows how I drew a selection rectangle around part of my image.

Fig. 9.11
I only need a small part of this image for my Web page.

— My selection box

Next, choose Image | Crop from the Paint Shop Pro menu bar. Only the selected area will remain. The resulting image will be a working file that is not saved until you choose File | Save As from the menu bar. Be sure to save often because you can only undo (Edit | Undo) one level of editing at a time.

Instead of using a rectangular or square shaped selection tool, you can also use the circle or ellipse shapes. When cropping with these two shapes, Paint Shop Pro crops the area you selected and places the cropped image into a rectangular shaped box because GIFs must be saved as rectangles.

Sculpting Your Image

The next step in creating a floating image is to sculpt away the unnecessary parts of your newly cropped image. Just like a sculptor, you want to whittle away the extra parts of the image so that you are left with the final image for display on your Web page. You sculpt your image so that the unnecessary part of your Web graphic is all the same color. For my image, I am sculpting around the head and making the background color of the image all white so that I can set white as transparent.

Sculpting around an image can be tedious and time consuming. Although you have cropped your image to a compact rectangle, you probably don't want the interference in the background of your image. For this example, I only want to display my head on my Web page. Therefore, I need to patiently cut away the excess part of the image until I am left with only the section of the photograph I want to use.

To sculpt, click the selection "lasso," which lets you select irregularly shaped areas. Using the lasso, mark the areas on the image that you want to "cut" away from your final product. Now choose Edit | Cut from the menu bar and Paint Shop Pro removes the selected area and replaces it with blank area. By default, your blank area is set at the background color defined in the Color Palette on the right hand side of the screen. Be careful not to select a background color that is part of the image itself. Otherwise your Web Browser might ignore parts of the image, not just the background. In general, white is an excellent color to use for transparent images.

Additionally, you may want to use the paintbrush tool to paint over smaller sections. I used a combination of the lasso and paintbrush to cut away all the extra parts of my image.

You can choose to zoom in on your image so that you can sculpt in detail. To zoom in on your photograph, choose <u>V</u>iew | Zoom <u>I</u>n from the menu bar. Figure 9.12 shows me whittling away part of the background wall from my photograph while zooming in for more detail. You'll find it helpful to constantly zoom in and zoom out to monitor your progress in the sculpting.

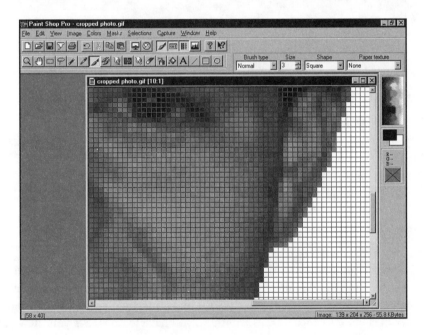

Fig. 9.12
I zoom in considerably when sculpting my photographs.

Sculpting is by far the most difficult step in creating a floating photograph for your Web page. Fortunately, Paint Shop Pro makes it easy for you to select and crop away unnecessary parts of your image. Once finished, move on to the next section. Take a look at figure 9.13 to see how my final image looks all sculpted and ready to use.

III

Advanced Techniques

Fig. 9.13
Similar to my original image, this photograph is ready to float onto the Web.

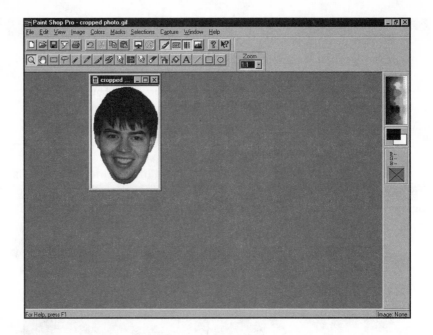

Finishing Touches

Now all you have to do is set your transparent color and save your GIF image. Earlier in this chapter, you learned how to select and set the proper background color to appear transparent. As you learned, identifying the correct background color can sometimes be difficult. When sculpting, however, there is no need to worry about identifying the correct background color—Paint Shop Pro has already done the work for you.

When you cut away each background section of the image, Paint Shop Pro replaces the cut away section with the background color set in the Color Palette. Paint Shop Pro has already identified and saved the background color as being transparent. This saves you the time and effort involved in identifying the correct color to appear transparent. All you have to do is save your new image. Choose File | Save As from the menu bar to bring up the Save As dialog box. Type in a new file name for your floating GIF.

> **Caution**
>
> Don't accidentally save your new image over your original GIF file. Use the Save As dialog box and rename your newly created floating GIF.

Click the Options button to bring up the File Preferences dialog box. Ensure that the option button **Set the transparency value to the background color** is marked and click OK. Save your image and you are ready to add it to your Web page.

Test Your Image

Once you are done creating your "floating" GIF, take a moment to test it with a WWW browser. Make sure that your background color is properly identified and that Netscape (or Internet Explorer) displays your image correctly.

Figure 9.14 shows my floating image twice—once as it should appear (bottom) and once as it looks when the background transparent color isn't set right (top). If your image doesn't display correctly, it's likely that an incorrect color was selected to be transparent. If you have this problem, return to step 8, which appears earlier in this chapter.

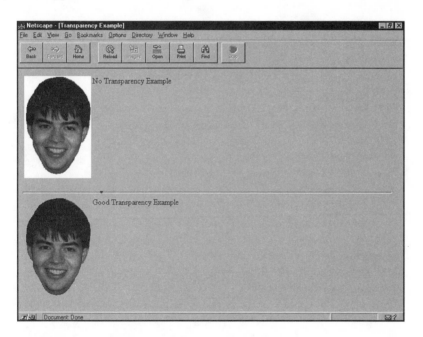

Fig. 9.14
The "floating" GIF looks slick when added to a Web page.

For more information on building the proper line of HTML to display your image in a WWW browser, see the section titled "Basic HTML Tags for Adding Images" in Chapter 1.

III

Advanced Techniques

CHAPTER 10

Moving Graphics: GIF Animation

There are several ways to add movement to a Web page. You can hire a programmer or spend a few months learning the Java language. You can use a pre-built applet or OLE component to play some sort of video or interactive media file. Or, you can ask all the visitors to your Web site to get a helper application or plug-in program to play your favorite media file format. All of these may be excellent solutions in many situations, but every one of them involves an investment of time and resources before you can even start to produce animation.

Wouldn't it be nice if you could just "snap together" three or four GIF images to make a simple animated graphic, without having to deal at all with any extra software components or media viewers? And wouldn't it be great if people using older Web browsers could automatically see at least the first frame of your animation, without you having to do any extra coding or producing of additional graphics files? And while we're wishing, how about an animation format that can save a cool animated icon in a 20Kb or smaller file?

> **Note**
>
> If you've never created an animation of any kind before, you may not realize that the illusion of animation is achieved by showing several still images (called "frames") in rapid succession.

Believe it or not, these Utopian dreams have already become a reality. In fact, multiframe animation was built into the GIF file format way back in 1989. The compression is very efficient and it's almost shamefully easy to make GIF animation. Every user of Netscape Navigator and Microsoft Internet Explorer (which means the vast majority of Internet surfers) can see animated GIFs without any additional software or add-ons. You can include this animation in a Web page exactly as if it were "ordinary" GIFs with the <IMG> tag. Most browsers will support GIF animation in their next releases. In the meantime, users of browsers other than Navigator or Explorer will always just see the first (or in some cases, the last) image in the animation.

Ease of creation and use makes GIF animation a great choice for simple, animated icons and any Web page graphics that can be spiced-up with a little motion. In this chapter, you'll learn how to create GIF animations and how to optimize them for the fastest possible display. This chapter will cover:

- **Building a GIF Animation**

  Learn to quickly assemble multiple images into an animation file that you can place on your Web pages just like any other GIF.

- **GIF Animation Tips and Tricks**

  Learn about palette controls and looping to make animation that plays forever without taking forever to download.

- **Optimizing GIF Animation for Speed and Size**

  Learn secrets that can often cut the size of your GIF animation files in half.

Building a GIF Animation

The CD-ROM accompanying this book includes an evaluation copy of Alchemy Mindworks' GIF Construction Set, a nifty little utility designed especially for assembling multi-image GIFs.

The first step in creating a GIF animation is to create a series of images to be displayed one after the other. You can use any graphics software you like to make the images. You don't even need to use software that supports GIF to make the images; GIF Construction Set can import BMP, JPEG, PCX, TIFF, and almost any other graphics file format you throw at it.

Tip

The fastest way to create a simple GIF animation with GIF Construction Set is to select File | Animation Wizard. This will start an "interview" which leads you through all the steps discussed next.

You can also automatically create scrolling text and a number of transition effects with the Edit | Banner and Edit | Transition commands. These commands provide an easy way to add some quick animation effects to still images.

In this chapter, however, I show you how to create animations "by hand," without using the Wizard or automatic effects. This will give you a head start when you want to use the advanced animation tricks discussed toward the end of the chapter.

The following numbered steps show you how to make a simple GIF animation. This animation will flip back and forth between two artistic renderings of the word "LOOK" that I created in Paint Shop Pro.

1. Before you assemble an animation with GIF Construction Set, you may want to open the images you'd like to include from another graphics program, so you can refer to them as you put the animation together. Figure 10.1 shows the two images for this example open in Paint Shop Pro with the GIF Construction Set program in the foreground.

> **Tip**
>
> You'll find it easier to build and modify animations if you give the images for each animation similar names. You might name the images for a dog animation dog1.gif, dog2.gif, dog3.gif, and so on.

2. To start a new animation, start GIF Construction Set and select File | New. At the top of the white area, HEADER GIF 89a Screen (640×480) should appear. This is the first "block" in the GIF file, to which you will be adding additional image blocks and control blocks that will be listed below it.

3. Click the Edit button and the dialog box in figure 10.1 appears. Enter the screen width and depth (height) of the largest image you want to use in the animation and click OK. (Not sure how big your images are? Paint Shop Pro displays the width and depth of the current image at the lower left corner of the screen.)

4. If you want the animation to loop continuously when viewed in Netscape Navigator, click the Insert button and then click Loop. This inserts a special control block telling it to immediately restart the animation every time it finishes. If you want to create an animation that plays only once and then stops (leaving the last image on display), skip this step.

5. Click Insert, then Image and choose the first image in the animation, as shown in figure 10.2. This is also the image that will be displayed by browsers that don't support GIF animation. If you want to go along

III

Advanced Techniques

with this example, select the **lookclr.gif** image in the **/look** directory of the CD-ROM.

Fig. 10.1
GIF Construction Set runs in a fairly small window, enabling you to see other applications—such as Paint Shop Pro— at the same time. Here, the Edit Header dialog box displays information.

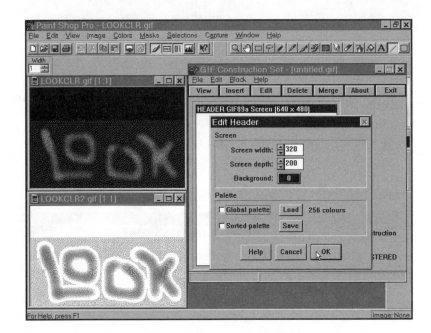

6. A dialog box will appear saying "The palette of the image you have imported does not match the global palette for this file." Later in this chapter, I'll explain the other options included in this dialog box, but for now, choose "Use a local palette for this image" and click OK.

Fig. 10.2
Even in Windows 95, GIF Construction Set uses a Windows 3.1 style file selection box. Tsk, tsk. (But then again, who really cares?)

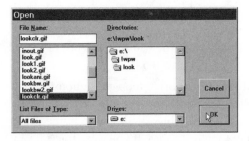

7. If you want the image you just inserted to be transparent, press the up arrow once or click with the mouse on LOOP, then click Insert, then CONTROL. This inserts a control block in front of the image.

Next click Edit to get the Edit Control Block dialog box shown in figure 10.3. Check Transparent colour and then click the little eyedropper icon button. The image is displayed and the cursor turns to an eyedropper. Click the tip of the eyedropper on the color you want to appear transparent when the image is displayed.

Before you click OK, be sure to select Background under the Remove by: selection list. (The other options are explained later in this chapter.)

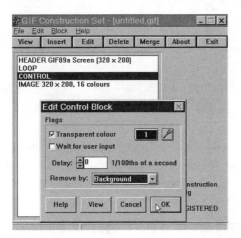

Fig. 10.3
Control blocks enable you to make images transparent or insert a time delay between images.

8. Repeat steps 5 through 7 for every image in the animation. Remember that the control block for an image has to appear *just above* the image block in the list. But you need to insert the image first and then go back to edit the control block to add transparency.

   A little confusing? Don't worry, you'll be an old pro at it by the end of this chapter. In the meantime, if you make a mistake, you can highlight any block and click Delete to get rid of it.

9. When all the images and control blocks are inserted in the right order, select File I Save As to save the animation (see fig. 10.4). Be sure to give it a name ending in .gif.

10. Using your favorite Web page editor, make an HTML document with an IMG tag referring to the .gif file you just saved as the SRC (an example tag might be: <IMG SRC="lookani.gif">). Load the document in Netscape Navigator version 2.0 or higher to see the results. You can also preview the animation within GIF Construction Set by clicking on View at any time during the construction process.

III

Advanced Techniques

Fig. 10.4

Save your file with the .gif extension.

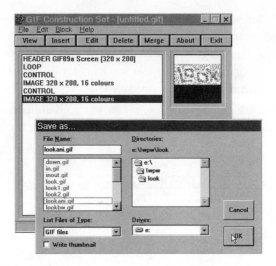

I obviously can't illustrate the animated effect of flipping back and forth between two images with a printed figure in a book. But you can load the **/look/look.htm** document on the CD-ROM if you'd like to see the action.

GIF Animation Tips and Tricks

Figure 10.5 shows a page I created for the CD-ROM to accompany my book *Web Page Wizardry* from Sams.net Publishing. *Web Page Wizardry* is an excellent choice if you want to learn about more advanced animation and multimedia techniques after you finish this book.

The pages shown in figures 10.5 through 10.7 are also on the CD-ROM included with this book, as **wpw/wpw.htm.** If you view the page with Netscape Navigator version 2.0 or higher, or with a Microsoft Internet Explorer 3.0, you'll notice that all the icons are animated: a vision appears in the crystal ball, the scepter flashes, the cauldron bubbles, the mirror revolves, and the book pages turn. These icons are actually five separate multi-image GIFs, and the HTML code for this snazzy action-filled page looks just like an ordinary static Web page (see listing 10.1).

Listing 10.1   The Web Page Wizardry Page (wpw.htm)

```
<HTML>
<HEAD><TITLE>Web Page Wizardry</TITLE></HEAD>
<BODY BACKGROUND="bubsmoke.jpg" BGCOLOR="black">
<CENTER>
<IMG SRC="wpwtitle.gif" LOWSRC="hat.gif"><P>
```

```
<A HREF="visions.htm"><IMG SRC="visions.gif" BORDER=0></A>
<A HREF="programs.htm"><IMG SRC="programs.gif" BORDER=0></A>
 <IMG SRC="spacer.gif"><IMG SRC="spacer.gif">
<A HREF="brews.htm"><IMG SRC="brews.gif" BORDER=0></A>
 <IMG SRC="spacer.gif"><IMG SRC="spacer.gif">
<A HREF="worlds.htm"><IMG SRC="worlds.gif" ALIGN="absmiddle"
➥BORDER=0></A>
<A HREF="pages.htm"><IMG SRC="pages.gif" BORDER=0></A><BR>

<A HREF="visions.htm"><IMG SRC="vistext.gif" BORDER=0></A>
<A HREF="programs.htm"><IMG SRC="prgtext.gif" BORDER=0></A>
<A HREF="brews.htm"><IMG SRC="brwtext.gif" BORDER=0></A>
<A HREF="worlds.htm"><IMG SRC="wrltext.gif" BORDER=0></A>
<A HREF="pages.htm"><IMG SRC="pagtext.gif" BORDER=0></A>
</CENTER>
</BODY>
</HTML>
```

> **Note**
>
> If this were a page on the Internet instead of a CD-ROM, I would have included ALT
> attributes so that users of very old browsers or very slow modems would see some
> text without having to wait for the graphics to download. For example, `<IMG`
> `SRC="wpwtitle.gif" ALT="Web Page Wizardry">`.

Fig. 10.5
At first glance, and
to non-Netscape
users, this looks
like a page full of
regular GIF images.

Fig. 10.6
Users of Netscape, however, will quickly notice that all the GIFs are actually multi-image animation.

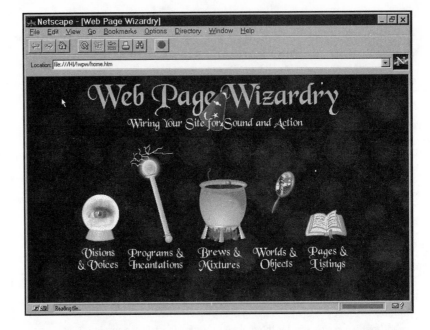

Fig. 10.7
Netscape gracefully handles the logistics of displaying five separate GIF animations all at once.

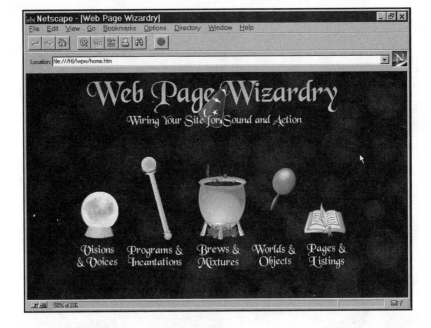

A Hand-Crafted Animation

I could have created all this animation in Paint Shop Pro or another shareware graphics program, but I decided to bring in the heavy artillery and create it in Adobe Photoshop instead. Not only does Photoshop offer more advanced drawing and coloring tools, but more importantly, it also lets you keep various parts of an image in separate layers that you can modify independently. This feature (which is also found in a number of other commercial graphics editors) makes drawing simple animation a breeze.

By way of example, let me explain how I created the spell book that flips its own pages. To start, I just sketched the first image from scratch and then drew five views of the turning page on separate layers, as shown in figure 10.8.

Note

To make "layered" animations like this in Paint Shop Pro, start by drawing the basic image (in this case the book), and using Edit I Copy and Edit I Paste I As New Image to create multiple copies of it. Then, add the details for each image (in this case the turning page) separately.

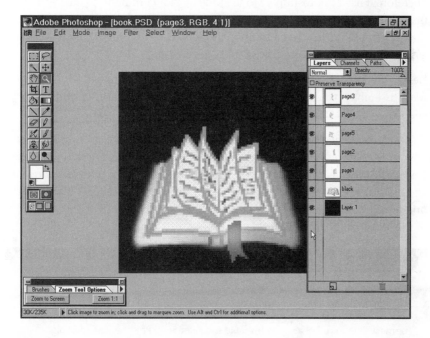

Fig. 10.8
Photoshop makes it easy to build animation because you can just draw the changes from frame to frame and use transparency to show or hide it at will.

After I drew all the pages, I turned on each layer one at a time (always keeping the book and background layers on) and used Photoshop's File | Save a Copy command to save each view as a separate true-color BMP file.

> **Tip**
>
> If you're wondering how I did the rotating mirror within Photoshop, I didn't. I used a 3D modeling program to build a three-dimensional model of the mirror and a keyframe animation of it rotating. Then I brought the images from that animation into Photoshop to add the magic window through which you can see the castle. You can find out more about creating 3D models and putting "virtual reality" scenes on your Web pages in the *Web Page Wizardry* book.

Handling Palettes

When I created the spell book, I knew that GIF Construction Set is able to import BMP files and dither them down to 256 colors. However, I also knew that I could get the best results by giving GIF Construction Set one file that was *already* dithered to 256 colors, so that GIF could use that file's colors as the global palette to which all other files in the animation could be matched. Therefore, I used Photoshop's Mode | Index Color command to change the first image in the sequence (the book with flat pages) to 256 colors and saved that in the GIF format. In Paint Shop Pro, you could achieve the same thing with the Colors | Decrease Color Depth command.

Next, I fired up GIF Construction Set and assembled the images—the same way I assembled the images in the step-by-step example earlier in this chapter.

The only difference between the present example and the earlier example is how I handled the global palette and the dithering of the imported BMP files. For the first image in the spell book GIF, I inserted the 256-color GIF file and chose "Use this image as the global palette," as shown in figure 10.9. For all other images, I inserted the true-color BMP files and chose "Dither this image to the global palette," as in figure 10.10.

> **Tip**
>
> In this case, the subtle gradations of color in these images look a lot better when dithered, so I was willing to put up with slightly larger file sizes that dithering creates.
>
> For most situations, however, you should use Paint Shop Pro's nearest color algorithm to change all images to 256 colors before bringing them into GIF Construction

Set, and then choose "Remap this image to the global palette" when importing them, rather than "Dither this image to the global palette." They might not look quite as pretty, but they'll often come out a lot smaller and faster.

On the other hand, when you need the absolute best possible quality and don't care so much about size or speed, you have the option of using a separate optimized palette of colors for each image. To do this, you choose "Use a local palette for this image" when you insert each image.

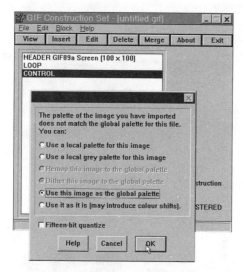

Fig. 10.9
For at least one image in your animation (usually the first one), you should select "Use this image as the global palette" after you insert the image.

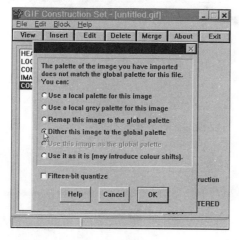

Fig. 10.10
Once you have a global palette from one image, you can reduce file size and improve display speed by remapping or dithering all other images to that palette.

Tips on Transparency

As demonstrated in the earlier "LOOK" example, you can make the background transparent by inserting a control block in front of each image and choosing Transparent colour and Remove by: Background when you edit the control block (see fig. 10.11). You can use the eyedropper tool (mentioned earlier) to pick the transparent color or you can click the number next to the eyedropper to pick the color directly from the global or local palette (see fig. 10.12).

Fig. 10.11

If you want the animation to have a transparent color, insert and edit a control block before each image.

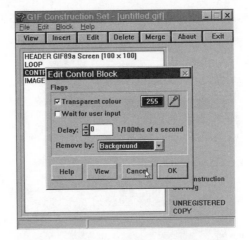

Fig. 10.12

To pull up this color-picking palette, click the number next to the eyedropper tool (255 in fig. 10.11).

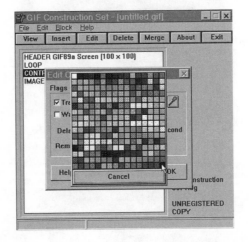

To make sure you pick the right color you want to be transparent, you can click the View button to preview the animation. Note that the background color used during the preview can be set by selecting File | Setup and picking a color from the Edit view mode background drop-down list box (see fig. 10.13). You may want to choose a contrasting color (in this example, white or gray) to check the transparency value, and then choose a color similar to your Web page background (in this example, black) to see what the animation will actually look like on the page.

Tip

Notice that the Setup dialog box also includes some controls to fine-tune the dithering of true-color images. You'll probably never need these, but if you're not happy with the results of a dithered image, this is where you go to fuss and fiddle with it.

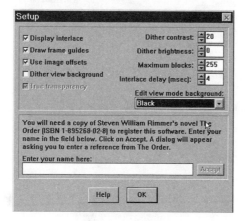

Fig. 10.13
The File | Setup dialog box lets you choose a preview background color and fine tune some other picky stuff.

Doing the Loop

In the first example in this chapter, I mentioned that you can make an animation continuously loop by clicking Insert, then LOOP in GIF Construction Set. However, there's one more thing you need to know to create a successful looped animation, and it isn't at all obvious. Because of the way that Netscape Navigator processes and displays multi-image GIF files, you will often find that the first frame of a looping animation is skipped or only half displayed, making a noticeable jerk or some other subtle-but-annoying effect.

The way to avoid this is to always repeat the first image at the end of the animation. This way, the "jerk" becomes invisible because it occurs between two identical images. For example, figure 10.14 shows the complete **pages.gif** animation. This actually contains only six separate images—the seventh one is a repeat of the first.

Repeating the first image does increase the size of the GIF file, so you may be willing to tolerate a little jerkiness to keep the size down. Also, in some animation such as the "LOOK" logo example, you never notice or care about the jerk anyway. So, it's a good idea to try the animation without the first image repeat to see if you're happy with the results. If you are, the only reason to consider repeating the first image is that a few older browsers will display only the last image in the animation. (Most older browsers, however, will display only the first image.)

Fig. 10.14
For smooth animation, it often helps to make the first and last images identical.

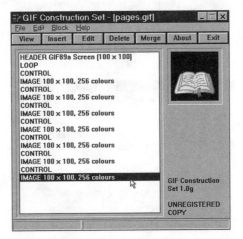

Tip

One more tip on looping: If you highlight the LOOP block and click the Edit button, you can set a number of iterations for the animation to repeat before stopping. This doesn't actually work in Netscape Navigator 2.0, but it does work in Navigator 3.0 and Microsoft Explorer 3.0.

Optimizing GIF Animation for Speed and Size

There are two ways to improve the speed and reduce the size of GIF animation. One way is to save only the part of the image that actually changes from one frame to the next and insert this smaller GIF file instead of replacing the whole image. The other way is to make transparent any part of the image that doesn't change. This can also dramatically reduce the size of the file because a solid region of transparency will compress much more efficiently than the same region filled with complex image data.

The most impressive application of these techniques is an animation in which a small moving character or object is superimposed over a complex backdrop. You can save the backdrop only once as the first image and then insert only the images of the small changing region for subsequent images. This can easily reduce the size of the animation file by a factor of 10 or more.

I'll use a less dramatic example, though, where we'll actually only shave about 6Kb off a 26Kb animation file. It should be quite clear how to apply the same technique to a larger file.

Cropping the Crystal

Like the spell book, the crystal ball animation was created as a number of separate image layers in Photoshop (see fig. 10.15). Instead of saving each frame in the animation as a layer, in this case I used the opacity slider to vary the transparency effects between layers as I swirled the "fog" layer around with the smudge brush. The exact same effect could be achieved in Paint Shop Pro by using the smudge brush on multiple copies of the original image.

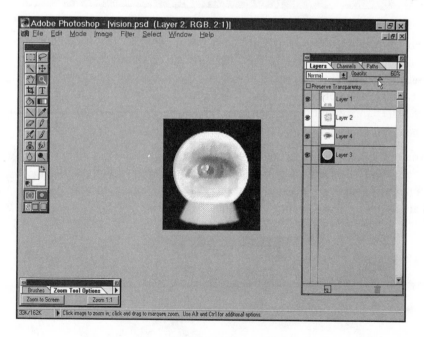

Fig. 10.15
The crystal ball animation was created by varying the opacity of the layers in a Photoshop image.

III

Advanced Techniques

However, only the first image of the series was saved in its entirety. I cropped off the bottom part (including the gold stand) of all the other images. Figure 10.16 shows the five images used to build the animation. Note that these include a cropped copy of the first image to put at the end of the animation.

Fig. 10.16
To make the file sizes smaller, I stored only the part of the animation that changes from frame to frame.

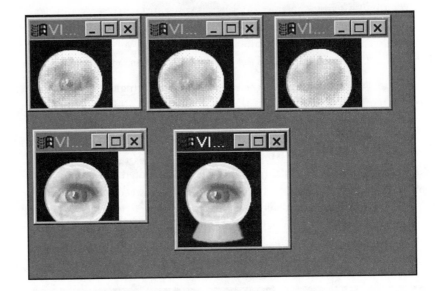

When I assembled these images in GIF Construction Set, I set each Edit Control Block to Remove by: Previous Image instead of Remove by: Background (see fig. 10.17). This keeps the previous image visible under any transparent areas—or areas not covered by the current image if the current image is smaller than any of the previous ones. This way, the gold stand from the first image remains unchanged when the smaller cropped frames are displayed.

You may also notice in figure 10.17 that I specified a Delay of 20/100 (or 1/5) of a second between animation frames. This slows the animation down enough so that the foggy haze seems to drift in and out, rather than snap back and forth like someone changing TV channels.

Fig. 10.17
By setting each Edit Control Block to Remove by: Previous Image, you can leave parts of a previously displayed frame visible.

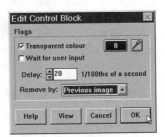

Tip

You can control where a smaller image appears over a larger one by highlighting the image block and clicking Edit (see fig. 10.18). In this example, both the Image left (horizontal offset) and Image top (vertical offset) values are 0, meaning that the top left corner of the image should be placed exactly over the top left corner of the entire animation. However, if you have a small object to place in the middle of a large backdrop, you can adjust these offsets to place the object just where you want it.

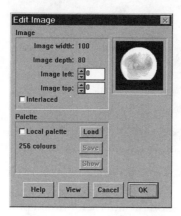

Fig. 10.18
You can use the Image left and Image top settings to place a smaller image in the middle of a larger one. (Here, no offset is needed so they are both set to 0.)

Emptying the Pot

The largest animation on the *Web Page Wizardry* home page is the bubbling cauldron. Because the big fat pot had to be dithered for the shading to look good, the animation weighs in at over 40Kb—about twice as large as the other multi-image GIFs on the page.

There's a sneaky way to cut that file size almost in half. In figure 10.19, I placed a blue rectangle over the unchanging (and biggest) part of each image, except for the first one. Then, when I pulled these images into GIF Construction Set, I set blue to be transparent and chose Remove by: Previous Image in the Edit Control Box, as I did for the crystal ball images.

Unfortunately, this sneaky stunt only works when you don't need to use the transparency to let the background of a Web page show around the edges of an image. (If I used the same black color to block out the pot as I used for the background around the top and bottom, parts of the steam, bubbles, and fire would not get erased properly between frames.)

Fig. 10.19

By blocking out
the unchanging
part of a large
image, you can
save a lot of space
in the GIF file.

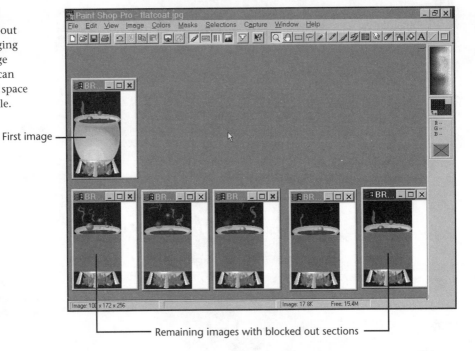

First image

Remaining images with blocked out sections

◄ Chapter 7,
"Making Your
Graphics
Lean," reveals a
number of
other ways to
reduce the size
and increase
the speed of
your GIF
graphics.

If I were posting this page on the Internet, I would probably choose to use a
solid black background on the page so I could use the optimized Remove by:
Previous Image version of this animation (26Kb) instead of the fully transparent Remove by: Background version (40Kb). But, since this is for CD-ROM, I
splurged and went with the fancy background and the 40Kb image. Even
with this move of reckless abandon, all the animation on the page still only
adds up to 120Kb, which is smaller than the static graphics on many Web
pages these days. ❖

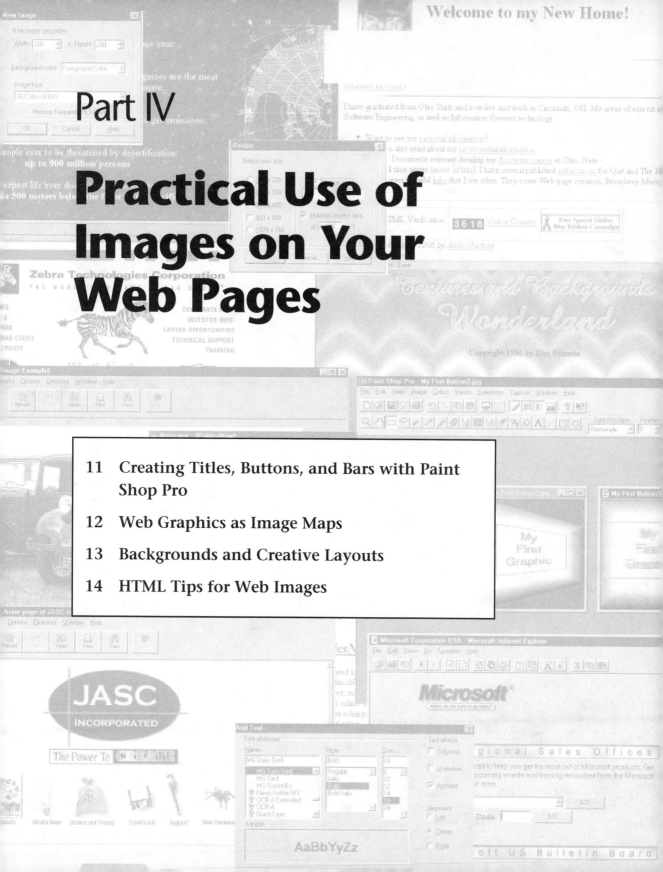

Part IV

Practical Use of Images on Your Web Pages

11   Creating Titles, Buttons, and Bars with Paint Shop Pro

12   Web Graphics as Image Maps

13   Backgrounds and Creative Layouts

14   HTML Tips for Web Images

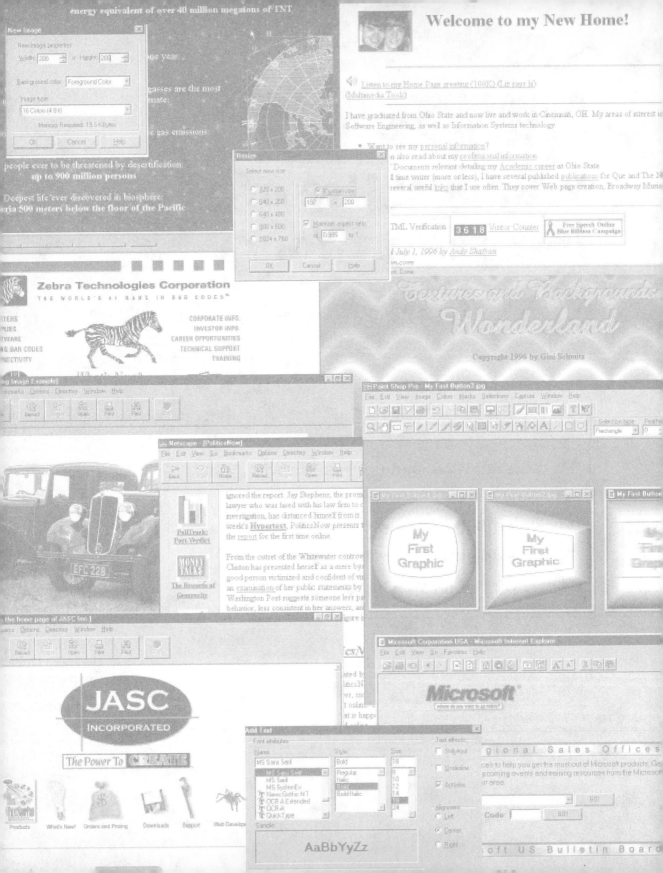

Creating Titles, Buttons, and Bars with Paint Shop Pro

As you have explored the Web, you've probably noticed that one of the most common uses of graphics is to help readers orient themselves in a vast homogeneous world-wide sea of pages. The role of graphics as a navigational aid is far more important on the Web than in a book or magazine, where there are physical cues to location.

Most Web page designers establish navigational aids by creating a set of icons, buttons, accents, and graphical titles for their pages, which are additional to any graphics that may accompany the text itself. Sometimes these icons are very generic—like a house which links you to a site's home page, or left and right arrows to leaf back and forth through a sequential series of pages. Generally, it's better to give your navigation icons a unique thematic look that reminds readers that the pages are all part of a single site.

In this chapter, I'll show you how the elements of several visually striking Web pages were created in Paint Shop Pro. You'll see how the techniques introduced in earlier chapters are put to work in real-world sites, and you will discover a few new techniques as well. Here's a brief outline of the topics covered in this chapter:

- **Making Your Own Buttons**

   You may be surprised at how easy it is to create sophisticated-looking 3D buttons and navigational graphics from scratch.

- **Matching Titles and Bars**

   Graphical headers and dividers set the mood of your site. Making them match your buttons and other accents is the key.

■ **Buttons and Titles that Work Together**

You can build interactive navigation toolbars and titles that fit together seamlessly—without messing with complicated image maps, frames or scripting.

■ **Icons and Graphical Accents**

Who says buttons have to look like buttons? Bold, effective icons for your pages can help users understand and remember your pages.

Making Your Own Buttons

A frightening number of people, when they notice that Paint Shop Pro has a "Buttonize" command on the Special Effects menu, start using it to create every button on their Web pages. And why not? It's quick, it's easy, and you can't argue with the fact that it makes something that looks an awful lot like a button.

This might, in fact, be a satisfactory approach if you're short on time and creativity—and if you don't mind your Web pages looking exactly like every other amateur Web page in the universe. But, since you bought this book, chances are that you're looking for something more than a quickie "me-too" page. Fortunately, it's almost as quick and easy to create truly unique buttons that communicate what *your* site is all about as it is to "Buttonize."

A Blinking Button

One way to add some pizazz to a button is to animate it using multi-image GIFs. (See Chapter 10, "Moving Graphics: GIF Animation," for details on how to put together a multi-image GIF.) Figure 11.1 shows one simple idea: I reduced the brightness of the bottom button to create the top button, and used GIF Construction Set to assemble the two images into a GIF animation.

When incorporated into a Web page, the result is a blinking button. A cheap trick, but it gets attention! (See fig. 11.2, **electric/welcome.htm** on the CD-ROM to view the button actually blink.)

> **Tip**
>
> Though I made this blinking button rather flashy (so to speak), please make any blinking graphics on your pages a bit less garish and annoying. Overuse of the <BLINK> tag has made many Web surfers extremely intolerant of anything that blinks, and getting visitors mad at you isn't usually what you are after with a Web page. Buttons that blink with a more subtle change in color will be more effective and less obnoxious.

Fig. 11.1
To create a blinking button, I selected Image | Special Effects | Buttonize to shade a white square, then darkened a copy of the image with Colors | Adjust | Brightness/Contrast.

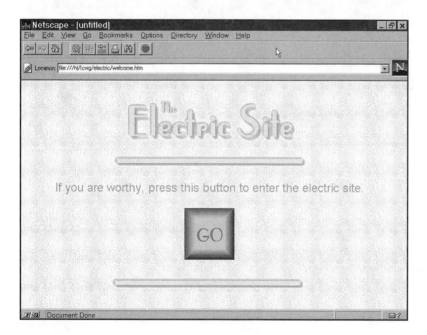

Fig. 11.2
When you view this document on the CD-ROM, you'll see the "GO" button blink brighter and darker every half second.

IV

Using Your Web Graphics

Special Effect Buttons

Blinking or not, the old square-button-with-a-word-in-the-middle look is definitely *tres cliché*. In this section, I outline a general formula you can follow to create an unlimited variety of professional-quality buttons without hiring (or becoming) a professional graphics artist. To illustrate the principles in action, I'll explain exactly how to create each of the four buttons shown in the right column of figure 11.3, step-by-step.

Fig. 11.3
Paint Shop Pro's special effects can help you produce a wide variety of button styles.

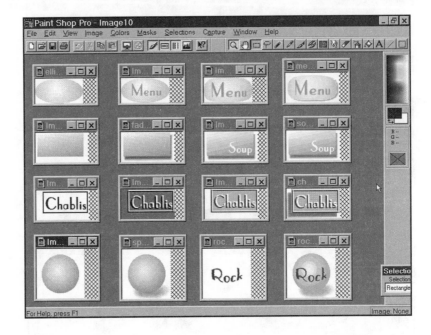

◀ For detailed coverage of all the special effects used in this chapter, refer to Chapter 6, "Filters, Deformations, and Special Effects."

The first—and most important—step in designing a button takes place in your imagination. What colors, shapes, and textures best express the mood and message of your Web site? In the examples for this chapter, I use the same color scheme (electric blue and white) and text font (Parisian) throughout every example to highlight the other differences between the buttons. Naturally, you will want to select a font (or, at most, two) and a color scheme that reflect the style you're after.

1. Select a shape

The first thing you need to decide on is a shape for your buttons. Iconic links (buttons that don't look like buttons) are discussed later in this chapter. For now, though, let's stick to easily recognized button shapes such as rectagles and ellipses. Each of the buttons in figure 11.3 started as a selection made with the rectangle, ellipse, or circle selection tool.

2. **Fill in or shade it**

   To make your shape stand out from the background, you need to fill it with some color. For a 3D-look with round buttons, use the fill bucket tool with Sunburst Gradient, as I did with the ellipse and sphere buttons in figure 11.3.

   A Linear Gradient usually looks better with rectangular buttons—as you can see on the Soup button in figure 11.3. I clicked Options in the fill bucket style palette to set the direction of the gradient to 350 degrees. Another option is to distinguish the outline of the button with a drawing tool, as I did with the rectangle drawing tool for the "Chablis" button in figure 11.3.

3. **Add a shadow2**

   The Image | Special Effects | Add Drop Shadow command can give almost any button more visual impact and "pushability." I used it to add a shadow to all the buttons in figure 11.3, with the exception of the sphere ("Rock" button). I added the sphere's shadow by hand with the brush tool for the specific three-dimensional effect I was after.

   Generally, you'll want to add a shadow before you label the button and then save the blank button as a full-color TIF or JPG file. That way you can use the same basic button many times simply by adding different labels. The exception to this rule is when you are going to distort or filter the entire button, including the text label. Then you'll need to wait and put the shadow on after you're done so its color and shape don't change in undesirable ways. The "Menu" button and "Chablis" button in figure 11.3 are examples of where I had to wait and add a last-minute shadow.

4. **Label it**

   Use the text tool to choose a font and put an appropriate label on your button. While the text is selected, you might consider using the fill bucket to shade the text with a gradient fill that contrasts with the button. To make the text transparent, fill it with the background color and make sure you save the file as a transparent GIF when you finish the rest of the steps below.

5. **Add a cool special effect**

   Any of the filters, distortions, and effects discussed in Chapter 6, "Filters, Deformations, and Special Effects," are available to make your button stand out and look smart. The buttons in figure 11.3 show just three of the infinite possibilities: I used Image | Deformations | Punch to warp the "Menu" button. For the "Chablis" button, I applied the Image | Special Filters | Emboss filter and then used Colors | Adjust | Brightness and Colors | Colorize to turn it light blue. After applying Image | Deformations | Circle twice to the word "Rock," I used Image | Arithmetic with the Darkest function to overlay it on the sphere.

Of course, not using a special effect may sometimes be the best special effect. For example, I didn't do any fancy image processing to the "Soup" button.

6. **Reduce the color depth**

Fancy buttons don't do much good if nobody can see them for 25 seconds after your Web page starts loading. A key move for keeping button graphic files small is to reduce the number of colors used as much as possible. Almost any good button should reduce nicely to 16 colors; select Colors | Decrease Color Depth | 16 Colors and choose Optimized Palette with the Nearest Color Reduction Method.

If you look closely, you'll notice some color "banding" in 16-color buttons that use gradient fills. But this slight aesthetic compromise is well worth the enhanced speed with which the buttons will come through your viewers' modems.

7. **Save as a transparent GIF**

Rectangular buttons with no shadow do not need to be transparent, but irregularly shaped buttons should be. That way, you can change the background on your Web pages any time you like without having to change the buttons.

To save a transparent GIF, select the eyedropper tool and click with the right mouse button on the region you want to be transparent. Then select File | Save As and choose GIF89A Noninterlaced. Click on the Options button and choose **Set the transparency value to the background color**. (You'll find more details on transparent GIFs in Chapter 9, "Creating Transparent GIFs.")

Tip

Occasionally, you may have a rectangular button with lots of gradually-changing colors that will save more efficiently and look better as a JPEG. Be warned, though, that the JPEG compression algorithm can blur text if you're not careful with the amount of compression.

---

8. **Touch up anything that looks amiss**

Often, you'll find an odd pixel or color shade that needs a bit of adjustment with the brush tool or Colors | Edit Palette command to look "just so."

Another common problem to watch out for with 16-color buttons is that parts of the button with colors similar to the background may become transparent when you intend them to be opaque. For example, the word "Soup" in figure 11.3 turned transparent when I reduced the image to 16 colors. To fix this problem, I selected a foreground color that looks almost as white as the background and used the color replacer tool to paint over the word "Soup."

By following these eight basic steps and adding your own choice of effects, you can create beautiful buttons that convey the unique flavor of your own Web pages.

Matching Titles and Bars

A Webmaster does not live by buttons alone. You'll almost certainly want some other matching graphics for your pages. Since the title is probably the first thing that people will look at on your page, you may want to make it a fancy graphic instead of (or in addition to) a text heading. In fact, aside from graphical buttons, fancy titles are probably the most common use of graphics on the Web.

Almost as common are graphical bars, rules, or page dividers. If your page contains a lot of text, a thematic bar or rule is a great way to provide a visual break to readers. And, whether your pages are text intesive or not, bars can add flair and help remind people where they are.

Figures 11.4 through 11.7 are pages from a fictitious Web site that I created for this chapter. For each of the four button styles you saw earlier in figure 11.3, I used similar shapes and effects to make matching titles and bars.

Figure 11.4 demonstrates how a little creativity can go a long way toward giving a page its own identity. By applying the exact same effects that I used to make the buttons, I made a title that conveys the same theme. Cutting and pasting one word over the other and using a slightly deeper shadow enhances the three-dimensional effect.

Similarly, cutting and pasting a line of shaded and shadowed dots fits the theme of the page better than simply drawing a horizontal line.

Fig. 11.4
Rules don't have
to follow the rules.
And who says
titles have to be
just text?

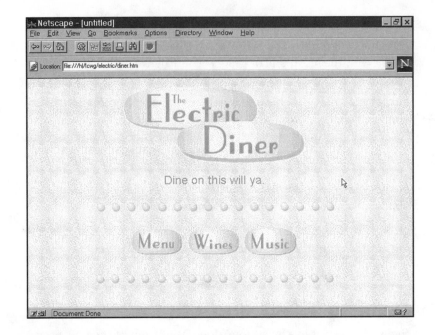

Tip

Another way to make a row of dots is to create an image of one dot and place it on the page several times, like this:

```
<IMG SRC="dot.gif"><IMG SRC="dot.gif"><IMG SRC="dot.gif">
```

This can reduce the size of the graphics file significantly, though it does make the HTML code for your Web page longer and slightly more difficult to maintain.

The title in figure 11.5 was a no-brainer once the buttons were designed. It uses precisely the same fill and shadow settings, which Paint Shop Pro remembers until you change them, even if you close down the program and start it up again. The only change in procedure was that I saved the title as a 256-color image instead of a 16-color image. The color banding in the large region of gradient fill would have been too pronounced with only 16 colors.

For a little visual variety, I used the Image | Special Effects | Cutout command to drop the rules into the page instead of using Add Drop Shadow to elevate them above the page.

The resulting Web page took only minutes to make, but looks sharp and loads fast.

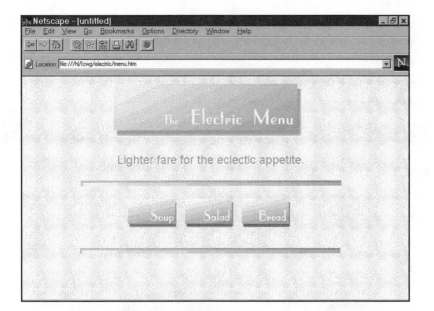

Fig. 11.5
The Cut Out effect can make something drop into the page, while drop shadows make elements stand out above the page.

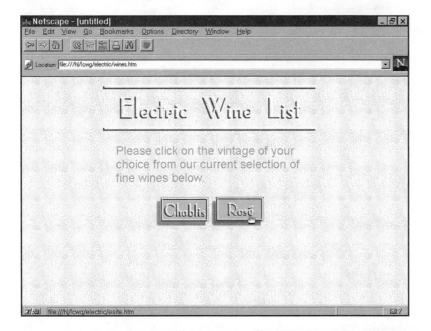

Fig. 11.6
Embossing gives titles and rules that oh-so-chic stamped-paper look.

Of course, titles don't have to look exactly the same as buttons to give a page visual consistency. In figure 11.6, I used the same Emboss and Colorize filters on the title as I did on the buttons. However, instead of adding a frame and drop-shadow, I simply made the background color transparent. This is a popular (and very easy) trick, which makes the title appear to have been literally embossed onto the page.

The horizontal rules above and below the title are actually separate graphics, which could be used anywhere on the page for dividers.

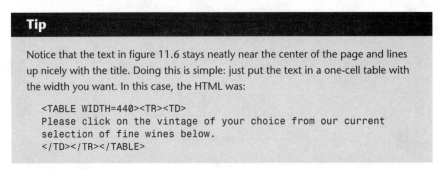

Tip

Notice that the text in figure 11.6 stays neatly near the center of the page and lines up nicely with the title. Doing this is simple: just put the text in a one-cell table with the width you want. In this case, the HTML was:

```
<TABLE WIDTH=440><TR><TD>
Please click on the vintage of your choice from our current
selection of fine wines below.
</TD></TR></TABLE>
```

Fig. 11.7

As long as you're careful not to get *too* wild, multiple effects can give your pages a singular personality.

If you choose to use multiple effects in a graphic, it can be tedious to repeat all the same steps when you want to make another matching image. To make the title in figure 11.7, for example, I played around a bit with Hot Wax Coating, Negative Image, and various color replacements and adjustments. When I finally got the result I liked, I would have been hard pressed to remember just what I'd done to arrive at it.

How, then, did I make the matching horizontal bar? Easy—I just cut out the letter "l" from the word "Electric" and pasted copies of it together to form a long vertical bar. Then I rotated it and added a drop shadow in the same direction as I had for the title. I actually find myself copying a letter "l" or "I" from text quite often to make a horizontal rule (e.g., refer to fig. 11.2). Dots from an "i" can make nice dotted bars, too.

Buttons and Titles that Work Together

No doubt you've heard the hoopla about Java, Shockwave, ActiveX, and half a hundred other buzzwords promising interactive magic on your Web pages. These cutting edge technologies are definitely the wave of the future, but the serious programming involved in creating a Java applet or ActiveX control is overkill for most Web pages today.

Many Web authors don't realize how much can be done with "plain old" graphics, without even using image maps. Of course, you aren't going to create an interactive stocks graph without some programming, but you can create buttons that work together and appear quite interactive.

Figure 11.8, the introductory page to the CD-ROM that comes with this book, is an example of buttons that fit together into a larger, cohesive graphic. The words "Graphics Software," "Example Web Pages," and "Reusable Graphics," all look like one large image, but they are actually three separate images placed right next to one another. Each of the three images is a link to one of the Web pages in figures 11.9 through 11.11.

Making "mock image maps" this way is much easier for you as a Web author than real image maps, since you don't have to figure out any coordinates, set up any server-side scripts, or try to predict how many visitors will be using browsers capable of handling client-side image maps. The links will even work in ancient text-based browsers if you include an ALT= attribute in each <IMG> tag.

On each of the pages in figure 11.9 through 11.11, one of the "buttons" becomes a "title" by substituting a more bold rendering of the same text. The other two are still navigation links. The net effect is similar to a toolbar or menu, in which the current page's title is highlighted. Navigating this site is very intuitive—not to mention fast, since most browsers keep recently loaded graphics in memory for quick access.

Fig. 11.8

What appears to be an image map (at the lower left) is actually three separate images placed side by side.

Fig. 11.9

Clicking "Graphics Software" in figure 11.8 brings you to this page.

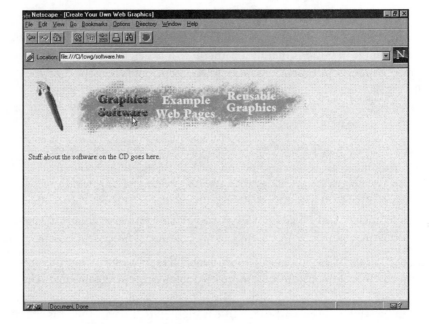

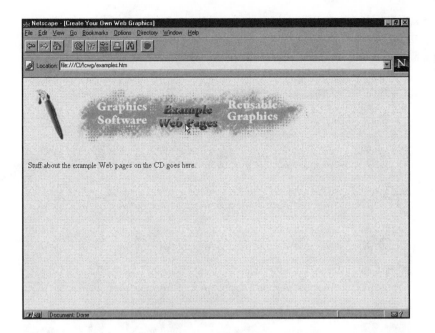

Fig. 11.10
Clicking "Example Web Pages" in figure 11.8 or 11.9 brings up this page.

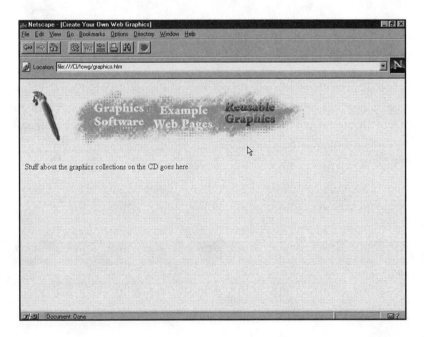

Fig. 11.11
Clicking "Reusable Graphics" in any other page at this site takes you here.

Figure 11.12 reveals the six images that make up all the navigational graphics in figures 11.9 through 11.11, and the master image out of which they were all created.

Fig. 11.12

By cutting the graphics in figures 11.9 through 11.11 into six pieces, the bandwidth requirements of this site were cut in half.

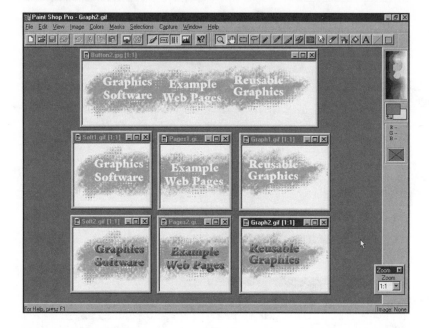

If each page used a separate image map, the images would total over 75K in size. Splitting them up and reusing the pieces cuts the total size to less than 40K. Since most of the images are in the cache after the first page loads, each subsequent page only needs to download a single 8K image instead of a 20K image map.

If this site were on the Internet instead of a CD-ROM, it would cut the typical waiting time for these pages to download via a 14.4K modem by 15 seconds per page!

Tip

For graphics to appear seamlessly next to one another, you must be careful not to put any spaces or line breaks between the <IMG> tags in your HTML document. For example, if you write this:

```
<IMG SRC="image1.gif">
<IMG SRC="image2.gif"> <IMG SRC="image3.gif">
```

there will be small spaces between the three images. But if you write:

```
<IMG SRC="image1.gif"><IMG
SRC="image2.gif"><IMG SRC="image3.gif">
```

the three images will have no space between them at all when displayed in Microsoft Internet Explorer, Netscape Navigator, and most other browsers.

Icons and Graphical Accents

Sometimes the best button isn't a button at all. It's an eye, or a fish, or a pot boiling over. Or, if you're willing to put together a few animation frames, how about a book that turns its own pages, a hopping kangaroo, or a winking Mona Lisa?

Figure 11.13 (**wpw/examples.htm** on the CD-ROM) should make the point that link icons can represent real items without requiring Leonardo to draw the artwork. I sketched all the icons on these pages with my trusty Microsoft mouse—and precious little artistic skill to back me.

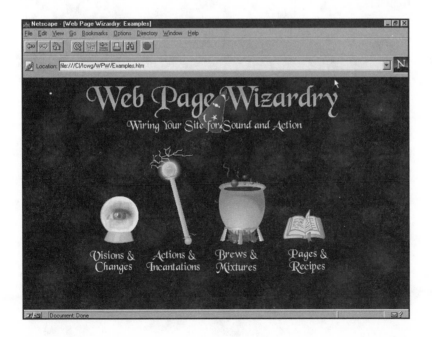

Fig. 11.13
Even these somewhat cartoony icons convey the mood of this page better than any carefully crafted "button" could.

Having a clear idea of what you're trying to represent counts for more on the Internet than steadiness of hand. Even if your mother failed to recognize your last self-portrait, you can use Paint Shop Pro's drawing tools to sketch a colorful little image that gets your point across better than plain text would.

Representational icons can also provide a visual tie-in between titles and the links that led to them, as shown in figures 11.14 through 11.16. The front page of this Web site (which comes on the CD-ROM issued with my book, *Netscape Unleashed*) incorporates colorful icons (see fig. 11.14) that are re-peated on the title graphic for each page (see figs. 11.15 and 11.16). The same theme is carried through to the horizontal bars that indicate the end of each page (bottom of fig. 11.16).

Fig. 11.14
Colorful thematic icons add spice to what might have otherwise been a dangerously boring page of buttons.

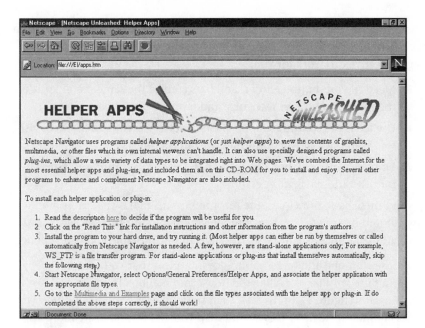

Fig. 11.15
Clicking the wire cutter icon in figure 11.14 takes you to this page, which incorporates the same image in its title.

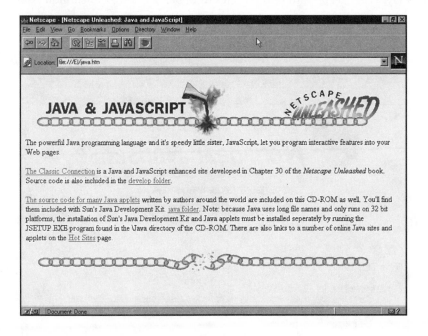

Fig. 11.16
Bold iconic images at the top of each page make it much easier to keep track of where you are within this complex site.

Even if you are building a Web site with a much different look and feel from the examples shown in this chapter, the same principles that make these pages effective can work for you:

- Make all your buttons, titles, and bars convey the same mood and theme so that visitors recognize and remember your site.

- Use icons or repeating graphical elements as "landmarks" to help visitors keep track of where they are within the site.

- Employ every trick you can to keep file sizes to a minimum, especially for titles and navigation graphics.

◀ Chapter 7, "Making Your Graphics Lean," includes many more tips on how to keep the size of your graphics files down.

Beyond these basic principles, the most important rule is that there aren't any cut-and-dry rules. The more unique you make your titles, accents, and navigation graphics, the more identifiable and memorable your site will be.

Of course, "unique and memorable" doesn't mean that you can't or shouldn't use familiar icons like the house and mailbox in figure 11.17 or the eye and ear in figure 11.18. In fact, such stereotypical symbols can help your pages communicate more clearly and help your visitors navigate more quickly. What keeps both of these sites from being boring is the unique way the stereotypes are rendered.

Fig. 11.17
Though the navigation symbols are stereotypical, the stylistic rendering and coloring still makes this site visually unique.

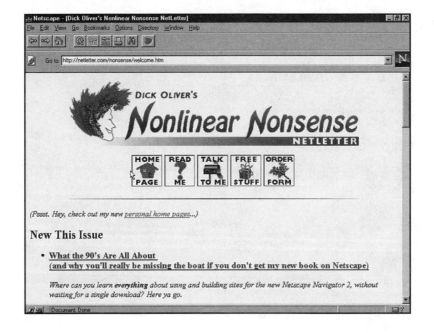

Fig. 11.18
Even a simple stylistic touch, like the brushstrokes I added to these scanned photos, can make a site more memorable.

IV

Using Your Web Graphics

Don't forget that the CD-ROM included with this book contains hundreds of professionally designed buttons, bars, backgrounds, and icons that you can use as inspiration and a starting point for your own Web pages. Whether you want to convey goofiness or grandeur, the techniques and tips presented in this chapter will help you make your site one that no visitor will easily forget. ❖

◀ Refer to Chapter 4, "Working with Existing Images," for tips on browsing and modifying the graphics files included on the CD-Rom.

CHAPTER 12

Web Graphics as Image Maps

Normally, images appear on your Web page as decoration, to make your site more colorful, fun, and enjoyable. In Chapter 11, you learned how to start putting your images to work for you by building buttons, bars, titles, and icons. Web graphics can serve as navigational tools, graphical information, and logical page separators.

Another popular way to use graphics on a Web page is as a clickable image map. Using *image maps*, you can link different areas of a single image to different HTML files. This lets visitors to your Web page navigate from page to page by using their mouse to select different areas of an image.

In this chapter, I'll show you how image maps work, what kinds of images do and do not work as image maps, and tools for creating your own image map. You will learn how to:

■ **Understand Image Maps and the Way They Work**

Clickable image maps are easy to use and they add a useful dimension to Web pages, as long as you understand exactly how they work when visitors stop by.

■ **Build a Simple Image Map for Your Web Page**

Nothing demonstrates how easy it is to create image maps as making one on your own—with the right tools.

■ **Decipher New HTML Tags that Support Client-Side Image Maps.**

Understand the new HTML tags that instruct Netscape how to interpret your image map.

■ **Link Sections of Images to Other HTML Files on the Web**

Learn how the mechanics of the HTML tags actually link different sections of a picture to separate HTML files.

How Image Maps Work

You already know how to link an image to another HTML file—I covered that way back in Chapter 1, "A Web Crawler's Beginning." By embedding the <IMG> tag inside of a Hypertext reference, you can create links from images:

```
<A HREF="ROME.HTML"> <IMG SRC="ROME.GIF"> </A>
```

This example, shown in figure 12.1, displays an image of the Coliseum in Rome on a Web page. Just like any regular Web graphic, it appears normal, but the small border around the image indicates that it is linked to another spot on the Internet. When visitors click the image, The Web browser automatically loads the file ROME.HTM.

Fig. 12.1

Linking an image to an HTML page is easy to do.

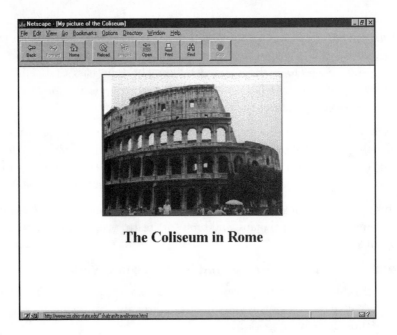

No matter where you click on the picture, the Web browser always links to ROME.HTM. This is where an image map can be useful. Using an image map, you can link *different* areas of an image to *different* HTML files, based on what section of the image is clicked.

This is an extremely useful technique because it lets visitors to your Web page get accustomed to a single image and navigate from page to page by clicking different sections of that image.

Look at the Magnavox home page (**http://www.magnavox.com**) for an excellent example of a cool Web graphic that is used as a server-side image map (see fig. 12.2). Here, the developers have included a picture of a remote control with several buttons drawn on it. Each section of the image takes you to a different spot on the Magnavox Web site. For example, clicking Company Info in the image brings up information about Magnavox, while you can easily imagine what kind of stuff appears when you click Fun & Games.

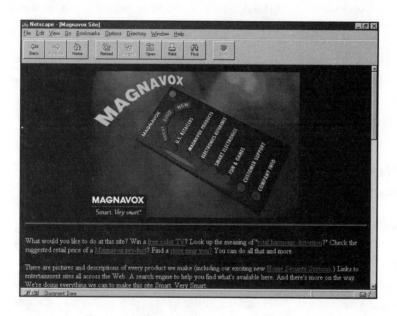

Fig. 12.2
Magnavox's image map is smart...very smart.

Graphics are often used as image maps because they enable a great looking picture to also serve a purpose for visitors who stop by. There are many good uses for image maps. For example, Italy might place a virtual map online. Using your mouse, you'd click whichever region or city of Italy you wanted to learn more about. Clicking Rome might bring up the Coliseum, and Pisa could link to that famous leaning tower. Or, Boeing might place a picture of its new 777 plane on the WWW. Visitors could click different parts of the cockpit to learn how the plane operates.

Virtually any existing Web graphic can become an image map—and image maps are easy to create. With the right tools (provided for you on the CD-ROM with this book), anyone can create and add an image map to their Web pages.

On the CD

Clickable image maps certainly are not new to the WWW. They have always been an option for your Web page if you knew the right steps to follow and had appropriate Web graphics.

Previously, to add a clickable image map to your Web page, you were dependent on your Web server software. Your server software controls all access to Web pages at a particular Internet site. To add an image map to your page, you had to find the right image, decide how each part of the image would link to a different HTML file, and then set up and customize your server properly. This was quite a hassle, even for those people who could understand every step—and some Web servers didn't permit image maps to run on them. Therefore, using image maps on Web pages was effectively limited to professional Web developers and larger companies; few individuals used image maps on personal Web pages. This type of image map is called a *server-side image map*.

Today, creating image maps is much easier. A new development called *client-side image maps* makes it much less difficult for individual Web page developers—like you—to add a clickable image map to a Web page.

Differences between Server-Side and Client-Side Image Maps

As I previously mentioned, *server-side image maps* have been around for a couple of years, but they are awkward to use. In this section, I'll explain exactly how server-side image maps run and why they're being pushed aside for newer technology.

Here's how a server-side image map works. Someone visits your home page and sees a neat image. After looking at the image for a while, they click one area (like one of the buttons on the Magnavox remote control), presumably to take them to a corresponding page of HTML. Netscape stores the coordinates that the user clicked and sends that information to the Web server. The server takes those coordinates and runs a separate program that translates those coordinates into a URL—the filename of the linked area clicked. Then the Web server sends that filename back to Netscape, which loads the file. As you probably gathered by now, server-side image maps aren't extremely efficient because of the many steps involved in using them. Also, if you have a Web server that is extremely popular, it uses all its time running the special program that translates pixel coordinates into an HTML file. This puts a heavier load on the Web server and slows access for everyone reading pages at that particular Web site.

Client-side image maps (called CSIM for short) are significantly simpler. As far as users can see, the same image appears on-screen, but what happens when they click the image is different. Instead of exchanging information with the Web server, Netscape automatically knows which HTML file to link to—and takes you there automatically. This process is significantly quicker to process (you don't have to wait for the Web server) and easier for Netscape to interpret.

Client-side image maps are more efficient, easier to create, and better for users who visit your Web pages. Eventually, client-side image maps will entirely replace image maps that are dependent on the Web server. More image maps are being created every day because of their relative ease of use.

> **Note**
>
> You can always tell whether you are using a server-side image map or a client-side one. Take a look at the status bar at the bottom of the Netscape screen while you move your mouse over an image map. If you see scrolling numbers, then you know it's a server-side image map (those pixel coordinates are sent to the server when you click). If you see a filename instead of coordinates, then you're using a client-side image map. Most people prefer seeing the filename in the status bar so they know exactly where a specific mouse click will lead them.

Creating a Client-Side Image Map

Now that you understand the difference between the two types of image map technologies, I'm going to show you how you can quickly build an image map on your Web page. I'll walk you step-by-step through the actual process of building and adding a client-side image map. You'll learn how to select the right kinds of images, link the different areas to separate HTML files, and add the correct tags to your Web page.

Finding a Good Image

The first step in creating an image map is to select or create a good image to use. You want to make sure that visitors who see the image understand that there are several different areas on the picture that they can select to link to different items. You need to select definitive images that have different regions which are easily delineated on-screen, and that make sense to visitors.

Figure 12.3 shows the image I'm going to use for this example, a client-side image map for the ACME Block Company.

Finding a good Web graphic to use as an image can be difficult and there is no single standard to decide if an image is good—or bad. Image maps can be created from virtually any graphic that can be added to your Web page.

Fig. 12.3
These big blocks make it easy for users to identify the different regions of the image map.

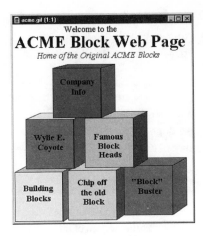

Icons, buttons, bars, pictures, and images of all types can be sectioned out and presented as an image map for visitors.

Not all images, however, make sense for use as image maps. In general, pictures make difficult image maps because they often lack clearly defined areas for the user to click. Recall my picture of the Coliseum earlier in the chapter (refer to fig.12.1)—that image wouldn't be a good image map because there aren't any well-defined areas other than the large image of the Coliseum. Try to always use graphics that have well defined sections to them so that users always know exactly where they are being linked to.

People and animals aren't *always* bad candidates for image maps, but you need to make sure that users will understand they can access different Web pages by clicking different parts of the image (for instance, body parts). Visit **http://www.cs.brown.edu/people/oa/Bin/skeleton.html** for a prime example of how a picture of a person (in this case, a skeleton) can be used as a client-side image map (see fig.12.4).

Planning the Map

Once you've selected an image, the next step is to logically divide it into different regions and define how you want the image map to work.

For my ACME block example, I want each block to be linked to a different Web page. This is where you need to understand how your site is set up and organized. Up to now, you've focused entirely on working with images. To create an image map, you need to be familiar with HTML and know the names of all the files to link into. Figure 12.5 shows how I want each part of the image to link to a different HTML file.

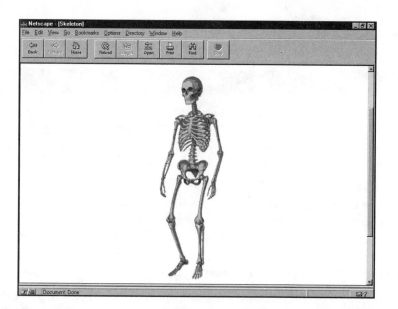

Fig.12.4
Now, where's that
funny bone?

IV

Using Your Web Graphics

Tip

Trying to figure out the complete path to your HTML files can be difficult. See
"Finding the Right Path" in Chapter 14, "HTML Tips for Web Images," for more
information.

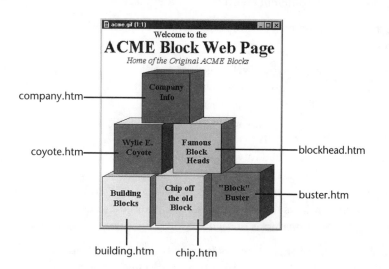

Fig. 12.5
Planning each link
from your image
map is an
important step.

Once you have a good idea of how to divide your image map, you're ready to move to the next step—adding the necessary HTML tags to your Web page.

> **Caution**
>
> Make sure that each HTML file your image links to exists. It's easy to forget to create one or more of the HTML files if you create your image map before they all exist.

Adding the Image to Your Web Page

With the correct image chosen, it's time to start learning the new HTML tags that support client-side image maps. Adding image maps is similar to adding regular images except that you need a new keyword and a couple of new tags. Fortunately, you won't be forced to learn very much new HTML —in a moment, we'll look at a new tool that saves you the hassle.

If adding the proper HTML yourself, you first need to embed the image into your Web page using the <IMG> tag with the USEMAP keyword:

```
<IMG SRC="BLOCKS.GIF" USEMAP="#ACME Block Image Map">
```

This tag tells your Web Browser how to display BLOCKS.GIF on the Web page. USEMAP tells the browser that the image is a client-side clickable image map, and to look for a named section that is named ACME Block Image Map in this HTML file. This named section of HTML tells the WWW browser how to interpret clicks on different coordinates of the image.

The # is very important because that's how Netscape recognizes named references within a file.

Your image appears in your Web page like normal. Now you're ready for the fun stuff. The next section teaches you how to tell Netscape which portions of an image link to which particular HTML files.

Mapping Your Image

With the image embedded in your Web page, your next step is to define each region on the image graphically. Think of each image as a large piece of graph paper on which you have to identify the exact *X* and *Y* coordinates for each section that links to an HTML file—the pixel coordinates. You have to specify the pixel dimensions of each section.

Fortunately, several easy-to-use tools exist that make it simple for you to specify each distinct section of the image map. One of the best, Map This!, is included on the CD-ROM accompanying this book. With Map This!, you use your mouse to draw each section on the image, and thereby create a link to an HTML file.

Now I'll step you through using Map This! to create a complete image map.

1. Start Map This!. You can run the program directly from the CD-ROM or copy it to your personal computer. A blank screen appears.

2. Choose File | New to create a new image map from scratch. The Make New Image Map dialog box appears (see fig. 12.6).

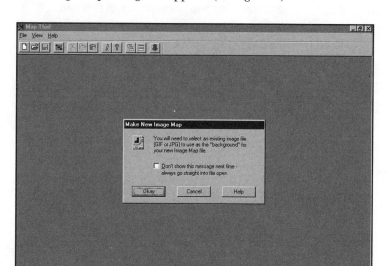

Fig. 12.6
First you need to tell Map This! which image you're mapping.

3. Click Okay to continue and reach the Open existing Image (GIF/JPG) file dialog box (see fig. 12.7) where you can specify the image you want to map.

Fig. 12.7
Select the image you want to map in this dialog box.

4. Select the image you want to map (Map This! currently supports only GIF and JPEG image formats—not PNG) and then click Open to bring up the mapping window shown in figure 12.8. Image maps work the same regardless of the image file type.

Use these icons to map
Rectangles, Circles, Polygons

Fig. 12.8
From here, you can map the image with your mouse.

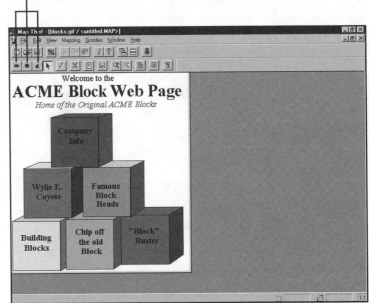

5. Once the image is opened, you can draw three types of shapes to indicate sections on your image: rectangles, circles, and polygons.

6. Draw as many different shapes and sections on your image as you need. For my ACME Block image, I have six different sections, one for each of the blocks. Figure 12.9 shows my image with the six sections marked.

7. Now, click the Show/Hide Area List icon on the toolbar to bring up the Area List dialog box (see fig. 12.10).

8. Select a listed area, and then click Edit | Edit Area Info from the menu bar or click the Pencil icon to bring up the Area Settings dialog box (see fig. 12.11). Here, type the URL of the file you want linked to this region. Click OK after you've typed the URL.

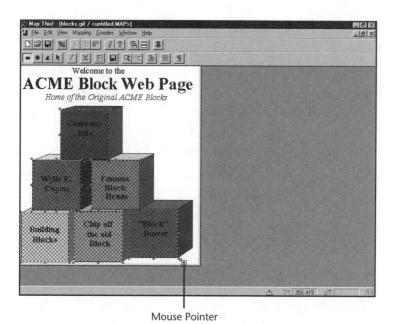

Mouse Pointer

Fig. 12.9
Notice the six rectangles drawn around the significant blocks on the image.

Show/Hide Area List icon

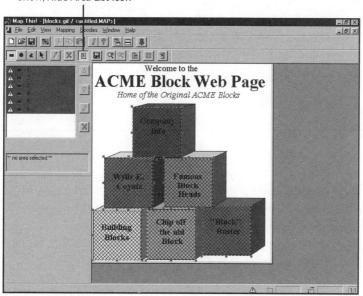

Fig. 12.10
From the Area List dialog box, you can link regions on the image to specific HTML files.

Fig. 12.11
For each area, you
have to tell Map
This! what you're
mapping.

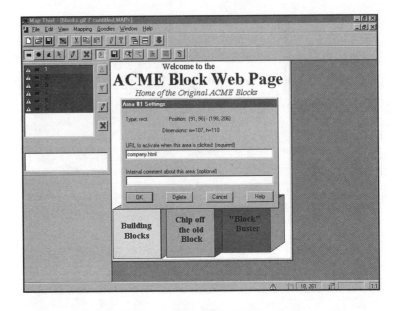

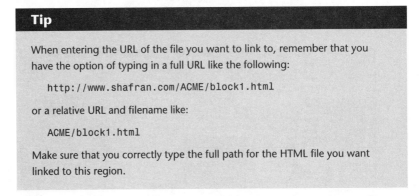

Tip

When entering the URL of the file you want to link to, remember that you
have the option of typing in a full URL like the following:

    `http://www.shafran.com/ACME/block1.html`

or a relative URL and filename like:

    `ACME/block1.html`

Make sure that you correctly type the full path for the HTML file you want
linked to this region.

▶ For a discussion
on relative
URLs, see
Chapter 14,
"HTML Tips for
Web Images."

9. Repeat Step 8 for every region defined on your image. After you finish,
your Area List dialog box lists each region along with the corresponding
linked file (see fig. 12.12).

10. Choose File | Save from the menu bar to bring up the Info about this
Mapfile dialog box (see fig. 12.13).

11. Enter the map's title, and make sure that the CSIM option button is
selected as the map file format. (Remember that CSIM stands for client-
side image map.) The NCSA and CERN option buttons are used when
creating server-side image maps. You should also type in a default URL
you want to link this image to, for users who click a part of the image
outside of the regions you've defined. I talk about default files later in
"Adding a Default Link."

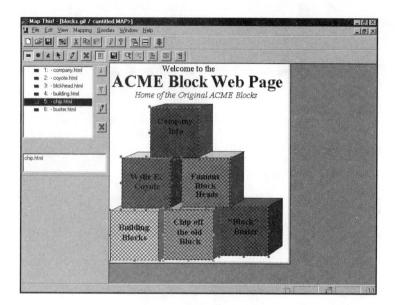

Fig. 12.12
My finished Area List dialog box—every region on the image map is now properly linked.

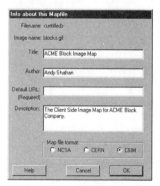

Fig. 12.13
Set your image map options here, and you're nearly finished.

Caution

For your image map to work properly, make sure that the title you type in the Info about this Mapfile dialog box corresponds exactly to what you entered following the USEMAP keyword earlier.

---

12. When you finish setting your image map options, click OK; Map This! prompts you to save the client-side image map to an HTML file. Name your file something useful, such as **blockmap.htm** for this example.

Here's a copy of my finished file:

```
<BODY>
<MAP NAME="ACME Block Image Map">
<!-- #$-:Image Map file created by Map THIS! -->
<!-- #$-:Map THIS! free image map editor by Todd C. Wilson -->
<!-- #$-:Please do not edit lines starting with "#$" -->
<!-- #$VERSION:1.20 -->
<!-- #$DESCRIPTION:The client-side Image Map for ACME Block
➥Company. -->
<!-- #$AUTHOR:Andy Shafran -->
<!-- #$DATE:Mon Mar 29 21:38:26 1996 -->
<!-- #$PATH:C:\ -->
<!-- #$GIF:blocks.gif -->
<AREA SHAPE=RECT COORDS="91,96,198,204" HREF=company.html>
<AREA SHAPE=RECT COORDS="29,206,136,314" HREF=coyote.html>
<AREA SHAPE=RECT COORDS="2,322,110,428" HREF=blckhead.html>
<AREA SHAPE=RECT COORDS="124,319,230,426" HREF=building.html>
<AREA SHAPE=RECT COORDS="161,205,269,311" HREF=chip.html>
<AREA SHAPE=RECT COORDS="247,310,355,416" HREF=buster.html>
</MAP>

</BODY>
```

That's the tough part! Now that you've successfully created your image map definition, all you have to do is add it to your HTML document—preferably, just below the <IMG> tag described in the previous section entitled "Adding the Image to Your Web Page." You now need to copy and paste the image map definition from your map file into your standard HTML file. That's it! You're all done. You've just created your own personalized client-side image map definition for your Web graphic.

Figure 12.14 shows what the example image map looks like in Netscape. Notice, as the mouse hovers over a particular block, how the status bar at the bottom of the screen indicates which HTML file you will be linked to if you click it.

Adding a Default Link

Another concern, besides overlapping regions, is what happens when a user clicks outside all established regions on your image map? You can specify a *default link* that is activated in this type of situation. Default links are nice because they make sure that visitors to your Web page are always linked to *some* page, regardless of where they click on the image.

When saving your image map, MapThis! Asks you to specify a default link URL. In this box you can specify the HTML file you want to load if a user clicks outside of the area where you've defined shapes.

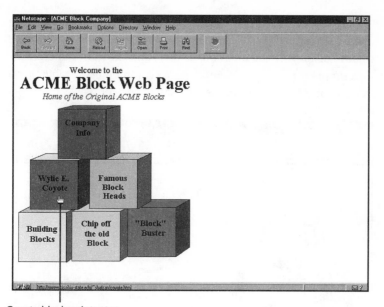

Fig. 12.14
Here's the finished
product—the
ACME Block image
map.

Coyote block pointer to
coyote.html file

Test the Image Map

Once you're finished creating the image map, make sure that you test it thoroughly with your Web browser. Test every region, one at a time, to make sure that your links have been created properly.

Many people overlook this step, assuming that there won't be any mistakes as long as they have followed the above steps exactly; however, typos, incorrect filenames, and other mistakes can easily create flaws in your image map.

This is extremely important. Making a cool graphic with Paint Shop Pro and putting time into the pixel definition is pointless if you aren't sure if it works properly.

Providing a Textual Alternative

Although virtually all new Web browsers support client-side image maps, it's always a good idea to provide some sort of textual alternative. This accommodates visitors to your page who are using a browser that doesn't read client-side image maps, or who don't want to wait for the entire image to download before selecting a region on the image map.

Figure 12.15 shows how I updated the ACME Block home page to have textual links as well as graphical ones. I used a two-column table with the left-hand column displaying the main image map, and the right-hand column showing a simple list of links. For more information on using tables and columns, see Chapter 13, "Backgrounds and Creative Layouts".

Fig. 12.15
This simple table provides an alternative to using my image map.

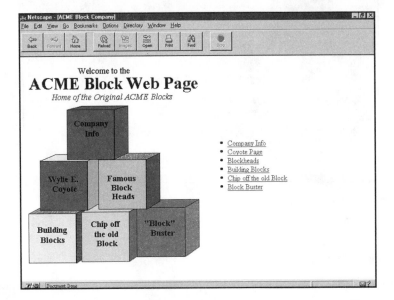

Image Map Design Considerations

In this section, I've consolidated several important tips you should keep in mind when you begin using client-side image maps in your Web pages. Some of them are information repeated from throughout this chapter, and others aren't. Basically, this is a last-minute checklist you should run through before you let everyone on the Web have access to your image maps:

■ **Be careful of file size**—Images that are mapped tend to have larger file sizes because they usually appear larger on the screen. Make sure that your image's file size isn't outrageous (for instance, above 100K); otherwise, visitors to your Web page will become impatient. If you find your image too large, practice some of the advanced file size trimming methods described in Chapter 7, "Making Your Graphics Lean."

■ **Use interlaced images**—*Interlaced images* are those that load in multiple levels, starting out fuzzy and slowly becoming more detailed. Interlaced images are ideal for image maps because as soon as visitors recognize which area they want to click, they don't have to wait for the whole image to appear. You can also learn more about interlaced images in Chapter 7.

■ **Define mapped areas clearly**—Make sure that you use an image that makes it easy for visitors to know which sections are mapped to other HTML files. It's easy for visitors to overlook small areas (or illogical areas) on an image map.

■ **Test your image twice**—I can't stress this enough. I've seen too many image maps that haven't been tested thoroughly. Usually, some regions link properly to files, but other regions don't. Nobody enjoys using an untested image map. ❖

CHAPTER 13

Backgrounds and Creative Layouts

Let's face it, after a few hours of surfing, most of the pages on the Web all start to look the same: the logo, the heading, the too-wide single column of text with cute little iconic images to the left every once in a while. And then there are those pages that are all one big graphic that take forever to download and contain only six words for you to read before you click yet another page that is all one big graphic that takes forever to download... It's enough to put you to sleep, even after that fifth cup of coffee.

This chapter demonstrates how creative use of backgrounds and layouts can ensure that Web surfers don't need to reach for the No-Doze in order to explore your site. It helps you pull together all the tools and techniques covered in this book to create a cohesive and attractive Web site. In this chapter, I'll cover these topics:

- **Making Seamless Background Tiles**

  Create backgrounds that set the perfect mood for your page—without making the text unreadable.

- **Using Tables to Lay Out Graphics**

  You may think of tables as a way to format numbers and text, but they can also be a powerful graphics design tool.

- **Tips and Tricks for Creative Designs**

  Pull all your graphics together into a site that visitors will be drawn to again and again.

Making Seamless Background Tiles

If eye-catching is what we're after, what better way to start than by catching an eye? Figure 13.1 is my two-year-old daughter's left eye, scanned with a cheap hand-scanner from a snapshot, and color-corrected a bit within Paint Shop Pro. (See Chapter 5, "Scanning and Enhancing Photos," for help with that sort of stuff.)

Fig. 13.1
The edges of this scanned photo don't fit together very well when tiled as a background.

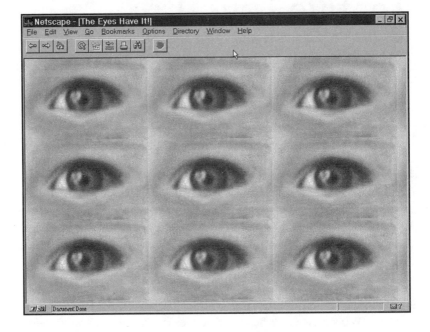

Seamless Backgrounds By Hand

The eye is pretty effective as an attention-getting background—but wouldn't it be slick if the tiles all fit together seamlessly? It may not be at all obvious how to turn this into a seamless background tile, so I'll explain it, step-by-step. Follow these steps to turn almost any interesting pattern or image into a repeating tile.

> **Tip**
>
> The following 11 steps do essentially the same thing as Paint Shop Pro's one-click Image | Special Effects | Create Seamless Pattern command. After I show you how to do it "the hard way," I'll show you the easy way. I'll also explain why this particular image (and many others) come out much better if you *don't* use the Create Seamless Pattern command.

The following instructions are specifically for Paint Shop Pro, but you can do the same thing in any good graphics editing program.

1. Open the graphics file you want to start with, and resize or crop it to suit the layout you have in mind. In this case, I chose a size that would tile nicely in a 640×480, 800×600, or 1024×768 window without the eye being cut in half on the right edge. (The image is 255×161 pixels.)

2. Select Image | Enlarge Canvas and double both the vertical and horizontal size of the canvas. This will leave room to arrange four copies of the image next to one another.

3. Using the rectangle selection tool, select the original image (in this case, the rectangle from 0,0 to 254,160). Paint Shop Pro displays the current location of the cursor at the bottom of the screen to help you get exactly the region you want.

4. Using the move selection tool, move a copy of the selection down as shown in figure 13.2.

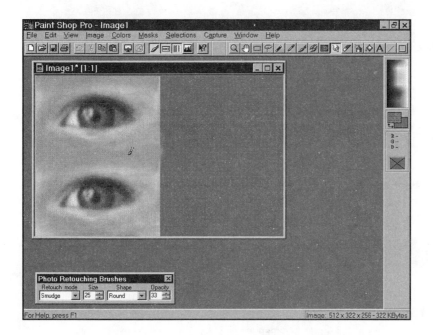

Fig. 13.2
To make a seamless tile, start by copying the image and smoothing the top and bottom edges together.

5. Using the smudge brush and/or the copy brush, smooth the transition at the edge between the two copies of the image.

6. Select the top part of the bottom image (here, the rectangle from 162,0 to about 350,255), and move it up to replace the top part of the top image. Now the top image will tile seamlessly in the vertical direction.

7. Repeat steps 3 through 6 for the horizontal direction; that is, move a copy of the top image to the right, smooth the edge between them, and copy the leftmost half back onto the original image (see fig. 13.3).

Fig. 13.3
Smooth the left and right edges together, being careful not to change the corners too much.

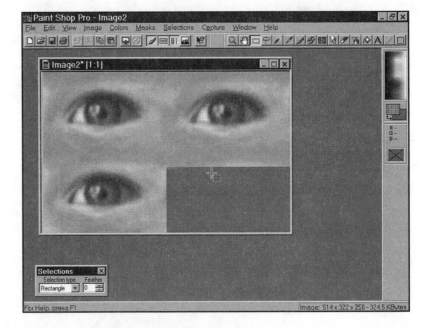

8. There still may be some abrupt color changes right at the corners of the image. To check for and correct these, copy the top left image down into the empty region at the bottom right. Use the smudge or copy brushes to smooth the corner at the center of the four images, then copy that corner carefully back up into the upper left.

9. Copy the top left image onto the clipboard, paste it into a new image file, and save it in the JPEG or GIF format.

10. Create a quick test document like this:

```
<HTML><BODY BACKGROUND="myimage.jpg"></BODY></HTML>
```

and open it into your Web browser, as shown in figure 13.4.

Note that most JPEG files will show barely visible seams between tiles—
even if you followed these steps perfectly—because the exact color information is distorted slightly during compression. Most people won't
even notice this subtle effect once the tile is on your page, but if it
bothers you, use a GIF image for tiling instead.

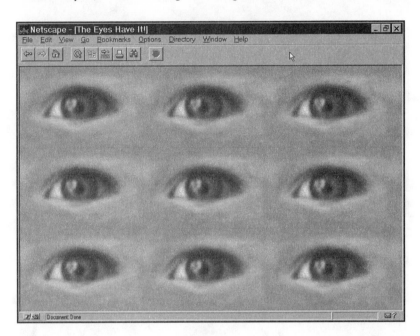

Fig. 13.4
JPEG images will
usually have barely
visible "cracks"
between tiles
due to the lossy
compression
algorithm.

11. Once you see the tile in your browser, you may see a few spots that
    need touching up in Paint Shop Pro before you pronounce your work a
    success.

You can use essentially the same process of copying and shuffling pieces of
an image to draw your own seamless tiles from scratch, or add artwork to existing tiles. Figure 13.5 is a simple example, created by painting a colored
stripe onto the image and its copies, then tweaking it as described here.
Figure 13.6 shows the result in Netscape.

Dramatic accents like this can make the subtle seams between JPEG tiles less
noticeable, too.

Fig. 13.5
When you get the
hang of tiling, you
can add any
number of artistic
effects to your
backgrounds.

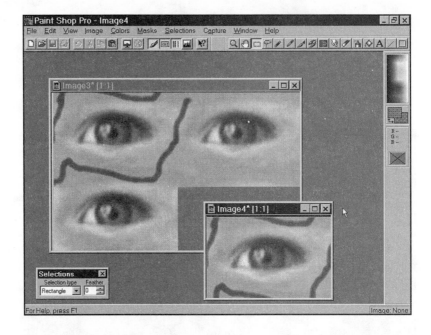

Fig. 13.6
The modified tile
in figure 13.5, as
seen in Netscape
Navigator.

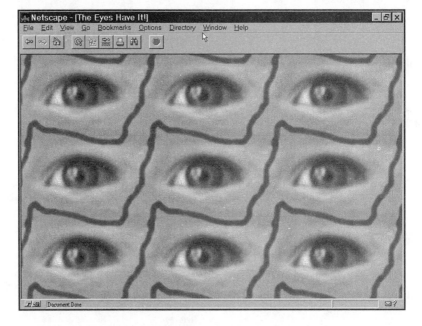

Seamless Backgrounds Automatically

If you made it through all the previous steps for creating a background tile by
hand, you're probably eager for the "easier way" that I promised to explain.

Paint Shop Pro actually has a special command for the sole purpose of creating seamless background tiles: you can simply select a rectangular region of any full-color image and Image | Special Effects | Create Seamless Pattern will do all the hard work for you.

The left image in figure 13.7 is a modified photo of a taro plant, and the two smaller images to its right are tiles taken from the same rectangular region of the taro leaf. They may look the same in figure 13.7, but figures 13.8 and 13.9 reveal the difference: one was simply cropped out of the larger image (see fig. 13.8) and does not make a very good background tile. The other was created with the Create Seamless Pattern command (see fig. 13.9) and tiles much more smoothly. With some color adjustment, it would make a very nice background for a Web page.

Tip

Watch for ugly "banding" that can present itself in the background if the tile pattern is too distinctive (the same light patch repeating over and over so that it paints a light stripe down the side of the page). Unless the background is theme related, subtlety should be the key.

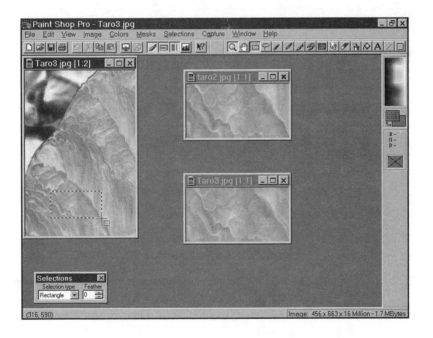

Fig. 13.7
The top image on the right was cut out of the larger image on the left. The bottom-right image was created with Paint Shop Pro's Create Seamless Background command.

Fig. 13.8
The top image from figure 13.7 doesn't make a very nice background tile because the edges are too abrupt.

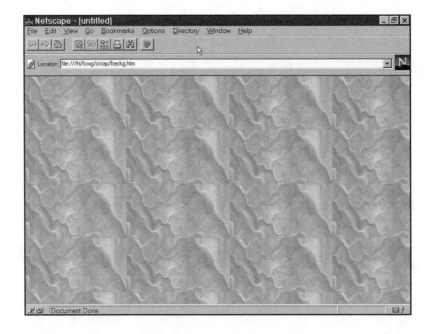

Fig. 13.9
The bottom image from figure 13.7 makes a better tile because its edges match up more smoothly.

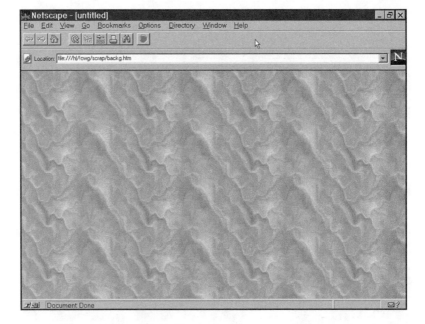

Unfortunately, the range of background images that Create Seamless Pattern works well with is fairly limited. For it to work at all, you must have an image which is at least twice as large as the background tile you want to create, and the area to make into a tile must be far enough from the edges of the original image that Paint Shop Pro can use the area around the selection to do its magic.

For the background tile to actually look good, the requirements of your original image are much more stringent. It must be a photo or full-color artwork with fairly gradual changes in color, and fairly low contrast. A scanned image of gravel or grass would work well, for example. The image of the eye presented earlier in this chapter, however, would get a bit mangled when the surrounding face was "faded" into it by the Create Seamless Pattern command. When the background you have in mind contains a high-contrast, recognizable image or pattern, you'll almost always achieve better success with the more labor intensive manual techniques, discussed earlier.

Hand-drawn Backgrounds

Figures 13.10 and 13.11 show two seamless backgrounds that the Create Seamless Background command wouldn't have been any help in creating. However, these were still quite easy to construct with Paint Shop Pro's other tools.

To make the chain-link fence in figure 13.10, I used the line and fill tools to make two crossed bars, then touched up the elbow with the paintbrush tool. I then cut and pasted four copies of the link around the original, and carefully cropped the image so that all four corners fell exactly on the center of the elbow. All this took a few minutes and some concentrated squinting at the screen, but a Bachelor's in Fine Arts was certainly not required (good thing, too: I majored in Engineering).

Despite the artsy theme of figure 13.11—which should look familiar if you've explored the CD-ROM that comes with this book—it took just about zero artistic skill to draw the canvas background (and not much more skill to draw the other elements on the page, for that matter). I simply picked an ivory color and painted a square with Paint Shop Pro's Paper Texture setting on the brush tool stylebar set to Canvas. And Voila! Canvas!

You can quickly make any of the other paper textures listed in the brush tool stylebar the same way. You can also make some very nice papers with the Image | Special Filters | Add Noise command, especially when combined with the Blur or Erode filters and Colorize command. Play around with the powerful tools that Paint Shop Pro provides and you'll be surprised at how easy it is to get some delightful results.

Fig. 13.10
You don't have to be Van Gogh to draw an interesting and effective background tile.

Fig. 13.11
Because Paint Shop Pro offers several canvas paper textures built into the brush tool, making a classy page like this is amazingly easy.

Using Tables to Lay Out Graphics

Tables are your most powerful tool for creative Web page layouts. The boring, conventional way to use tables is for tabular arrangements of text and numbers. But the real fun begins when you make the borders of your tables invisible and use them as guides for arranging graphics and columns of text any old which way you please.

> **Tip**
>
> Tables were once only visible to users of Netscape Navigator. But, now that the current version of Microsoft Internet Explorer (and the next version of every other major browser) supports tables, you can use tables without the fear that they will turn into a mushy mish-mash of text before the eyes of non-Netscapers.

Laying It Out on the Table

In figure 13.12, I've arranged some scanned handwriting and type of various sizes and colors into a table. I left the borders visible so I could make sure everything was placed the way I wanted; but, before putting this on a Web page, I would use the TABLE BORDER=0 command to make the lines invisible.

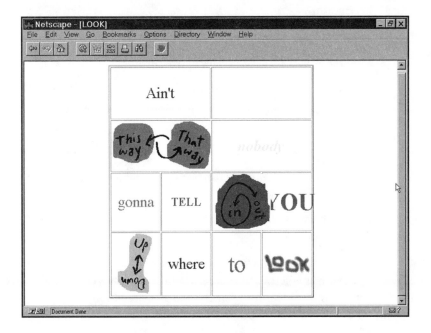

Fig. 13.12
Tables can include text, graphics, or a combination of both.

Listing 13.1 contains the HTML to make the table in figure 13.12.

Listing 13.1   Making a Table for Text and Graphics

```
<TABLE BORDER=2>
<TR VALIGN="middle" COLSPAN=2>
  <TD ALIGN="center" WIDTH=200 COLSPAN=2>
    <FONT SIZE=6 COLOR="blue">Ain't</FONT></TD>
  <TD ALIGN="center" WIDTH=200 COLSPAN=2>
    <IMG SRC="space100.gif"></TD>
</TR>
<TR VALIGN="middle">
  <TD ALIGN="left" WIDTH=200 COLSPAN=2>
    <IMG SRC="thisthat.gif" USEMAP="#thisthat" BORDER=0></TD>
  <TD ALIGN="center" WIDTH=200 COLSPAN=2>
    <FONT SIZE=6 COLOR="yellow"><I><B>nobody</B></I></FONT></TD>
</TR>
<TR VALIGN="middle">
  <TD ALIGN="center" WIDTH=100>
    <FONT SIZE=6 COLOR="fuchsia">gonna</FONT></TD>
  <TD ALIGN="center" WIDTH=100>
    <FONT SIZE=5 COLOR="green"><B>TELL</B></FONT></TD>
  <TD ALIGN="center" WIDTH=100>
    <IMG SRC="inout.gif" USEMAP="#inout" BORDER=0></TD>
  <TD ALIGN="center" WIDTH=100>
    <FONT SIZE=7 COLOR="teal"><B>YOU</B></FONT></TD>
</TR>
<TR VALIGN="middle">
  <TD ALIGN="center" WIDTH=100>
    <IMG SRC="updown.gif" USEMAP="#updown" BORDER=0></TD>
  <TD ALIGN="center" WIDTH=100>
    <FONT SIZE=6 COLOR="purple">where</FONT></TD>
  <TD ALIGN="center" WIDTH=100>
    <FONT SIZE=7 COLOR="gray">to</FONT></TD>
  <TD ALIGN="center" WIDTH=100>
    <IMG SRC="look2.gif"></TD>
</TR>
</TABLE>
```

In case you're not familiar with the HTML syntax for tables, here's a quick rundown of how all the code works.

The <TABLE> and </TABLE> tags always start and end a table, and the BORDER attribute sets the border width.

A <TR> and </TR> tag enclose each row in a table and accept the VALIGN attribute, which controls whether the contents of the row are vertically aligned to the "middle," "top," or "bottom." You could also use HEIGHT to set an exact height for the row in pixels, but in this example, I just let the browser automatically figure out the right height based on the tallest item in the row.

Each cell in the table starts with `<TD>` and ends with `</TD>`. The `ALIGN` attribute sets the horizontal alignment within the cell to either "center," "left," or "right." I used `WIDTH` to set the cell widths to exactly 200 or 100 pixels, and `COLSPAN` to indicate that each cell in the top two rows should span two columns.

That's all there is to it! I did use a few sneaky tricks: a totally transparent 100×100-pixel image called `space100.gif` to fill an empty cell, and an image too big to fit in its cell (more on that shortly).

Nested Tables

Now suppose you want to add a column of text to the page, placed to the right of the table in figure 13.12. No current extension to HTML allows you to wrap text to the right (or left) of a table—but that doesn't mean there isn't a way to do it! You can create another table, like the one shown in figure 13.13, and insert the table in figure 13.12 within a cell in that new table.

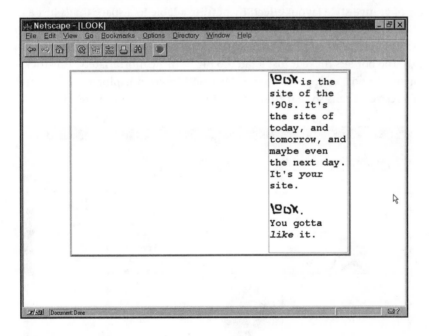

Fig. 13.13
To wrap text to the right or left of a table, create another table and insert the first one inside it.

The code to create a nested table with the arrangement shown in figures 13.13 and 13.14 is shown in listing 13.2.

Listing 13.2   Creating Nested Tables

```
<TABLE BORDER=4>
<TR VALIGN="middle">
<TD WIDTH=400>
```
(the table code in Listing 13.1 goes here)
```
</TD>
<TD WIDTH=160>
<IMG SRC="look1.gif" ALIGN="bottom">
<FONT SIZE=5><TT><B>is the site of the '90s.
It's the site of today, and tomorrow, and maybe even the next day.
It's <I>your</I> site.<P>
<IMG SRC="look1.gif">.<BR> You gotta<BR> <I>like</I> it.</B></TT><P>
</TD>
</TR>
</TABLE>
```

Figure 13.14 shows the two tables from figures 13.12 and 13.13 put together. It also demonstrates a handy "bug" that you can use on purpose to create a sort of grunge-style layout effect: By putting a table in a space that's just a little too small to hold it, you can make text or images from one cell overlap into another. (Though both the table and the space to put it in are 400 pixels wide, the borders make it just a tad too big to fit.) Unfortunately, this trick only works on Netscape Navigator. Microsoft Internet Explorer will automatically resize all cells so that they fit together properly, as in figure 13.15.

Fig. 13.14

Putting a table where it won't quite fit within another table can create an overlapping post-modern effect in Netscape Navigator.

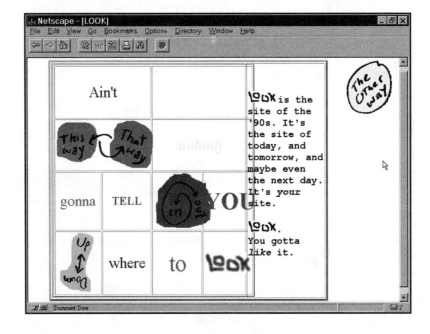

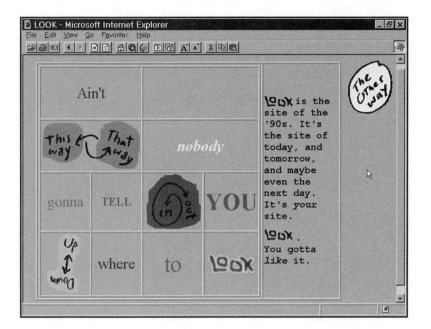

Fig. 13.15
Microsoft Internet
Explorer is a little
more fussy than
Netscape Naviga-
tor and adjusts the
size of all cells to
hold any oversized
content. (This is
the same HTML
page shown in
fig. 13.14.)

As an added touch, you'll notice that I inserted yet another graphic to the
right of the nested table in figures 13.14 and 13.15 by placing the following
tag *before* all of the table code:

```
<IMG SRC="other.gif" ALIGN="right" BORDER=0>
```

The image appears on the far right-hand margin and all graphics, text, or
tables that follow are automatically placed to the left of it.

The finished "LOOK" page, complete with borderless table layouts, is depicted in figure 13.16. But, if you look at this page on the CD-ROM (it's
/look/look.htm), you'll see more than any figure in a book could show! The
logo at the top of the page is animated in flashing colors and each of the
handwritten images is a clickable image map.

◀ Chapter 12,
"Web Graphics
as Image
Maps," explains
how to set up
the clickable
image maps,
and Chapter
10, "Moving
Graphics: GIF
Animation,"
reveals how the
animated GIF
images were
produced.

Tip

Note that Microsoft Internet Explorer 3.0 and Netscape Navigator 3.0 now allow you
to specify a separate background for each cell in a table by placing the BGCOLOR= or
BACKGROUND= attributes in a <TR> or <TD> tag, just as you would use these attributes
in the <BODY> tag.

Fig. 13.16
When the borders of the tables are hidden and a wild background is added, the result is an unquestionably unique look!

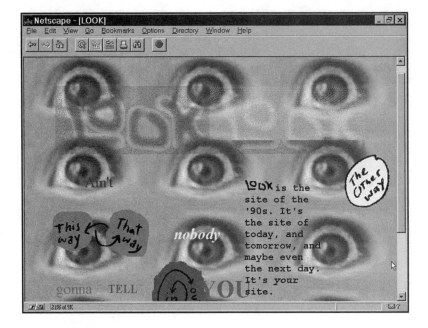

▶ Chapter 14, "HTML Tips for Web Images," includes many more tips for laying out graphics and text.

Microsoft Internet Explorer 3.0 and Netscape Navigator 2.0 (or later) support frames, which are similar to tables except that each frame contains a separate HTML page and can be updated independently of the others. A complete frame sample site can be found in the /maple directory folder on the *Web Page Wizardry* CD-ROM.

Tips and Tricks for Creative Design

This chapter—and this whole book—have given you a wide range of techniques for creating Web page graphics, and many examples of Web pages that the authors specifically created as examples. Now your task is to adapt those techniques to make your pages unique in a totally different direction. To help you take that leap, here are a few final pointers for designing and laying out your pages:

■ Maintain a consistent color scheme and visual flavor throughout your site. Resist the temptation to use *all* of Paint Shop Pro's fantastic tools at once, and stick to a few "signature" effects that express the theme of your pages.

■ Keep any graphics that substitute for text small so they load and display first. Try to make sure that any larger graphics are not essential for reading the page, keeping in mind that they'll appear more slowly.

- When possible, use the same graphics repeatedly on a page and throughout your site. This speeds display because they only need to be loaded once.

- It's fine for background images to be bold and eye-catching, but not if it means that your text is difficult to read. Either make sure that your text falls over quiet regions of the background or stick to subdued colors and designs for your background tiles.

- Make almost all the actual text content of your pages "real text," not graphics, so visitors can use their browser's Find command to search it for keywords. And, more importantly, Internet search indexes will index your pages according to their text content so potential visitors can find them easily.

- Even if you want a much more business-like look than the wild examples in this chapter, multicolumn text and a unique layout can make your pages stand out from the crowd of "me-too" pages on the Internet.

In this book, you've seen how to make highly expressive graphics. Now it's up to you to put them together into eye-catching pages that communicate your unique message to the world. ❖

IV

Using Your Web Graphics

HTML Tips for Web Images

Throughout this entire book, you've learned a great deal about making cool graphics for your Web pages. You've seen how to draw unique shapes, create neat buttons and icons, scan photos directly into your Web page, and even make spectacular special effects such as GIF animation. By this point, you should be an expert in image creation and understand the ins and outs of building efficient graphics for the Internet.

While all of these details are important when it comes to *creating* your Web graphics, there's another important piece of the puzzle to learn when *using* your graphics on Web sites. All Web pages are built with HTML, Hypertext Markup Language. HTML has many important features that affect how graphics appear on your site.

This chapter introduces you to many advanced HTML tips and Web techniques that'll come in handy when creating Web sites. You'll see that understanding the dimensions of Paint Shop Pro is only one part of creating effective graphics for a Web site. These HTML features will be extremely useful when trying to control exactly how your images appear on a Web site, including size and placement. In this chapter, I will show you how to:

■ **Define Your Image Size**

HTML allows you to control the exact height and width an image should appear (in pixels), allowing you significant flexibility in your image's appearance, without resizing or editing the actual file.

■ **Use Tables and Frames with Graphics**

Two common HTML structures Web developers use are tables and frames. Learn how you can integrate Web graphics with these two features to create an effective Web site.

- **Successfully Find your Images**

  One of the most common problems encountered when adding images to Web sites is pointing to an incorrect image file. See how you can build the correct and complete file path to your Web graphics.

- **Get Familiar with Page Layout Tips**

  Graphics designers have been creating effective looking fliers, newspapers, and books for years. Take advantage of some of their easy-to-use secrets when putting together your complete Web page.

Controlling Your Image's Appearance

By this point in the book, you should be able to create all sorts of fantastic and impressive graphics for your Web site. Whether you scanned in a photo, built a set of home page buttons and icons, or created your own dazzling background images, you've spent countless hours making just the right images for your site.

When it comes to adding these graphics to your Web page, most Web developers simply use the <IMG> tag, as described in the section titled "Basic HTML Tags for Adding Images" in Chapter 1, "A Web Crawler's Beginning." With a basic understanding of HTML, you are able to add an image to your Web page and control the alignment with which it is placed.

In this section, I talk about some more advanced HTML concepts that will likely enhance the way images are used at your site. You'll learn how to use some more advanced HTML keywords and tags, and how images integrate with other HTML tags, such as tables and frames.

Height and Width HTML Tags

In Chapter 7, "Making Your Graphics Lean," you learned how to resize and crop your image within Paint Shop Pro. Resizing your image allows you to reduce the overall file size and make an image fit slightly better on a Web page.

◀ For more information on pixels and how they work with Web graphics see "Understanding Pixel Size" in Chapter 3, "Creating Simple Graphics."

Besides using Paint Shop Pro, you can also directly control the size and appearance of your image with special HTML keywords. PSP allows you to make changes to your actual GIF or JPEG file, saving the image with its new pixel sizes. Using HTML sizing techniques, you only affect the way the image appears on a Web page without making physical changes to your graphic.

You can control the size your image appears on screen with the HEIGHT and WIDTH keywords that work within the <IMG> tag. Both HEIGHT and WIDTH can be assigned pixel values that subsequently control the sizing of an image on a page. For example, to see an image appear 200 pixels tall and 400 pixels wide, I'd use the following line of HTML:

```
<IMG SRC="ANDYLIZ.GIF" HEIGHT=200 WIDTH=400>
```

You can resize an image to almost any set of coordinates. Figure 14.1 shows an image in several different sizes.

Fig. 14.1
Here's the same image in several different sizes.

One great advantage to using the HEIGHT and WIDTH keywords is that they allow you to use an image multiple times on the same Web page, but with different results. A button or bar can be stretched and sized in different ways to fit on a particular Web page. Real benefits are derived when you use an image multiple times on a single page because visitors only have to download it once, saving a lot of time. Your Web browser uses the image from the computer's cache, or memory, to display it, rather than downloading the image again.

Caution

Using the HEIGHT and WIDTH keywords doesn't change the amount of time it takes to download and view a Web graphic. Even if you display an image using very small HEIGHT and WIDTH coordinates, visitors still have to wait the same amount of time as

(continues)

(continued)

they would when observing the full size version. However, the rest of the Web page will load quicker because your Web browser knows exactly how large the image will be. This allows the browser to place text and other images on your Web page immediately, without waiting for the image to be downloaded. If you want to use HEIGHT and WIDTH to get additional performance benefits on a Web page, your best bet is to create smaller, resized versions of your graphics and embed the new versions on your site.

Buffering Your Image

Another important way of controlling your image's appearance is to set the horizontal and vertical buffer space that appears around each graphic. Often, you'll find that your WWW browser will place images and text closer together than you prefer, as shown in figure 14.2.

Fig. 14.2
A little buffer space around the image would be nice.

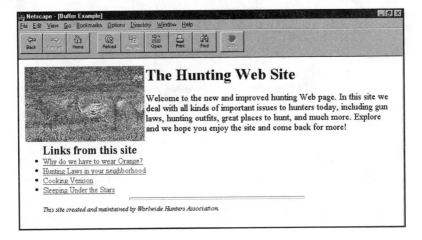

Without a small buffer, headlines and graphics may run together or two images placed side by side may be indistinguishable. To counter this problem, use the HSPACE and VSPACE keywords in your <IMG> tag. HSPACE affects the horizontal buffer space to the left of the image and VSPACE refers to the buffer size above and below the image.

Much like HEIGHT and WIDTH, described in the last section, HSPACE and VSPACE require you to type in the number of pixels you want to use as a buffer around your image. To fix the previous example, I simply added a 20 pixel buffer area to the sides of the image and a small 10 pixel buffer on the vertical axis (see fig. 14.3):

```
<IMG SRC="DEER.JPG" HSPACE=20 VSPACE=10>
```

Fig. 14.3
This page looks better because of the slight buffer change around the image.

Using Tables with Graphics

Tables are an important feature of HTML that allow Web developers to organize information on their pages in a column and row format. Often, tables are used to compare and contrast information or are used in the design of a Web page.

When displaying Web graphics, tables can be used in a special way to organize and set off important images on a page. Working with tables is easy—you simply need to learn a handful of tags, including <TABLE>, <TD>, and <TR>. You organize a table by designating information you want to appear in each cell of data for each row within the table. For example, to create a simple two-row by two-column table, use the following HTML (see fig. 14.4):

```
<TABLE BORDER=1>
    <TR>
        <TD>Row 1 - Column 1</TD>
        <TD>Row 1 - Column 2</RD>
    </TR>
    <TR>
        <TD>Row 2 - Column 1</TD>
        <TD>Row 2 - Column 2</RD>
    </TR>
</TABLE>
```

Fig. 14.4

Here's a very simple table.

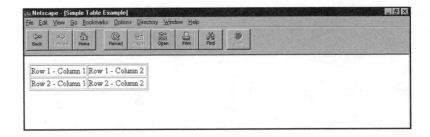

Tables are very flexible to work with when you are building a Web page with graphics. Below, I've listed a few situations in which you may want to consider using tables on your Web site.

■ **Image Grid**—When you want to display many different images on a single page, try using a table to control their appearance on-screen. Figure 14.5 shows a table that makes it easy to organize and separate each of the images used.

Fig. 14.5

Tables help keep track when you use many different images on a page.

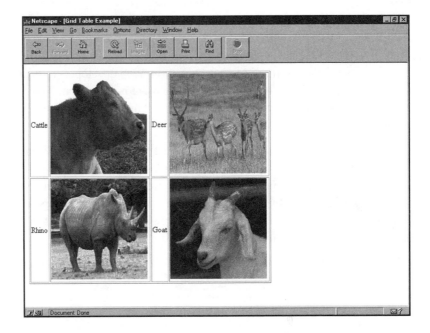

■ **Attention Grabber**—Sometimes you'll have an image that you want to draw extra attention to—perhaps an image serving as a large head-line at the top of the page. These images are usually as important as the textual headlines themselves. Figure 14.6 shows a single image within a single cell table that uses a thick border (the border is a thickness of 50 in this example).

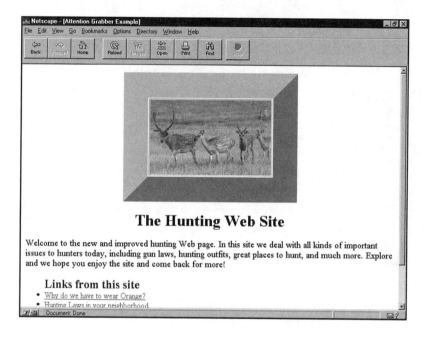

Fig. 14.6
You can't miss this image when browsing the Web!

In this small section, I only touched the tip of the iceberg in describing how tables can be used. There are many more keywords and table-related tags that can improve the effectiveness of your images and Web page. For a more complete reference to using tables effectively on your Web site, check out *Creating and Enhancing Netscape Web Pages, Bestseller Edition.*

Introducing Frames

Another frequently used method of structuring Web pages is with the use of frames. Frames allow you to split up the browser window into multiple areas, each displaying a separate HTML file. Frames have many different uses and possibilities when it comes to working with Web graphics.

Probably the most popular use of frames is to keep a standard header or footer on the screen when exploring a Web site. Figure 14.7 shows an example of my Web page framed with a simple image in the top frame. This image is a small GIF that is a large color image being used as a headline (instead of text placed with the <H1> tags). No matter which page is explored in your site, this header is always visible. As you explore the Web, you will find that places use frames in this manner to keep their logo or headline ever present.

Fig. 14.7
Frames keep a logo
always visible at a
Web site.

Top frame with
title logo

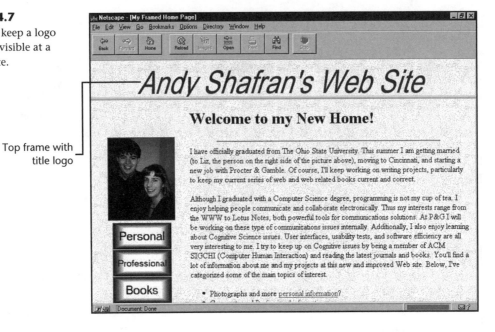

Like tables, frames also have virtually unlimited use and flexibility on Web
sites. The HTML used in frames isn't complicated, but it can be tricky. If you
want to use frames on your Web site, look at *Creating and Enhancing Netscape
Web Pages, Bestseller Edition*, for a complete guide to integrating this technology into your site.

Finding the Right Image Path

The most basic way to add an image to a Web page is to use the <IMG> tag and
simply specify which GIF or JPG file you want to display. For example, to display a file named ANDYLIZ.GIF on a Web page, I'd build the following line of
HTML:

```
<IMG SRC="ANDYLIZ.GIF">
```

By just listing the file name in the <IMG> tag, you are telling your WWW
Browser to look in the same sub-directory as the HTML file for ANDYLIZ.GIF.

Often, you'll want to reference an image that is saved in a different sub-
directory from your HTML file. To do that, you must understand how to
properly build the link to another sub-directory or even to a different drive
on your computer.

Link to a Sub-directory

For example, let's say ANDYLIZ.GIF is instead saved in a sub-directory called PICTURES. In this case, your tag would be:

```
<IMG SRC="PICTURES/ANDYLIZ.GIF">
```

Remember that the path to your Web graphic depends on where your HTML file is stored. The path concept works the same even if your image is saved in a sub-directory of a sub-directory. For example, if ANDYLIZ.GIF is saved in a sub-directory called PICTURES, which is in a sub-directory called WWW, your tag would be:

```
<IMG SRC="WWW/PICTURES/ANDYLIZ.GIF">
```

One Directory Above

Similarly, sometimes your images might be saved in a directory one level above where your HTML file is located. In this case you'd use the <IMG> tag like this:

```
<IMG SRC="../ANDYLIZ.GIF">
```

Link to a Different Drive

Sometimes you'll want to add an HTML reference to an image that is stored on a different drive from your current HTML file. In this situation, finding the proper path is a little bit more complicated. For example, if my file was saved on the **D:** drive, I'd use the following tag:

```
<IMG SRC="FILE:///D:\ANDYLIZ.GIF">
```

Of course, you can even point to a file saved in a sub-directory of a different drive:

```
<IMG SRC="FILE:///D:\PICTURES\ANDYLIZ.GIF">
```

> **Note**
>
> Linking to images on a different drive is only useful when building Web pages on your personal computer. Internet Service Providers (ISPs) usually require that your entire collection of files for your Web site be in one system of directories and sub-directories, with no access to other drives.

Images Elsewhere on the WWW

Another useful technique available is to display an image that is saved at a completely different Web site. This powerful trick enables you to use images that are saved anywhere in the world, just by listing the correct URL in the <IMG> tag.

Let's say you wanted to "borrow" a button from my personal Web site. Instead of copying the image through Netscape, you simply want to use the actual file that I use. To use this button on your Web page, you'd add the following line of HTML:

```
<IMG SRC=" http://www.shafran.com/links.jpg">
```

This line of HTML tells your WWW browser that, when loading your page, it should go to **www.shafran.com** and download **links.jpg**. Your Web browser (such as Internet Explorer or Netscape) makes it very easy to point to an image at a different file location. If you're browsing the Web with Netscape and you find an image you want to use, simply click your right-mouse button on top of the image (see fig. 14.8) and choose Copy Image Location. Netscape copies the full URL of the image into your computer's clipboard so you can simply paste it into your HTML file. Internet Explorer doesn't allow you to copy the URL into your clipboard, but you can create an Internet Shortcut to the image and save the image on your personal computer.

Fig. 14.8
Linking to images elsewhere on the Net is easy.

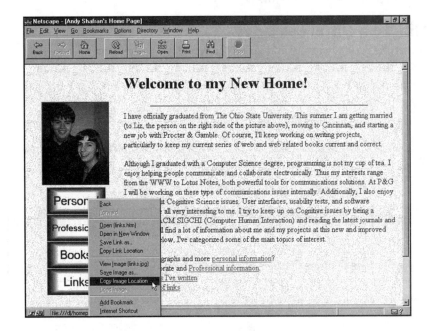

There are several drawbacks in linking to images elsewhere on the WWW. I outline each of them so you are aware of possible problems that may occur.

- **Performance**—When you link to an image at another site, visitors who stop by have to download your entire page of HTML and graphics, then wait for the Web browser to connect to the other site and download the images stored there. Often, this can be a real bottleneck and can significantly slow down the amount of time it takes to see your Web page.

- **Files Change**—Every so often, Web sites are updated and changed by replacing old graphics and files with new ones. When you link to another site, you are at the mercy of that Web developer to maintain the particular image you are using. If that image changes or is deleted, it no longer appears on your Web page—a real bummer!

- **Server Considerations**—When linking to an image at another site, you place an increased workload on the second WWW server. While initially it isn't a big deal for a few people to link to the image on my site, imagine if thousands of people had Web pages that did! My poor Web server would be swamped because other people are using my images!

- **Legal Issues**—One of the hottest topics among Web developers nowadays is the issue of copyright. Images that are on another page are not automatically yours for the picking. They have been painstakingly drawn, scanned, and created by someone else, and may be copyrighted. On the Internet, copyright laws haven't had a very clear precedent set. Using images from other sites on your own Web page may create problems for your Web site if you have not received permission.

Sometimes there will be no way around linking to an image at another site. For example, I have a built-in graphical Web counter on my home page as shown in figure 14.9.

This counter is created and incremented by a WWW server elsewhere on the Internet. Every time someone stops by my home page, their WWW Browser goes out and explores **http://www.digits.com** and downloads a simple GIF that shows their visitor number.

In general, if you want to use an image from another Web site, it's best to send e-mail asking for permission to use the images. Many individuals don't mind sharing their graphics, but some large companies do. Once you obtain permission, simply save the image to your personal Web site and use it like any standard GIF or JPEG.

Fig. 14.9
Created and
maintained on
another Web site,
all I did was add a
single <IMG> tag.

My Counter

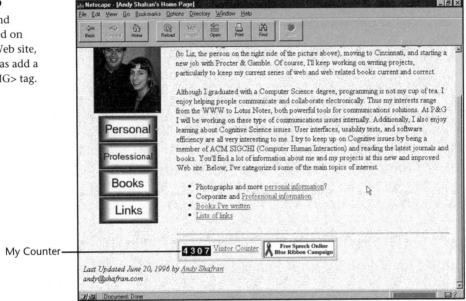

Fixing a Broken Image Pointer

If you are confused as to how all these file references work, don't worry; you're in good company. Using the incorrect path when adding an image to a Web page is one of the largest problems Web developers have for all sites, large and small.

When you are pointing to the wrong place for an image file, Web browsers display a simple "broken image" icon on the page where the original image would have appeared. Figure 14.10 shows how the "broken image" icon appears in Netscape.

When you see this icon on your Web page, you know that the WWW browser simply could not find and download the image or that the Web server did not send the image to your computer within the allotted time. Most likely, you have a typo in your image's file name or have incorrectly set the image's path to the wrong location. If you see this icon when browsing the Web, try reloading that particular page to see if it is a server problem or if the image path is incorrect.

Don't let all of your hard work in creating great Web graphics go to waste. If you see this icon on your pages, track down the problem immediately so visitors can experience all of the glory of your Web graphics.

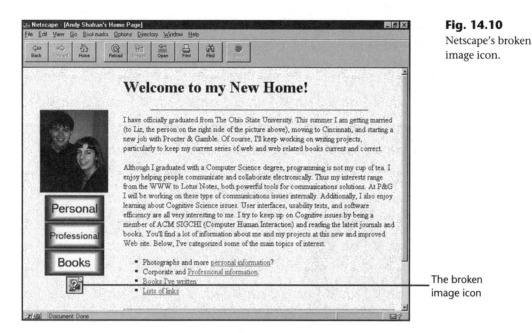

Fig. 14.10
Netscape's broken
image icon.

The broken
image icon

Image Design Suggestions

So far in this chapter, you've learned several different technical specifications
to be aware of when incorporating your graphics into a Web page. In this section, I'm going to switch gears and demonstrate how several important design considerations can affect your Web page's appearance, no matter how
great your images are.

Don't worry if you forget to use some of these design techniques; they are of-
fered only as a guideline. I've included them so that you can be aware of how
professional Web developers evaluate their sites and make small, but significant improvements that most people might not notice.

Image Visioning

Borrowed from the newspaper industry, image visioning helps control the direction of a visitor's eye through your Web page. Image visioning is the technique of placing and using a graphic on a Web page so that the visitor's eyes
will naturally focus on the highlight of the page, instead of away from it.

You'll see these practices all the time in your local newspaper. It's how editors
decide which side of the paper to place photographs and drawings on. Here's
an example of what I mean. Figure 14.11 is a simple Web page. Notice how I

placed the image on the left side of the screen, but placed the headline and text on the right side. That's because the image points towards the right. When you look at this image, your eyes automatically follow the line of vision provided by the image (cow) and you are naturally drawn into the text and headline.

Fig. 14.11
This picture draws your eyes towards the text on the right.

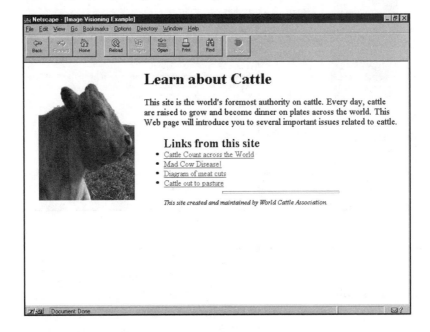

Now, look at this same Web page with the image on the right hand side of the screen (see fig. 14.12). It just doesn't have the same effect. Most people don't even notice this subtle placement of the image unless they are comparing two example pages, as in this situation.

You want to draw visitors *into* your Web page. That helps ensure that they'll read the page instead of leaving quickly. Image visioning ensures that visitors will follow the line of vision in a graphic.

Site Consistency

Another important detail for using Web graphics on a page is maintaining a consistent look throughout your entire site. Consistency is important because it allows visitors to become familiar with your set of pages. For example, Chapter 11, "Creating Titles, Buttons, and Bars with Paint Shop Pro," taught you how to create all sorts of different icons for your site. You also learned that icons are important navigational aids that let visitors meander through your set of pages. If you have navigational icons on one page, it's a good idea to use them on all pages. That way visitors will recognize the icons and know how to maneuver through your set of pages.

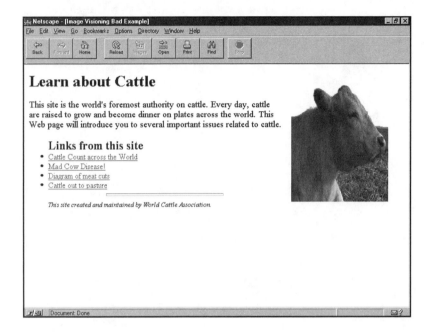

Fig. 14.12
Not quite the same effect, is it?

This is also important when creating a set of pages on a related topic. On my Web site (**http://www.shafran.com**) I have a set of support pages for each published book. There are a half dozen different pages that are all related. It's important that each page in the set maintain a consistent look.

I use the same format on each page. I start with a headline at the top next to the book cover, followed by a sub-headline, and then the full page of information. At the bottom of each page, I use the same standard links so visitors will know how to get through the site. I also use the same image in the background of the pages. Figures 14.13 and 14.14 show two example pages.

Consistency is important when you create graphics because it makes your pages fit with one another. Imagine serving dinner at your home with each guest drinking from a different type of glass. One uses a mug, another a flute, yet someone else has a plastic cup. Sure, everyone gets to drink, but using a set of the same glasses just looks better. Apply the same concept to your Web site. Making your pages look similar will make visitors enjoy your site more.

Fig. 14.13
Here's a page from
my Web site.

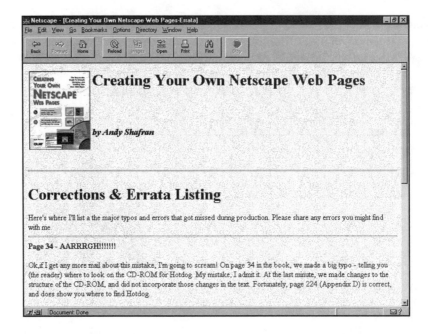

Fig. 14.14
Different page, but
consistent
appearance.

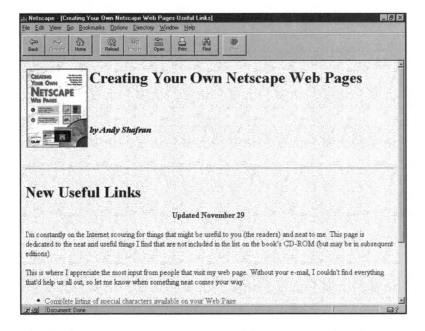

IV

Using Your Web Graphics

Color Coordination

Everyday, you wake up and get ready to go to work. Along the way, you must make conscious decisions about which clothing to wear. When you put on light blue pants, surely the orange striped shirt stays in the closet. Matching and color coordinating your clothes is something most people are capable of; it's an easy and quick daily decision.

The same concept works on the WWW. When creating cool graphics and images of all colors, it's a good idea to match the color of text on your page so that it fits with your style or theme. For example, if you create a Web page about the Ohio State Buckeyes, you might want to use scarlet and gray text, while Michigan fans would stick with maize (yellow) and blue.

Coordinating text color on your page is important and very effective. Figure 14.15 shows a simple home page on the Web (**http://rhf.bradley.edu/ ~lissa/**). At this site, the developer has a dark picture of a red rose and a very dark (black) background image. She coordinated her text color to be a light red so it matched with the image at the top. Without the matching colors, her page would be rather blasé and boring.

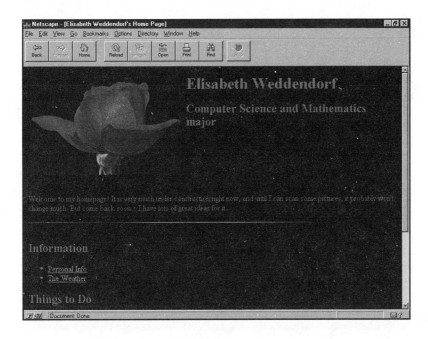

Fig. 14.15
This rosey site really scores on the color coordination scale.

Changing your text color to match your graphics is easy. You simply surround the specific text with the `<FONT COLOR=>` tag. So, to mark a sentence as red, I'd use this tag:

```
<FONT COLOR=RED>This is red text</FONT>
```

Your Web browser recognizes 16 different colors that you can specify by name, just like Red was used above:

Black	Maroon	Green	Olive
Navy	Purple	Teal	Gray
Silver	Red	Lime	Yellow
Blue	Fuchsia	Aqua	White

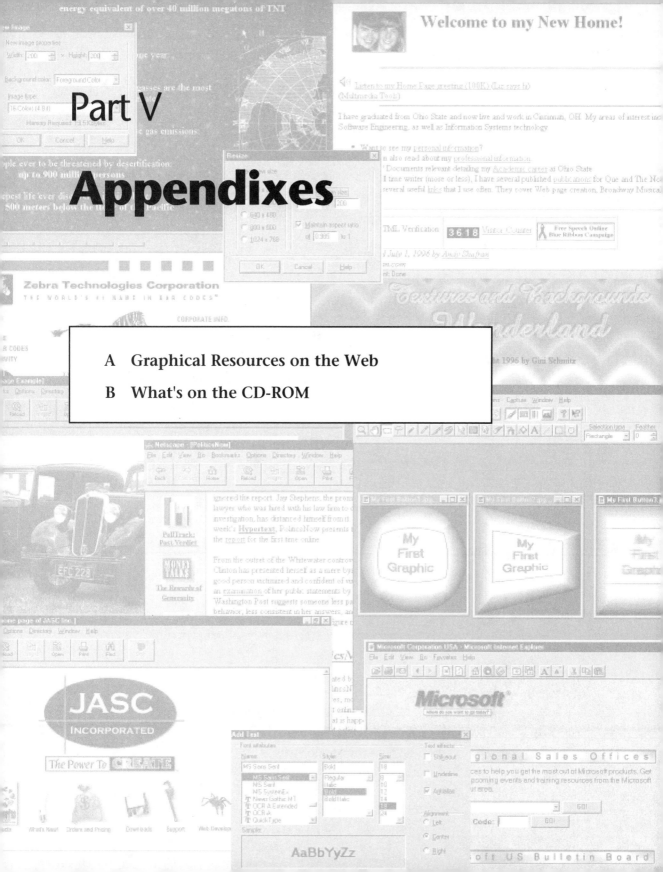

Part V

Appendixes

A   Graphical Resources on the Web

B   What's on the CD-ROM

APPENDIX A

Graphical Resources on the Web

This Appendix is a guide to many different WWW pages that you'll find useful when creating your own Web graphics. The links are organized in several categories to make them easier to use and explore. You'll also find a version of this list on the CD-ROM, in HTML format—meaning you can visit each site by clicking your mouse instead of typing them in one by one.

The Home Page for this book
http://www.shafran.com/graphics

JASC, Inc. (makers of Paint Shop Pro)
http://www.jasc.com

To order Paint Shop Pro
http://www.jasc.com/order.html

On the CD

Graphics Related Tools

Most of this book consists of using existing tools and programs to make your life easier when using Web Graphics. This section lists the home page for all of the tools and programs I mention in the book.

Map This! Home Page
http://galadriel.ecaetc.ohio-state.edu/tc/mt/

Asymetrix's Web3D home page
http://web3d.asymetrix.com

Asymetrix home page
http://www.asymetrix.com

Carberry Technology FIGleaf multiple image format plug-in

http://www.ct.ebt.com/figleaf.html

GIF Construction Set

http://www.mindworkshop.com/alchemy/alchemy.html

Graphics and Image Information

Beside tools and programs, there is a bounty of useful information for Web graphics developers. Check out these links for technical format references and useful caches of information for all readers.

The PNG graphic format information center
http://quest.jpl.nasa.gov/PNG/

Comprehensive list of colors available for your Web page
http://www.infi.net/wwwimages/colorindex.html

"User Interface Task Centered Design" by Lewis and Rieman
ftp://ftp.cs.colorado.edu/pub/cs/distribs/clewis/HCI-Design-Book/

Frequently Asked Questions about JPEG images
http://www.cis.ohio-state.edu/hypertext/faq/usenet/jpeg-faq/part2/faq.html

Netscape's comprehensive list of plug-ins
http://home.netscape.com/comprod/products/navigator/version_2.0/plugins/index.html

WWW Browsers

Without a Web browser, you cannot surf the Web. New versions of Web browsers are constantly being developed, so it is a good idea to stop by your browser's home page and make sure you are current.

Netscape Home Page (download current Netscape version from here)
http://home.netscape.com

Microsoft Internet Explorer
http://www.microsoft.com/windows/ie

Lynx—Text only browser
http://www.cc.ukans.edu/about_lynx/about_lynx.html

Cool Sites I Use

To emphasize a point in a book, I often use an existing Web page to serve as an example. Most of these sites are excellent examples of how graphics can really make a difference between a good page and a bad one. Check out these sites to see colorful and exciting pit stops on the Web.

Politics Now!
http://www.politicsnow.com

Airplane On-line
http://www.airplane.com

Image Newsgroup
news:comp.infosystems.www.authoring.images

Que's home page (the publisher of this book)
http://www.mcp.com/que

CompuServe Incorporated
http://www.compuserve.com

Clickable human skeleton
http://www.cs.brown.edu/people/oa/Bin/skeleton.html

An interactive tour through the Louvre
http://watt.emf.net/wm/paint/auth/michelangelo/

Collections of Images to Use

You don't always have to do all of the difficult work yourself. There are literally millions of images and graphics available on the Web for you to use. Here's just a smattering of places to look when trying to find that one perfect image.

Yahoo's List of Image Sites
http://www.yahoo.com/Computers_and_Internet/ Multimedia/Pictures/

Kodak Collection of Images to use
http://www.kodak.com/digitalImages/samples/ imageIntro.shtml

Hundreds of free and small icons to use
http://www2.cybernex.net/~jen/webpages/bullets/ bullets.html

The Graphics Library (definitive source of free images and backgrounds)
http://www.inin.co.uk/images/gl/index.html

Scanner Developers

When you have a photograph or picture that you want to save electronically, you have to enlist the help of a computer scanner. No longer prohibitively priced, scanners are now becoming common equipment for all Web developers who have an interest in innovative graphics.

Logitech Home Page
http://www.logitech.com/logitech/214e.htm

Hewlett-Packard Home Page
http://www.dmo.hp.com/peripherals/scanners/main.html

Umax Technologies
http://www.umax.com/scandir2.html

Mustek Scanners
http://www.mustek.com

Search Utilities

The following sites provide useful search utilities:

Lycos
http://lycos.cs.cmu.edu

InfoSeek
http://www.infoseek.com/

Nexor
http://pubweb.nexor.co.uk/public/archie/servers.html

Nevada SCS
http://www.scs.unr.edu/veronica.html

What's on the CD-ROM

The CD-ROM included with this book is loaded with valuable programs, utilities, and samples. This appendix gives you a brief overview of the contents of the CD. For a more detailed look at these resources, load the CD-ROM and browse the contents.

Paint Shop Pro

The CD-ROM contains a complete shareware copy of the latest version of Paint Shop Pro. Paint Shop Pro is the best all around computer program available for creating professional caliber graphics. Paint Shop Pro provides truly impressive graphics file manipulation, edits, and conversions into over 30 different file types, with an easy to use and intuitive interface. An award winning piece of software from JASC, Inc., Paint Shop Pro allows you to evaluate it for 30 days before you are required (if interested) to purchase it for $54.00.

Other Graphics Programs

Several other programs are included on the CD-ROM for your use. These programs include software to create image maps and GIF animations, and to manipulate images. Load the CD-ROM and browse the contents to access these programs:

- GIFCon
- Lview Pro
- Map Edit
- Map This!
- Web Hotspots

Web Graphics Collections

Several Web graphics collections are included on the CD-ROM. These samples will help you get started immediately with pre-made electronic artwork. Buttons, lines, directional controls, and other graphics are available for instant use on your Web pages. You can manipulate these samples with the included programs to give your Web pages a unique look. You can also use them as a starting point to create your own graphics.

Examples from this Book

Many of the graphics described in the book can also be found on the CD-ROM. These examples include not only images taken from chapter illustrations, but also sample Web pages. The sample pages will give you a feel for how all of the graphical elements on a Web page can work together to draw attention to your site and give it that polished look. ❖

Index

Symbols

\# (pound signs) in client-side image map URLs, 238

A

<A HREF> tag (thumbnails), 142
adding
  images to Web pages, 24-25
    alternate text, 26-28
    client-side image maps, 238
    text to images, 40
airbrush tool (Paint Shop Pro), 67
ALIGN= keyword (<IMG> tag), 26
aligning
  images, 25-26, 51
  nested tables, 263
  text, 220
alternate text, 26-28
  client-side image maps, 245-246
  GIF animation, 197
America Online photo scanning, 94

animation (GIFs), 191-192
  alternate text, 197
  blinking buttons, 212
  building, 192-196
  example, 196-197
  file names, 193
  file size, reducing, 204-208
  layered animation, 199-200
  looping, 193, 203-204
  matching colors, 200-201
  speed, optimizing, 204-208
  transparent images, 194-195
    backgrounds, 202-203
Archie search, 73-74
Asymetrix Web site, 287

B

backgrounds, 19, 251-253
  color
    adjusting, 85
    GIF animation, 202-203
    new images, 53, 59
  Create Seamless Pattern command (Paint Shop Pro), 254-257
  customizing, 84-85

  drawing, 257
  embossing images, 110-111
  GIF animation (transparent GIFs), 202-203
  photograph backgrounds, removing, 104-107
  saving backgrounds, 71
  smoothing image edges, 252
  table cells, 263
  see also transparent GIFs
bars (horizontal rules), 217-221
black-and-white images, 158-160
  creating, 163-169
    converting color images, 165
    new images, 163-165
    reducing to 16 colors (shades), 165-169
  dithering, 167
  file size
    converted images, 165
    new images, 164
  overlaying images (Low Resolution keyword), 169-170
  spotting with color, 171-172

when to use, 160-163
artistic emphasis,
160-161
performance
considerations,
162-163
theme coordination,
161-162
**Black-and-White Photo
Gallery Web site, 158**
<BLINK> tag, 212
**blinking buttons
(GIF animation), 212**
borders
image buffers, 270-271
tables, 259
broken image icons, 278
browsers
saving background
images, 71
Netscape plug-ins, 24
transparent GIF
treatment, 176-177
Web sites, 288
buffering images, 270-271
**buttons, 41, 129-130,
212-217**
blinking (GIF
animation), 212
color depth, 216
fill, 215
label text, 215
matching titles, 221-225
shadow, 215
shape, 214
special effects, 215-216
touching up, 217
transparent GIFs, 216

C

**Carberry Technology
(FIGleaf plug-in)
Web site, 288**

cells (tables), 261
backgrounds, 263
overlapping
(nested tables), 262
<CENTER> tag, 51
centering
images (screen
resolution), 51
text, 220
see also aligning images
chisel effect, 130
**client-side image maps,
234-235**
(pound signs) in
URLs, 238
adding images to Web
pages, 238
choosing images, 235-236
default links, 244
design considerations,
246
file size, 246
interlaced images,
246-247
mapping images, 238-244
titling maps, 242-243
URLs, 242
planning, 236-238
testing, 245
text alternatives, 245-246
color, 119-127
backgrounds
adjusting, 85
GIF animation,
202-203
see also transparent
GIFs
black-and-white images,
171-172
buttons, 216
colorizing images, 121
converting color images
to black and white, 165
coordination, 283-284

depth
decreasing, 126-127,
166-167
increasing, 41
dithering, 167
drawing shapes, 59-61
file size, 145-147
reducing colors,
147-151
GIF animations
backgrounds, 202-203
matching colors,
200-201
greyscale, 121
negatives, 121
new images, 40
backgrounds, 53
image type, 53-55
number of colors, 53-55
black-and-white
images, 165-169
reducing, 147-151
photographs
brightness/contrast,
96-97
equalizing, 102-104
gamma correction, 98
HSL (Hue/Saturation/
Luminance)
correction, 100-102
RGB (Red/Green/Blue)
correction, 101-102
tonal correction,
99-100
posterizing images,
124-126
solarizing, 123
thin lines, 83
Web page schemes, 264
Web site, 288
**combining images,
115-119**
**compressing JPEGs,
151-153**

consistency within Web sites, 280-281

counters, 277

creating new images, 39-41, 48
  background color, 53
  black-and-white, 163-165
  image type, 53-55
  saving new images, 56-59
  size, 49-53
  transparent GIFs, 178-181
    setting transparent colors, 182-183

cropping images, 42, 142-144
  floating photographs, 184-186

customizing images
  adding text, 40
  buttonizing, 41
  color, 40
    depth, 41
  cropping, 42
  deforming, 43
  resizing, 42-43

cutout effect (Paint Shop Pro), 130

D-E-F

decreasing color depth, 126-127
  black-and-white images, 166-167

deforming images, 43, 114-117

dithering, 167

drawing
  backgrounds, 257
  shapes, 59
    airbrush tool, 67
    colors, 59-61
    eraser tool, 68
    flood fill tool, 68

lines, 61-62
ovals, 63-64
paintbrush tool, 64-66
rectangles, 62
retouch tool, 68

drop shadow effect, 127-129

equalizing histograms, 102-103

eraser tool (Paint Shop Pro), 68

example Web sites, 289

existing images
  backgrounds, customizing, 84-85
  CD-ROM, 77-78
  finding on the Internet, 70-71
    Archie, 73-74
    saving, 71
    Veronica, 74-76
    Web sites, 288-289
  resizing, 82-84
  screen shots, capturing, 78-81

FIGleaf Web site, 288

files
  formats, 20-24
    GIF (Graphical Interchange Format), *see* GIFs
    JPEG (Joint Photographic Experts Group), *see* JPEGs
    Netscape plug-ins, 24
    PCD (Kodak PhotoCD), 94
    PNG (Portable Network Graphics), 23
  naming, 57
  size, 136-137
    client-side image maps, 246

color, 145-151
converted images, 165
cropping images, 142-144
GIF animation, 204-208
JPEGs, 146, 151-153
new black-and-white images, 164
overlaying images (Low Resolution keyword), 169-170
pixels, 53
resizing images, 138-140
thumbnails, 141-142

filters (photographs), 110-114

finding graphics on the Internet, 70-71
  Archie, 73-74
  saving graphics, 71
  Veronica, 74-76
  Web sites, 288-289

floating photographs, 183-189
  cropping images, 184-186
  finishing touches, 188-189
  saving, 188-189
  scanning, 184
  sculpting images, 186-187
  testing, 189

flood fill tool (Paint Shop Pro), 68

foregrounds colors (new images), 59

frames, 264, 273-274

G

gamma correction (photographs), 98

GIF Construction Set, 192
blinking buttons, 212
commands
Animation Wizard
(File menu), 192
Banner
(Edit menu), 192
Loop
(Insert menu), 203
New (File menu), 193
Save As
(File menu), 195
Setup (File menu), 203
Transition
(Edit menu), 192
dialog boxes
Edit Header, 193-194
Setup, 203
GIF animations, 192-196
loops, 193, 203-204
matching colors, 200
optimizing animation
speed, 204-208
reducing file size,
204-208
scrolling text, 192
transparent
backgrounds,
202-203
transparent images,
194-195
Web site, 288
GIFs (Graphical
Interchange Format),
21-22
animation, 191-192
alternate text, 197
blinking buttons, 212
building, 192-196
example, 196-197
file names, 193
layered animation,
199-200
looping, 193
loops, 203-204

matching colors,
200-201
reducing file size,
204-208
speed, optimizing,
204-208
transparent
backgrounds,
202-203
transparent images,
194-195
black-and-white images,
165
see also black-and-
white images
color
creating, 55
reducing, 147-151
interlaced, 57-58,
154-155
saving new images as,
57-58
size, 145-151
transparent, 174-177
browser treatment,
176-177
buttons, 216
creating new images,
178-181
existing images, 182
floating photographs,
see floating
photographs
GIF animation,
194-195
setting transparent
colors, 182-183
Gopher, 16
Graphical Interchange
Format, *see* **GIFs**
graphics
backgrounds, *see*
background graphics
black and white, 158-160
converting color
images, 165

creating new images,
163-165
dithering, 167
file size, 164-165
overlaying images
(Low Resolution
keyword), 169-170
reducing to 16 colors
(shades), 165-169
spotting with color,
171-172
when to use, 160-163
design considerations
color coordination,
283-284
consistency, 280-281
image visioning,
279-280
finding on the Internet,
70-71
Archie, 73-74
saving graphics, 71
Veronica, 74-76
Web sites, 288-289
formats, 20-24
GIF (Graphical
Interchange Format),
see GIFs
JPEG (Joint
Photographic Experts
Group), *see* JPEGs
Netscape plug-ins, 24
PCD (Kodak
PhotoCD), 94
PNG (Portable
Network Graphics),
23
icons, 17
broken images, 278
link icons, 225-229
Web site, 289
load time, 136-137
photographs, *see*
photographs
resizing, 82-84

screen shots, capturing, 78-81
tables, 271-273
   image grids, 272
Graphics Library Web site, 289
greyscale images, 121, 165-169
   converting color images, 165
      photographs, 96
   special effects, 129
grids (images), 272

H

height of images (HEIGHT keyword), 268-270
Hewlett-Packard Web site, 290
histograms, 96-97
   brightness/contrast correction, 97
   equalizing, 103
   gamma correction, 98
   stretching, 103
   tonal corrections, 99-100
home pages,
   see World Wide Web, pages, sites
horizontal rules, 217-221
hot wax tinting, 130
HSL (Hue/Saturation/ Luminance) correction (photographs), 100-102
HTML tags
   <A HREF>, 142
   <BLINK>, 212
   <CENTER>, 51
   <IMG>, 25-26, 169-170, 195, 224, 232, 238, 268-271, 274
   <TABLE>, 260, 271

<TABLE BORDER=>, 259
<TD>, 261, 271
<TR>, 260, 271

I

icons, 17
   broken images, 278
   link icons, 225-229
   Web site, 289
image maps, 232-234
   client-side, 234-235
      # (pound signs) in URLs, 238
      adding images to Web pages, 238
      choosing images, 235-236
      default links, 244
      design considerations, 246-247
      file size, 246
      interlaced images, 246-247
      mapping images, 238-244
      planning, 236-238
      testing, 245
      text alternatives, 245-246
   mock image maps, 221
   server-side, 234-235
images
   adding to Web pages, 24-25
   aligning, 25-26
      centering, 51
   alternate text, 26-28
   backgrounds,
      see backgrounds
   black and white, 158-160
      converting color images, 165
      creating new images, 163-165

      dithering, 167
      file size, 164-165
      overlaying images (Low Resolution keyword), 169-170
      reducing to 16 colors (shades), 165-169
      spotting with color, 171-172
      when to use, 160-163
   broken image icons, 278
   buffering, 270-271
   CD-ROM, 77-78
   color, *see* color
   combining, 115-119
   creating with Paint Shop Pro, 39-41, 48
      background color, 53
      image type, 53-55
      naming, 57
      size, 49-53
   cropping, 42
   deforming, 43, 114-117
   design considerations
      color coordination, 283-284
      consistency, 280-281
      image visioning, 279-280
   drop shadow effect, 127-129
   filters, 110-114
   finding on the Internet, 70-71
      Archie, 73-74
      saving, 71
      Veronica, 74-76
      Web sites, 288-289
   formats, 20-24
      GIF (Graphical Interchange Format), *see* GIFs
      JPEG (Joint Photographic Experts Group), *see* JPEGs

Netscape plug-ins, 24
PCD (Kodak
PhotoCD), 94
PNG (Portable
Network Graphics),
23
grids, 272
height, 268-270
interlaced, 154-155
client-side image
maps, 246-247
layering, 115-119
linking, 274-278
other drives, 275
other level directories,
275
other Web sites, 28,
275-277
sub-directories, 275
troubleshooting, 278
overlaying (Low
Resolution keyword),
169-170
resizing, 42-43, 82-84,
138-140
color, 145-151
cropping, 142-144
HEIGHT and WIDTH
keywords (<IMG>
tag), 268-270
JPEG compression,
151-153
thumbnails, 141-142
saving, 56-59
GIF format, 57-58
JPEG format, 58-59
Web pages, 71
screen shots, capturing,
78-81
sizing new images, 49-53
special effects
buttonizing, 129-130
chiselling, 130
cutout, 130
hot wax tinting, 130

thumbnails, 141-142
width, 268-270
see also GIFs; JPEGs; PNGs
<IMG> tag, 25
GIF animation, 195
image maps, 232, 238
keywords
ALIGN=, 26
HEIGHT, 268-270
HSPACE, 270-271
LOWSRC, 169-170
SRC=, 274
USEMAP, 238
VSPACE, 270-271
WIDTH, 268-270
spaces, 224
InfoSeek search engine, 70
**interlaced images, 57-58,
154-155**
client-side image maps,
246-247
Internet, 70-71
Archie, 73-74
Gopher, 16
saving graphics, 71
Veronica, 74-76
World Wide Web, *see*
World Wide Web
**Internet Explorer
Web site, 288**
**isolating subjects from
photograph backgrounds,
104-107**

J-K

**JASC Inc. (Paint Shop
Pro makers), 32**
**JPEGs (Joint Photographic
Experts Group), 22-23**
compressing, 151-153
creating
colors, 55
paper texture, 66

FAQ (Frequently Asked
Questions) Web site,
288
file size, 146
progressive, 58-59,
154-155
resizing, 140
see also resizing images
saving new images as,
58-59
standard, 58

Kodak
Collection of Images Web
site, 289
PhotoCD service, 94

L

layering images, 115-119
lines
color of thin lines, 83
drawing, 61-62
links, 28, 274-278
icons, 225-229
images, *see* image maps
other drives, 275
other level directories,
275
other Web sites, 275-277
sub-directories, 275
thumbnails, 141-142
troubleshooting, 278
loading time, 136-137
HEIGHT and WIDTH
keywords (<IMG> tag),
270
Logitech Web site, 290
**loops (GIF animation),
203-204**
**Low Resolution keyword
(LOWSRC=), 169-170**
**Lycos search engine,
70, 290**
Lynx Web site, 288

M

MapThis! utility
creating client-side image maps, 239-244
dialog boxes
Area List, 240-241
Area Settings, 240, 242
Make New Image Map, 239
Open existing Image (GIF/JPG) file, 239
Web site, 287
mapping images, 238-244
titling image maps, 242-243
URLs, 242
Microsoft Internet Explorer Web site, 288
modem speed, 136-137
monitor resolution, 49-51
centering images, 51
Mustek Scanners Web site, 290

N

negative images, 121
nested tables, 261-264
overlapping cells, 262
source code, 262
Netscape
plug-ins, 24
Web site, 288
saving backgrounds with Netscape Navigator, 71
Web site, 288
Nevada SCS Web site, 290
new images, 39-41, 48
background color, 53
black-and-white, 163-165
drawing, 59
airbrush tool, 67
colors, 59-61
eraser tool, 68

flood fill tool, 68
lines, 61-62
ovals, 63-64
paintbrush tool, 64-66
rectangles, 62
retouch tool, 68
image type, 53-55
naming, 57
saving, 56-59
GIF format, 57-58
JPEG format, 58-59
size, 49-53
transparent GIFs, 178-181
setting transparent colors, 182-183
Nexor Web site, 290

O-P

ovals, drawing, 63-64
overlaying images (Low Resolution keyword), 169-170

Paint Shop Pro (PSP), 32-33
backgrounds, 251-253
Create Seamless Pattern command, 254-257
customizing, 84-85
drawing, 257
smoothing image edges, 252
black-and-white graphic
converting color images, 165
new images, 163-165
reducing to 16 colors (shades), 165-169
browsing the CD-ROM images, 77-78
buttons, 41
color depth, 216
fill, 215
label text, 215

shadow, 215
shape, 214
special effects, 215-216
touching up, 217
transparent GIFs, 216
capturing screen shots, 78-81
color, 40, 119-127
colorizing images, 121
depth, 41, 126-127
dithering, 167
greyscale, 121
negatives, 121
posterizing images, 124-126
reducing, 147-151
solarizing, 123
Color Palette, 38, 59-60
combining images, 115-119
commands
Acquire (File menu), 92
Add Drop Shadow (Special Effects sub-menu), 128-129, 215
Add Noise, 257
Browse (File menu), 77
Buttonize (Special Effects sub-menu), 41, 129
Capture, 79
Chisel (Special Effects sub-menu), 130
Colorize, 121
Copy (Edit menu), 80
Create Seamless Pattern, 250
Crop (Image menu), 42, 144, 186, 188
Cutout (Special Effects sub-menu), 130, 218
Decrease Color Depth, 126, 147, 166
Deformations (Image menu), 43

Equalize, 103
Gamma Correction
  (Colors menu), 85
Grey Scale (Colors
  menu), 121, 165
Help Topics
  (Help menu), 44
Histogram Window,
  96
Hot Wax (Special
  Effects sub-menu),
  130
Increase Color Depth
  (Color menu), 41
Negative Image
  (Colors menu),
  83, 121
New (File menu), 39,
  48, 163, 178-182
Paste (Edit menu), 80
Posterize, 114, 124
Resample
  (Image menu), 83
Resize (Image menu),
  42, 138
Save As (File menu),
  155, 188
Solarize, 123
Stretch, 103
Undo (Edit menu), 43
Update (File menu), 78
Zoom In/Out
  (View menu), 182
copying images, 80
creating images,
  39-41, 48
  background color, 53
  image type, 53-55
  size, 49-53
cropping images, 42,
  143-144
deforming images,
  114-117
dialog boxes
  Add Text, 40-41
  Capture Setup, 79
  Color, 60-61

Decrease Color Depth,
  147-148, 166-167
Edit Palette, 60-61,
  163-164
File Preferences,
  151-152, 180-183
Image Arithmetic,
  115-118
New Image, 39, 48-49,
  163, 178
Resize, 138-139
Save As, 41, 56, 155,
  180, 188
drawing shapes, 59
  colors, 59-61
  lines, 61-62
  ovals, 63-64
  rectangles, 62
embossing images,
  110-111
filters, 110-114
floating photographs
  cropping images,
    184-186
  finishing touches,
    188-189
  saving, 188-189
  sculpting images,
    186-187
help system, 44
histograms, 96-97
images, deforming, 43
installing, 33-34
JPEG compression,
  151-153
layering images, 115-119
  layered animation,
    199
naming new images, 57
paper textures
  (backgrounds), 257
registering, 35-36
resampling images, 83
resizing images, 42-43,
  82-84, 138-140

saving images, 41, 56-59
  GIF format, 57-58
  JPEG format, 58-59
scanned photographs,
  91-92, 94-104
  brightness/contrast,
    96-97
  equalization, 102-104
  gamma correction, 98
  HSL (Hue/Saturation/
    Luminance)
    correction, 100-102
  removing
    backgrounds,
    104-107
  RGB (Red/Green/Blue)
    correction, 101-102
  tonal correction,
    99-100
sizing images, 49-53
  screen resolution,
    50-51
special effects, 127-130
  buttons, 129-130
  chiselling, 130
  cutout effect, 130, 218
  drop shadow,
    127-129, 215
  hot wax tinting, 130
  seamless patterns, 250
starting, 33
Style Bar, 37-38
text
  button labels, 215
  font attributes, 179
Tool Palette, 37
Toolbar, 37-38
  adding scanning
    buttons, 92
tools
  airbrush, 67
  eraser, 68
  flood fill, 68
  lasso, 104, 186
  magic wand, 104
  paintbrush, 64-66
  retouch, 68

transparent GIFs
creating new images,
178-181
existing images, 182
setting transparent
colors, 182-183
undoing, 64
**paths (image links),
274-278**
different drives, 275
other level
directories, 275
other Web sites, 275-277
counters, 277
drawbacks, 276-277
legal issues, 277
sub-directories, 275
troubleshooting, 278
PCD (PhotoCD) files, 94
photographs, 18
backgrounds, removing,
104-107
brightness/contrast,
96-97
choosing suitable
photos, 90
color, 119-127
colorizing images, 121
decreasing color
depth, 126-127
greyscale, 96, 121,
165-169
negatives, 121
posterizing images,
124-126
solarizing, 123
combining, 115-119
converting to
greyscale, 96
deforming images,
114-117
embossing, 110-111
equalizing, 102-104
filters, 110-114
floating photographs,
183-189

cropping images,
184-186
finishing touches,
188-189
saving, 188-189
scanning, 184
sculpting images,
186-187
testing, 189
gamma correction, 98
histograms, 96-104
HSL (Hue/Saturation/
Luminance) correction,
100-102
Kodak's PhotoCD
service, 94
layering images, 115-119
old-fashioned effect, 121
RGB (Red/Green/Blue)
correction, 101-102
scanning
Paint Shop Pro, 91-92
scanning services, 94
tonal correction, 99-100
Photoshop GIF animation
layered animation,
199-200
matching colors, 200-201
pictures, *see* **photographs**
pixel sizing, 49-53
file size, 53
screen resolution, 49-51
centering images, 51
plug-ins (Netscape)
image formats, 24
Web site, 288
**PNGs (Portable Network
Graphics), 23**
**posterizing images,
124-126**
**pound signs (#) in
client-side image map
URLs, 238**
**progressive JPEGs, 58-59,
154-155**
PSP, *see* **Paint Shop Pro**

Q-R

rectangles, drawing, 62
resampling images, 83
**resizing images, 42-43,
82-84, 138-140**
color, 145-147
reducing, 147-151
cropping, 142-144
HEIGHT and WIDTH
keywords (<IMG> tag),
268-270
JPEGs, 140
compression, 151-153
resampling, 83
thumbnails, 141-142
**resolution (monitors),
49-51**
**retouch tool (Paint Shop
Pro), 68**
**RGB (Red/Green/Blue)
correction (photographs),
101-102**
rows (tables), 260
rules (horizontal), 217-221

S

saving
floating photographs,
188-189
new images
GIF format, 57-58
JPEG format, 58-59
Web page graphics, 71
scanned images
choosing suitable
photos, 90
color, 119-127
colorizing images, 121
decreasing color
depth, 126-127
greyscale, 121
negatives, 121
posterizing, 124-126
solarizing, 123

combining, 115-119
deforming, 114-117
filters, 110-114
floating photographs, 184
layering, 115-119
Paint Shop Pro, 91-92
scanners Web site, 290
scanning services, 94
TWAIN interface, 92
screens
resolution, 49-51
centering images, 51
screen shots, capturing, 78-81
scrolling text, 192
search engines, 70
Web sites, 290
server-side image maps, 234-235
shadow, 127-129
buttons, 215
shapes, drawing with Paint Shop Pro, 59
airbrush tool, 67
colors, 59-61
eraser tool, 68
flood fill tool, 68
lines, 61-62
ovals, 63-64
paintbrush tool, 64-66
rectangles, 62
retouch tool, 68
shareware, 32-33
sizing images, 52-53, 82-84
resampling, 83
resizing images, 138-140
cropping, 142-144
HEIGHT and WIDTH keywords (<IMG> tag), 268-270
JPEG compression, 151-153
reducing color, 147-151
thumbnails, 141-142

solarizing images, 123
source code (saving backgrounds with Netscape Navigator), 71
special effects, 127-130
buttons, 129-130
labels, 215-216
chiselling, 130
cutout effect, 130, 218
drop shadow, 127-129, 215
hot wax tinting, 130
seamless patterns, 250
standard JPEGs, 58
stretching histograms, 103-104

T-U-V

<TABLE> tag, 260, 271
<TABLE BORDER=> tag, 259
tables, 259-264
borders, 259
cells, 261
backgrounds, 263
graphics, 271-273
image grids, 272
nested, 261-264
overlapping cells, 262
source code, 262
rows, 260
tags (HTML)
<A HREF>
thumbnails, 142
<BLINK>, 212
<CENTER>, 51
<IMG>, 25
ALIGN= keyword, 26
GIF animation, 195
HEIGHT keyword, 268-270
HSPACE keyword, 270-271
image maps, 232, 238

Low Resolution keyword (LOWSRC=), 169
spaces, 224
SRC= keyword, 274
USEMAP keyword, 238
VSPACE keyword, 270-271
WIDTH keyword, 268-270
<TABLE>, 260, 271
<TABLE BORDER=>, 259
<TD>, 261, 271
<TR>, 260, 271
text
adding to images, 40
alternate, 26-28
client-side image maps, 245-246
GIF animation, 197
button labels, 215
centering, 220
font attributes (transparent GIFs), 179
scrolling, 192
Web page design, 265
Texture and Background Wonderland Web site, 70
thumbnails, 141-142
CD-ROM images, 77
titles
matching bars, 217-221
matching buttons, 221-225
tonal corrections (photographs), 99-100
<TR> tag, 260, 271
transparent GIFs, 174-177
browser treatment, 176-177
buttons, 216
creating
existing images, 182
new images, 178-181
setting transparent colors, 182-183

floating photographs, 183-189
  cropping images, 184-186
  finishing touches, 188-189
  saving, 188-189
  scanning, 184
  sculpting images, 186-187
  testing, 189
GIF animation, 194-195
  backgrounds, 202-203
TWAIN interface (scanners), 92

Umax Technologies Web site, 290

Veronica, 74-76

W-X-Y-Z

Web3D Web site, 287
width of images, 268-270
World Wide Web, 14-16
browsers, *see* browsers
pages
  adding image maps, 238
  animation, *see* animation
  color coordination, 283-284
  color schemes, 264
  consistency, 280-281
  design considerations, 264-265
  frames, 264, 273-274
  loading time, 136-137, 270
  Low Resolution keyword (LOWSRC=), 169-170

source code, 71
tables, 259-264, 271-273
saving graphics, 71
searching for graphics
  Archie, 73-74
  Veronica, 74-76
sites
  Asymetrix, 287
  Black-and-White Photo Gallery, 158
  browsers, 288
  Carberry Technology (FIGleaf plug-in), 288
  color, 288
  example sites, 289
  FIGleaf, 288
  GIF Construction Set, 288
  graphics information, 288
  Graphics Library, 289
  graphics tools, 287-288
  Hewlett-Packard, 290
  icons, 289
  InfoSeek search engine, 70
  Internet Explorer, 288
  JASC Inc. (Paint Shop Pro makers), 32
  JPEG FAQ (Frequently Asked Questions), 288
  Kodak Collection of Images, 289
  Logitech, 290
  Lycos search engine, 70
  Lynx Web browser, 288
  MapThis!, 287
  Microsoft Internet Explorer, 288

  Mustek Scanners, 290
  Netscape, 288
  Nevada SCS, 290
  Nexor, 290
  plug-ins (Netscape), 288
  PNGs, 23
  scanners, 290
  search engines, 290
  Texture and Background Wonderland, 70
  Umax Technologies, 290
  Web3D, 287
  Yahoo! search engine, 70

Before using any of the software on this disc, you need to install the software you plan to use. See Appendix B, "What's on the CD-ROM," for directions. If you have problems with this CD-ROM, please contact Macmillan Technical Support at (317) 581-3833. We can be reached by e-mail at **support@mcp.com** or by CompuServe at **GO QUEBOOKS**.

Read This Before Opening Software